From Zero to Java Hero

Master The Art of Java Programming

JARREL E.

First published by Indy Pub 2023

Library of Congress Control Number: 2023921320

First edition

ISBN: 9798868945045

Contents

Forward

"From Zero to Java Hero" is not just a book; it is a transformative journey for individuals aspiring to navigate the vast realm of Java programming. As I reflect on the content within these pages, I am struck by the author's commitment to providing a comprehensive and accessible guide. Whether you are a newcomer to the world of coding or a seasoned developer seeking to broaden your skill set, this book serves as a valuable companion.

Preface

Welcome to "From Zero to Java Hero," a comprehensive guide designed to transform you into a proficient Java developer. This book is crafted with a singular purpose—to empower individuals, regardless of their prior coding experience, to master the intricacies of Java programming.

As the landscape of technology evolves, Java remains a stalwart in the realm of programming languages. Its versatility, platform independence, and extensive ecosystem make it a compelling choice for both beginners and seasoned developers. Whether you're embarking on a new career path or seeking to enhance your existing skills, this book is your roadmap to Java mastery.

Key Features:

- **Progressive Learning Modules:** The book follows a structured approach, gradually building your understanding of Java concepts. Each chapter builds upon the foundation laid in the previous, ensuring a smooth and logical progression.
- **Hands-On Exercises:** Theory is important, but practical application solidifies learning. Throughout the

book, you'll find hands-on exercises that challenge you to apply what you've learned, reinforcing your understanding and proficiency.

- **Real-World Examples:** Java is widely used in diverse applications, from web development to mobile applications. Real-world examples and case studies peppered throughout the book provide insights into how Java is employed in practical scenarios.
- **Comprehensive Coverage:** From the fundamentals of Java syntax to advanced topics like multithreading and design patterns, this book leaves no stone unturned. It serves as a comprehensive reference for both novice and experienced developers.

Who Should Read This Book:

- **Programming Novices:** If you're new to programming, this book provides a gentle and structured introduction to Java, laying a solid foundation for your coding journey.
- **Experienced Developers:** Even if you're well-versed in other programming languages, "From Zero to Java Hero" serves as a valuable resource for quickly grasping Java's nuances and leveraging its unique features.
- **Students and Professionals:** Whether you're a student studying computer science or a professional looking to upskill, the content is tailored to meet your learning needs.

How to Use This Book:

- **Sequential Approach:** For beginners, it is recommended to follow the chapters in sequence, as each chapter builds upon the knowledge gained in the previous ones.
- **Reference Guide:** For experienced developers, use the book as a reference guide. Dive into specific chapters or topics as needed to enhance your Java skills.

Dedication

To my dearest son Sean and beloved daughter Shamim,

This book is dedicated to you with immense love and gratitude. Throughout the countless hours spent researching, coding, and refining the content within these pages, your unwavering support has been my guiding light.

Sean, your curiosity and zest for learning inspire me daily. May this book be a testament to the importance of lifelong learning and the pursuit of one's passions.

Shamim, your resilience and creativity are a source of endless joy. As you navigate your own journey, may the knowledge within these chapters serve as a foundation for your own pursuits and ambitions.

In the tapestry of life, family is the thread that weaves through every experience, every challenge, and every triumph. Your presence is not only cherished but forms the very fabric of this endeavor.

May the principles and skills explored in "From Zero to

Java Hero" serve as a beacon of inspiration for both of you. As you grow and embark on your unique paths, know that this book stands as a testament to the importance of perseverance, curiosity, and the pursuit of excellence.

With all my love,

Overview

Java programming language was originally developed by Sun Microsystems which was initiated by James Gosling and released in 1995 as core component of Sun Microsystems' Java platform (Java 1.0 [J2SE]).

The latest release of the Java Standard Edition is Java SE 8. With the advancement of Java and its widespread popularity, multiple configurations were built to suit various types of platforms. For example: J2EE for Enterprise Applications, J2ME for Mobile Applications.

The new J2 versions were renamed as Java SE, Java EE, and Java ME respectively. Java is guaranteed to be **Write Once, Run Anywhere**.

Java is:

- **Object Oriented:** In Java, everything is an Object. Java can be easily extended since it is based on the Object model.
- **Platform Independent:** Unlike many other programming languages including C and C++, when Java is com-

piled, it is not compiled into platform specific machine, rather into platform independent byte code. This byte code is distributed over the web and interpreted by the Virtual Machine (JVM) on whichever platform it is being run on.

- **Simple:** Java is designed to be easy to learn. If you understand the basic concept of OOP Java, it would be easy to master.
- **Secure:** With Java's secure feature it enables to develop virus-free, tamper-free systems. Authentication techniques are based on public-key encryption.
- **Architecture-neutral:** Java compiler generates an architecture-neutral object file format, which makes the compiled code executable on many processors, with the presence of Java runtime system.
- **Portable:** Being architecture-neutral and having no implementation dependent aspects of the specification makes Java portable. Compiler in Java is written in ANSIC with a clean portability boundary, which is a POSIX subset.
- **Robust:** Java makes an effort to eliminate error prone situations by emphasizing mainly on compile time error checking and runtime checking.
- **Multithreaded:** With Java's multithreaded feature it is possible to write programs that can perform many tasks simultaneously. This design feature allows the developers to construct interactive applications that can run smoothly.
- **Interpreted:** Java byte code is translated on the fly to native machine instructions and is not stored anywhere. The development process is more rapid and analytical

since the linking is an incremental and light-weight process.

- **High Performance:** With the use of Just-In-Time compilers, Java enables high performance.
- **Distributed:** Java is designed for the distributed environment of the internet.
- **Dynamic:** Java is considered to be more dynamic than C or C++ since it is designed to adapt to an evolving environment. Java programs can carry extensive amount of run-time information that can be used to verify and resolve accesses to objects on run-time.

History of Java

James Gosling initiated Java language project in June 1991 for use in one of his many set- top box projects. The language, initially called 'Oak' after an oak tree that stood outside Gosling's office, also went by the name 'Green' and ended up later being renamed as Java, from a list of random words.

Sun released the first public implementation as Java 1.0 in 1995. It promised **Write Once, Run Anywhere** (WORA), providing no-cost run-times on popular platforms.

On 13 November, 2006, Sun released much of Java as free and open source software under the terms of the GNU General Public License (GPL).

On 8 May, 2007, Sun finished the process, making all of

Java's core code free and open- source, aside from a small portion of code to which Sun did not hold the copyright.

Tools You Will Need

For performing the examples discussed in this book, you will need a Pentium 200-MHz computer with a minimum of 64 MB of RAM (128 MB of RAM recommended).

You will also need the following softwares:

- Linux 7.1 or Windows xp/7/8 operating system
- Java JDK 8
- Microsoft Notepad or any other text editor

This book will provide the necessary skills to create GUI, networking, and web applications using Java. First let's write our first Java code.

```
public class MyFirstJavaProgram
{
public static void main(String []args) {
System.out.println("Hello World");
}
}
```

Environment Setup

Setting up a Java development environment is an essential step in your journey to becoming a Java programmer. Below, I'll provide a professional, step-by-step guide to setting up your Java environment. Please note that this guide assumes you're working on a typical development machine running Windows, macOS, or Linux.

Step 1: Install Java Development Kit (JDK)

- Download the latest version of the Java Development Kit (JDK) from Oracle's website or another trusted source. Make sure to choose the version compatible with your operating system (Windows, macOS, or Linux).
- Follow the installation instructions provided for your specific operating system.

Step 2: Set up Environment Variables

- After installing the JDK, you need to set up environment variables to point to the JDK installation directory.
- On Windows:
- Right-click on "This PC" or "My Computer" and select

"Properties."

- Click on "Advanced system settings" on the left.
- Click the "Environment Variables" button.
- Under "System variables," find "Path" and click "Edit." Add the path to your JDK's "bin" directory (e.g., "C:\Program Files\Java\jdk1.8.0_241\bin").
- On macOS and Linux:
- Open a terminal.
- Edit your shell configuration file (e.g., **.bashrc** or **.zshrc**) and add the following line:

```ruby
rubyCopy code
export PATH=$PATH:/path/to/your/jdk/bin
```

- Use the **source** command to reload your shell configuration:

```bash
bashCopy code
source ~/.bashrc
```

Step 3: Verify Java Installation

- Open a terminal or command prompt.
- Type the following command to check if Java is properly installed:

```
Copy code
java -version
```

- You should see information about the installed Java version.

Step 4: Choose an Integrated Development Environment (IDE)

- While you can write Java code in a simple text editor, it's highly recommended to use an Integrated Development Environment (IDE) for a more productive experience. Some popular Java IDEs include Eclipse, IntelliJ IDEA, and NetBeans. Download and install your preferred IDE.

Step 5: Create a Java Project

- Open your chosen IDE and create a new Java project. You can follow the IDE's specific project creation wizard.

Step 6: Write and Run Your First Java Program

- Create a new Java class within your project.
- Write a simple "Hello, World!" program to ensure everything is set up correctly.
- Run your program to see the output.

With these steps, you've successfully set up your Java development environment. You can now start writing, compiling, and running Java code as you work on your journey to becoming a Java hero.

Basic Syntax

When we consider a Java program, it can be defined as a collection of objects that communicate via invoking each other's methods. Let us now briefly look into what do class, object, methods, and instance variables mean.

- **Object** - Objects have states and behaviors. Example: A dog has states - color, name, breed as well as behavior such as wagging their tail, barking, eating. An object is an instance of a class.
- **Class** - A class can be defined as a template/blueprint that describes the behavior/state that the object of its type supports.
- **Methods** - A method is basically a behavior. A class can contain many methods. It is in methods where the logic is written, data is manipulated and all the actions are executed.
- **Instance Variables** - Each object has its unique set of instance variables. An object's state is created by the values assigned to these instance variables.

First Java Program

Let us look at a simple code that will print the words **Hello World**.

```
public class MyFirstJavaProgram {
/* This is my first java program.
* This will print 'Hello World' as the output
*/
public static void main(String []args) {
System.out.println("Hello World"); // prints
Hello World
}
}
```

Let's look at how to save the file, compile, and run the program. Please follow the subsequent steps:

- Open notepad and add the code as above.
- Save the file as: MyFirstJavaProgram.java.
- Open a command prompt window and go to the directory where you saved the class. Assume it's C:\.
- Type 'javac MyFirstJavaProgram.java' and press enter to compile your code. If there are no errors in your code, the command prompt will take you to the next line(Assumption : The path variable is set).
- Now, type ' java MyFirstJavaProgram ' to run your program.
- You will be able to see ' Hello World ' printed on the window.

```
C:\>javac MyFirstJavaProgram.java
C:\> java MyFirstJavaProgram
Hello World
```

Basic Syntax

About Java programs, it is very important to keep in mind the following points.

- **Case Sensitivity** – Java is case sensitive, which means identifier Hello and **hello** would have different meaning in Java.
- **Class Names** – For all class names the first letter should be in Upper Case.

If several words are used to form a name of the class, each inner word's first letter should be in Upper Case.

Example: *class MyFirstJavaClass*

- **Method Names** – All method names should start with a Lower Case letter.

If several words are used to form the name of the method, then each inner word's first letter should be in Upper Case.

Example: *public void myMethodName()*

- **Program File Name** – Name of the program file should

exactly match the class name.

When saving the file, you should save it using the class name (Remember Java is case sensitive) and append '.java' to the end of the name (if the file name and the class name do not match, your program will not compile).

Example: Assume 'MyFirstJavaProgram' is the class name. Then the file should be saved as *'MyFirstJavaProgram.java'*

- **public static void main(String args[])** - Java program processing starts from themain() method which is a mandatory part of every Java program.

Java Identifiers

All Java components require names. Names used for classes, variables, and methods are called **identifiers**. In Java, there are several points to remember about identifiers. They are as follows:

- All identifiers should begin with a letter (A to Z or a to z), currency character ($) or an underscore (_).
- After the first character, identifiers can have any combination of characters.
- A key word cannot be used as an identifier.
- Most importantly, identifiers are case sensitive.
- Examples of legal identifiers: age, $salary, _value, 1_value.
- Examples of illegal identifiers: 123abc, -salary.

Java Modifiers

Like other languages, it is possible to modify classes, methods, etc., by using modifiers. There are two categories of modifiers:

- **Access Modifiers:** default, public , protected, private
- **Non-access Modifiers:** final, abstract, strictfp

We will be looking into more details about modifiers in the next chapter.

Java Variables

Following are the types of variables in Java:

- Local Variables
- Class Variables (Static Variables)
- Instance Variables (Non-static Variables)

Java Arrays

Arrays are objects that store multiple variables of the same type. However, an array itself is an object on the heap. We will look into how to declare, construct, and initialize in the upcoming chapters.

Java Enums

Enums were introduced in Java 5.0. Enums restrict a

variable to have one of only a few predefined values. The values in this enumerated list are called enums. With the use of enums it is possible to reduce the number of bugs in your code.

For example, if we consider an application fora fresh juice shop, it would be possible to restrict the glass size to small, medium, and large. This would make sure that it would not allow anyone to order any size other than small, medium, or large.

Example

```
class FreshJuice {
enum FreshJuiceSize{ SMALL, MEDIUM, LARGE }
FreshJuiceSize size;
}
public class FreshJuiceTest {
public static void main(String args[]){
FreshJuice juice = newFreshJuice();
juice.size = FreshJuice.FreshJuiceSize.MEDIUM;
System.out.println("Size: " + juice.size);
}
}
```

The above example will produce the following result:

Size: MEDIUM

Note: Enums can be declared as their own or inside a class. Methods, variables, constructors can be defined inside enums as well.

Java Keywords

The following list shows the reserved words in Java. These reserved words may not be used as constant or variable or any other identifier names.

Comments in Java

Java supports single-line and multi-line comments very similar to C and C++. All characters available inside any comment are ignored by Java compiler.

```java
public class MyFirstJavaProgram{
/* This is my first java program.
* This will print 'Hello World' as the output
* This is an example of multi-line comments.
*/
public static void main(String []args){
// This is an example of single line comment
/* This is also an example of single line
comment. */ System.out.println("Hello World");
}
}
```

Using Blank Lines

A line containing only white space, possibly with a comment, is known as a blank line, and Java totally ignores it.

Inheritance

In Java, classes can be derived from classes. Basically, if you need to create a new class and here is already a class that has some of the code you require, then it is possible to derive your new class from the already existing code.

This concept allows you to reuse the fields and methods of the existing class without having to rewrite the code in a new class. In this scenario, the existing class is called the **superclass** and the derived class is called the **subclass**.

Interfaces

In Java language, an interface can be defined as a contract between objects on how to communicate with each other. Interfaces play a vital role when it comes to the concept of inheritance.

An interface defines the methods, a deriving class (subclass) should use. But the implementation of the methods is totally up to the subclass.

Objects & Classes

Java is an Object-Oriented Language. As a language that has the Object-Oriented feature, Java supports the following fundamental concepts:

- Polymorphism
- Inheritance
- Encapsulation
- Abstraction
- Classes
- Objects
- Instance
- Method
- Message Parsing

In this chapter, we will look into the concepts - Classes and Objects.

- **Object** - Objects have states and behaviors. Example: A dog has states - color, name, breed as well as behaviors – wagging the tail, barking, eating. An object is an instance of a class.

- **Class** - A class can be defined as a template/blueprint that describes the behavior/state that the object of its type support.

Objects in Java

Let us now look deep into what are objects. If we consider the real-world, we can find many objects around us, cars, dogs, humans, etc. All these objects have a state and a behavior. If we consider a dog, then its state is - name, breed, color, and the behavior is - barking, wagging the tail, running. If you compare the software object with a real-world object, they have very similar characteristics.

Software objects also have a state and a behavior. A software object's state is stored in fields and behavior is shown via methods. So in software development, methods operate on the internal state of an object and the object-to-object communication is done via methods.

Classes in Java

A class is a blueprint from which individual objects are created. Following is a sample of a class.

```
public class Dog{
String breed;
int ageC
String color;
void barking(){
}
```

```
void hungry(){
}
void sleeping(){
}
}
```

A class can contain any of the following variable types.

- **Local variables:** Variables defined inside methods, constructors or blocks are called local variables. The variable will be declared and initialized within the method and the variable will be destroyed when the method has completed.
- **Instance variables:** Instance variables are variables within a class but outside any method. These variables are initialized when the class is instantiated. Instance variables can be accessed from inside any method, constructor or blocks of that particular class.
- **Class variables:** Class variables are variables declared within a class, outside any method, with the static keyword.

A class can have any number of methods to access the value of various kinds of methods. In the above example, barking(), hungry() and sleeping() are methods.

Following are some of the important topics that need to be discussed when looking into classes of the Java Language.

Constructors

When discussing about classes, one of the most important sub topic would be constructors. Every class has a constructor. If we do not explicitly write a constructor for a class, the Java compiler builds a default constructor for that class.

Each time a new object is created, at least one constructor will be invoked. The main rule of constructors is that they should have the same name as the class. A class can have more than one constructor.

Following is an example of a constructor:

```
public class Puppy{
public Puppy(){
}
public Puppy(String name){
// This constructor has one parameter, name.
}
}
```

Java also supports Singleton Classes where you would be able to create only one instance of a class.

Note: We have two different types of constructors. We are going to discuss constructors in detail in the subsequent chapters.

How to Use Singleton Class?

The Singleton's purpose is to control object creation, limiting the number of objects to only one. Since there is only one Singleton instance, any instance fields of a Singleton will occur only once per class, just like static fields. Singletons often control access to resources, such as database connections or sockets.

For example, if you have a license for only one connection for your database or your JDBC driver has trouble with multithreading, the Singleton makes sure that only one connection is made or that only one thread can access the connection at a time.

Implementing Singletons

Example 1

The easiest implementation consists of a private constructor and a field to hold its result, and a static access or method with a name like getInstance().

The private field can be assigned from within a static initializer block or, more simply, using an initializer. The getInstance( ) method (which must be public) then simply returns this instance –

```
// File Name: Singleton.java
public class Singleton {
private static Singleton singleton = new
Singleton( );
/* A private Constructor prevents any other
```

```
 * class from instantiating.
 */
private Singleton(){ }
/* Static 'instance' method */
public static Singleton getInstance( ) {
return singleton;
}
/* Other methods protected by singleton-ness */
protected static void demoMethod( ) {
System.out.println("demoMethod for singleton");
}
}
```

Here is the main program file, where we will create a singleton object:

```
// File Name: SingletonDemo.java
public class SingletonDemo {
public static void main(String[] args) {
Singleton tmp = Singleton.getInstance( );
tmp.demoMethod( );
}
}
```

This will produce the following result –

demoMethod for singleton

Example 2

Following implementation shows a classic Singleton design pattern:

```
public class ClassicSingleton {
private static ClassicSingleton instance = null;
private ClassicSingleton() {
// Exists only to defeat instantiation.
}
public static ClassicSingleton getInstance() {
if(instance == null) {
instance = new ClassicSingleton();
}
return instance;
}
}
```

The ClassicSingleton class maintains a static reference to the lone singleton instance and returns that reference from the static getInstance() method.

Here, ClassicSingleton class employs a technique known as lazy instantiation to create the singleton; as a result, the singleton instance is not created until the getInstance() method is called for the first time. This technique ensures that singleton instances are created only when needed.

Creating an Object

As mentioned previously, a class provides the blueprints for objects. So basically, an object is created from a class. In Java, the new keyword is used to create new objects.

There are three steps when creating an object from a class:

- **Declaration:** A variable declaration with a variable

name with an object type.

- **Instantiation:** The 'new' keyword is used to create the object.
- **Initialization:** The 'new' keyword is followed by a call to a constructor. This call initializes the new object.

Following is an example of creating an object:

```java
public class Puppy{
public Puppy(String name){
// This constructor has one parameter, name.
System.out.println("Passed Name is :" + name );
}
public static void main(String []args){
// Following statement would create an object
myPuppy
Puppy myPuppy = new Puppy( "tommy" );
}
}
```

If we compile and run the above program, then it will produce the following result:

Passed Name is :tommy

Accessing Instance Variables and Methods

Instance variables and methods are accessed via created objects. To access an instance variable, following is the fully qualified path:

```
/* First create an object */
ObjectReference = new Constructor();

/* Now call a variable as follows */
ObjectReference.variableName;

/* Now you can call a class method as follows */
ObjectReference.MethodName();
```

Example

This example explains how to access instance variables and methods of a class.

```
public class Puppy{
int puppyAge;
public Puppy(String name){
// This constructor has one parameter, name.
System.out.println("Name chosen is :" + name );
}
public void setAge( int age ){
puppyAge = age;
}
public int getAge( ){
System.out.println("Puppy's age is :" + puppyAge
);
return puppyAge;
}
public static void main(String []args){
/* Object creation */
Puppy myPuppy = new Puppy( "tommy" );
/* Call class method to set puppy's age */
myPuppy.setAge( 2 );
/* Call another class method to get puppy's age */
myPuppy.getAge( );
```

```
/* You can access instance variable as followsas
well */ System.out.println("Variable Value :" +
myPuppy.puppyAge );
   }
}
```

If we compile and run the above program, then it will produce the following result:

Name chosen is :tommy

Puppy's age is :2

Variable Value :2

Source File Declaration Rules

As the last part of this chapter, let's now look into the source file declaration rules. These rules are essential when declaring classes, *import* statements and *package* statements in a source file.

- There can be only one public class per source file.
- A source file can have multiple non-public classes.
- The public class name should be the name of the source file as well which should be appended by **.java** at the end. For example: the class name is *public class Employee{}* then the source file should be as Employee.java.
- If the class is defined inside a package, then the package statement should be the first statement in the source file.
- If import statements are present, then they must be

written between the package statement and the class declaration. If there are no package statements, then the import statement should be the first line in the source file.

- Import and package statements will imply to all the classes present in the source file. It is not possible to declare different import and/or package statements to different classes in the source file.

Classes have several access levels and there are different types of classes; abstract classes, final classes, etc. We will be explaining about all these in the access modifiers chapter.

Apart from the above mentioned types of classes, Java also has some special classes called Inner classes and Anonymous classes.

Java Package

In simple words, it is a way of categorizing the classes and interfaces. When developing applications in Java, hundreds of classes and interfaces will be written, therefore categorizing these classes is a must as well as makes life much easier.

Import Statements

In Java if a fully qualified name, which includes the package and the class name is given, then the compiler can easily locate the source code or classes. Import statement is a way of giving the proper location for the compiler to find that particular class.

For example, the following line would ask the compiler to load all the classes available in directory java_installation/-java/io:

```
import java.io.*;
```

A Simple Case Study

For our case study, we will be creating two classes. They are Employee and EmployeeTest.

First open notepad and add the following code. Remember this is the Employee class and the class is a public class. Now, save this source file with the name Employee.java.

The Employee class has four instance variables - name, age, designation and salary. The class has one explicitly defined constructor, which takes a parameter.

```
import java.io.*;
public class Employee{
String name;
int age;
String designation;
double salary;
// This is the constructorof the class Employee
public Employee(String name){
this.name = name;
}
// Assign the age of the Employee to the variable
```

```
age. public void empAge(int empAge){
age = empAge;
}
/* Assign the designation to the variable
designation.*/
public void empDesignation(String empDesig){
designation = empDesig;
}
/* Assign the salary to the variable    salary.*/
public void empSalary(double empSalary){
salary = empSalary;
}
/* Print the Employee details */
public void printEmployee(){
System.out.println("Name:"+ name );
System.out.println("Age:" + age );
System.out.println("Designation:" + designation );
System.out.println("Salary:" + salary);
}
}
```

As mentioned previously in this book, processing starts from the main method. Therefore, in order for us to run this Employee class there should be a main method and objects should be created. We will be creating a separate class for these tasks.

Following is the *EmployeeTest* class, which creates two instances of the class Employee and invokes the methods for each object to assign values for each variable.

Save the following code in EmployeeTest.java file.

```java
import java.io.*;
public class EmployeeTest{
public static void main(String args[]){
/* Create two objects using constructor */
Employee empOne = new Employee("James Smith");
Employee empTwo = newEmployee("Mary Anne");
// Invoking methods for each object created
empOne.empAge(26);
empOne.empDesignation("Senior Software Engineer");
empOne.empSalary(1000); empOne.printEmployee();
empTwo.empAge(21);
empTwo.empDesignation("Software Engineer");
empTwo.empSalary(500); empTwo.printEmployee();
} }
```

Now, compile both the classes and then run *EmployeeTest* to see the result as follows:

```
C:\>javac Employee.java
C:\> javac EmployeeTest.java C:\> java
EmployeeTest Name:James Smith
Age:26
Designation:Senior Software Engineer
Salary:1000.0
Name:Mary Anne
Age:21
Designation:Software Engineer
Salary:500.0
```

What is Next?

In the next chapter, we will discuss the basic data types in Java and how they can be used when developing Java applications.

Basic Datatypes

Variables are nothing but reserved memory locations to store values. This means that when you create a variable you reserve some space in the memory.

Based on the data type of a variable, the operating system allocates memory and decides what can be stored in the reserved memory. Therefore, by assigning different datatypes to variables, you can store integers, decimals, or characters in these variables.

There are two data types available in Java:

- Primitive Datatypes
- Reference/Object Datatypes

Primitive Datatypes

There are eight primitive datatypes supported by Java. Primitive datatypes are predefined by the language and named by a keyword. Let us now look into the eight primitive data types in detail.

byte:

- Byte data type is an 8-bit signed two's complement integer
- Minimum value is -128 (-2^7)
- Maximum value is 127 (inclusive)(2^7 -1)
- Default value is 0
- Byte datatype is used to save space in large arrays, mainly in place of integers, since a byte is four times smaller than an integer
- Example: byte a = 100 , byte b = -50

short:

- Short datatype is a 16-bit signed two's complement integer
- Minimum value is -32,768 (-2^15)
- Maximum value is 32,767 (inclusive) (2^15 -1)
- Short datatype can also be used to save memory as byte data type. A short is 2 times smaller than an integer
- Default value is 0
- Example: short s = 10000, short r = -20000

int:

- Int datatype is a 32-bit signed two's complement integer
- Minimum value is - 2,147,483,648 (-2^31)
- Maximum value is 2,147,483,647(inclusive) (2^31 -1)
- Integer is generally used as the default data type for integral values unless there is a concern about memory.

- The default value is 0
- Example: int a = 100000, int b = -200000

long:

- Long datatype is a 64-bit signed two's complement integer
- Minimum value is -9,223,372,036,854,775,808 (-2^63)
- Maximum value is 9,223,372,036,854,775,807 (inclusive) (2^63 -1)
- This type is used when a wider range than int is needed
- Default value is 0L
- Example: long a = 100000L, long b = -200000L

float:

- Float datatype is a single-precision 32-bit IEEE 754 floating point
- Float is mainly used to save memory in large arrays of floating point numbers
- Default value is 0.0f
- Float datatype is never used for precise values such as currency
- Example: float f1 = 234.5f

double:

- double datatype is a double-precision 64-bit IEEE 754 floating point
- This datatype is generally used as the default data type

for decimal values, generally the default choice
- Double datatype should never be used for precise values such as currency
- Default value is 0.0d
- Example: double d1 = 123.4

boolean:

- boolean datatype represents one bit of information
- There are only two possible values: true and false
- This datatype is used for simple flags that track true/-false conditions
- Default value is false
- Example: boolean one = true

char:

- char datatype is a single 16-bit Unicode character
- Minimum value is '\u0000' (or 0)
- Maximum value is '\uffff' (or 65,535 inclusive)
- Char datatype is used to store any character
- Example: char letterA ='A'

Reference Datatypes

- Reference variables are created using defined constructors of the classes. They are used to access objects. These variables are declared to be of a specific type that cannot be changed. For example, Employee, Puppy, etc.
- Class objects and various type of array variables come under reference datatype.

- Default value of any reference variable is null.
- A reference variable can be used to refer any object of the declared type or any compatible type.
- Example: Animal animal = new Animal("giraffe");

Java Literals

A literal is a source code representation of a fixed value. They are represented directly in the code without any computation.

Literals can be assigned to any primitive type variable. For example:

```
byte a = 68;
char a = 'A'
```

byte, int, long, and short can be expressed in decimal(base 10), hexadecimal(base 16) or octal(base 8) number systems as well. Prefix 0 is used to indicate octal, and prefix 0x indicates hexadecimal when using these number systems for literals. For example:

```
int decimal = 100; int octal = 0144; inthexa =
0x64;
```

String literals in Java are specified like they are in most other languages by enclosing a sequence of characters between a pair of double quotes. Examples of string literals are:

```
"Hello World" "two\nlines"
"\"This is in quotes\""
```

String and char types of literals can contain any Unicode characters. For example:

```
char a = '\u0001'; String a = "\u0001";
```

Java language supports few special escape sequences for String and char literals as well.

They are:

Notation	Character represented
\n	Newline (0x0a)
\r	Carriage return (0x0d)
\f	Formfeed (0x0c)
\b	Backspace (0x08)
\s	Space (0x20)
\t	tab
\"	Double quote
\'	Single quote
\\	backslash
\dddd	Octal character (ddd)
\uxxxx	Hexadecimal UNICODE character (xxxx)

This chapter explained the various data types. The next topic explains different variable types and their usage. This will give you a good understanding on how they can be used in the Java classes, interfaces, etc.

Variable Types

A variable provides us with named storage that our programs can manipulate. Each variable in Java has a specific type, which determines the size and layout of the variable's memory; the range of values that can be stored within that memory; and the set of operations that can be applied to the variable.

You must declare all variables before they can be used. Following is the basic form of a variable declaration:

```
data type variable [ = value][, variable [=
value] ...] ;
```

Here *data type* is one of Java's datatypes and *variable* is the name of the variable. To declare more than one variable of the specified type, you can use a comma-separated list.

Following are valid examples of variable declaration and initialization in Java:

```
int a, b, c;         // Declares three
ints, a, b, and c. inta = 10, b = 10; // Example
of initialization
byte B = 22; // initializes a byte type variable
B.
double pi = 3.14159; // declares and assigns a
value of PI.
char a = 'a';        // the char variable a iis
initialized with value 'a'
```

This chapter will explain various variable types available in Java Language. There are three kinds of variables in Java:

- Local variables
- Instance variables
- Class/Static variables

Local Variables

- Local variables are declared in methods, constructors, or blocks.
- Local variables are created when the method, constructor or block is entered and the variable will be destroyed once it exits the method, constructor, or block.
- Access modifiers cannot be used for local variables.
- Local variables are visible only within the declared method, constructor, or block.
- Local variables are implemented at stack level internally.
- There is no default value for local variables, so local variables should be declared and an initial value should

be assigned before the first use.

Example

Here, *age* is a local variable. This is defined inside *pupAge()* method and its scope is limited to only this method.

```
public class Test{
public void pupAge(){
int age = 0;
age = age + 7;
System.out.println("Puppy age is : " + age);
}
public static void main(String args[]){ Test test
= new Test(); test.pupAge();
}
}
```

This will produce the following result:

Puppy age is: 7

Example

Following example uses *age* without initializing it, so it would give an error at the time of compilation.

```
public class Test{
public void pupAge(){
int age;
age = age + 7;
System.out.println("Puppy age is : " + age);
}
```

```
public static void main(String args[])
{
Test test = new Test();
test.pupAge();
}
}
```

This will produce the following error while compiling it:

Test.java:4:variable number might not have been initialized age= age + 7;

∧

1 error

Instance Variables

- Instance variables are declared in a class, but outside a method, constructor or any block.
- When a space is allocated for an object in the heap, a slot for each instance variable value is created.
- Instance variables are created when an object is created with the use of the keyword 'new' and destroyed when the object is destroyed.
- Instance variables hold values that must be referenced by more than one method, constructor or block, or essential parts of an object's state that must be present throughout the class.
- Instance variables can be declared in class level before or after use.
- Access modifiers can be given for instance variables.
- The instance variables are visible for all methods, constructors and block in the class. Normally, it is recom-

mended to make these variables private (access level). However, visibility for subclasses can be given for these variables with the use of access modifiers.

- Instance variables have default values. For numbers, the default value is 0, for Booleans it is false, and for object references it is null. Values can be assigned during the declaration or within the constructor.
- Instance variables can be accessed directly by calling the variable name inside the class. However, within static methods (when instance variables are given accessibility), they should be called using the fully qualified name. *ObjectReference.VariableName.*

Example

```java
import java.io.*;
public class Employee{
// this instance variable is visible for any
child class. public String name;
// salary variable is visible in Employee class
only. private double salary;
// The name variable is assigned in the
constructor. public Employee (String empName){
name = empName;
}
// The salary variable is assigned a value.
public void setSalary(double empSal){
salary = empSal;
}
// This method prints the employee details.
public void printEmp(){
System.out.println("name : "+ name );
System.out.println("salary :" + salary);
}
```

```
public static void main(String args[]){ Employee
empOne = new Employee("Ransika");
empOne.setSalary(1000);
empOne.printEmp();
}
}
```

This will produce the following result:

name : Ransika salary :1000.0

Class/static Variables

- Class variables also known as static variables are declared with the *static* keyword in a class, but outside a method, constructor or a block.
- There would only be one copy of each class variable per class, regardless of how many objects are created from it.
- Static variables are rarely used other than being declared as constants. Constants are variables that are declared as public/private, final, and static. Constant variables never change from their initial value.
- Static variables are stored in the static memory. It is rare to use static variables other than declared final and used as either public or private constants.
- Static variables are created when the program starts and destroyed when the program stops.
- Visibility is similar to instance variables. However, most static variables are declared public since they must be available for users of the class.

- Default values are same as instance variables. For numbers, the default value is 0; for Booleans, it is false; and for object references, it is null. Values can be assigned during the declaration or within the constructor. Additionally, values can be assigned in special static initializer blocks.
- Static variables can be accessed by calling with the class name *ClassName.VariableName*.
- When declaring class variables as public static final, then variable names (constants) are all in upper case. If the static variables are not public and final, the naming syntax is the same as instance and local variables.

Example

```java
import java.io.*;
public class Employee{
// salary variable is a private static variable
private static double salary;
// DEPARTMENT is a constant
public static final String DEPARTMENT =
"Development ";
public static void main(String args[]){
salary = 1000;
System.out.println(DEPARTMENT + "average
salary:"+ salary);
}
}
```

This will produce the following result:

Development average salary:1000

Note: If the variables are accessed from an outside class, the constant should be accessed as Employee.DEPARTMENT

Modifier Types

Modifiers are keywords that you add to those definitions to change their meanings. Java language has a wide variety of modifiers, including the following:

- Java Access Modifiers
- Non Access Modifiers

Java Access Modifiers

Java provides a number of access modifiers to set access levels for classes, variables, methods, and constructors. The four access levels are:

- Visible to the package, the default. No modifiers are needed.
- Visible to the class only (private).
- Visible to the world (public).
- Visible to the package and all subclasses (protected).

Default Access Modifier– No Keyword

Default access modifier means we do not explicitly declare

an access modifier for a class, field, method, etc.

A variable or method declared without any access control modifier is available to any other class in the same package. The fields in an interface are implicitly public static final and the methods in an interface are by default public.

Example

Variables and methods can be declared without any modifiers, as in the following examples:

```
String version = "1.5.1";
boolean processOrder() {
return true;
}
```

Private Access Modifier – Private

Methods, variables, and constructors that are declared private can only be accessed within the declared class itself.

Private access modifier is the most restrictive access level. Class and interfaces cannot be private.

Variables that are declared private can be accessed outside the class, if public getter methods are present in the class.

Using the private modifier is the main way that an object encapsulates itself and hides data from the outside world.

Example

The following class uses private access control:

```
public class Logger { private
String format; public
String getFormat() {
return this.format;
}
public void setFormat(String format) {
this.format = format;
}
}
```

Here, the *format* variable of the Logger class is private, so there's no way for other classes to retrieve or set its value directly.

So, to make this variable available to the outside world, we defined two public methods: *getFormat()*, which returns the value of format, and *setFormat(String)*, which sets its value.

Public Access Modifier - Public

A class, method, constructor, interface, etc. declared public can be accessed from any other class. Therefore, fields, methods, blocks declared inside a public class can be accessed from any class belonging to the Java Universe.

However, if the public class we are trying to access is in a different package, then the public class still needs to be imported. Because of class inheritance, all public methods and variables of a class are inherited by its subclasses.

Example

The following function uses public access control:

```
public static void main(String[] arguments) {
// ...
}
```

The main() method of an application has to be public. Otherwise, it could not be called by a Java interpreter (such as java) to run the class.

Protected Access Modifier – Protected

Variables, methods, and constructors, which are declared protected in a superclass can be accessed only by the sub-classes in other package or any class within the package of the protected members' class.

The protected access modifier cannot be applied to class and interfaces. Methods, fields can be declared protected, how-ever methods and fields in a interface cannot be declared protected.

Protected access gives the subclass a chance to use the helper method or variable, while preventing a non related class from trying to use it.

Example

The following parent class uses protected access control, to allow its child class override *openSpeaker()* method:

```
class AudioPlayer {
protected boolean openSpeaker(Speaker sp) {
// implementation details
}
}
class StreamingAudioPlayer {
boolean openSpeaker(Speaker sp) {
// implementation details
}
}
```

Here, if we define *openSpeaker()* method as private, then it would not be accessible from any other class other than *AudioPlayer*. If we define it as public, then it would become accessible to all the outside world. But our intention is to expose this method to its subclass only, that's why we have used *protected* modifier.

Access Control and Inheritance

The following rules for inherited methods are enforced:

- Methods declared public in a superclass also must be public in all subclasses.
- Methods declared protected in a superclass must either be protected or public in subclasses; they cannot be

private.
- Methods declared private are not inherited at all, so there is no rule for them.

Java Non-Access Modifiers

Java provides a number of non-access modifiers to achieve many other functionalities.

- The *static* modifier for creating class methods and variables.
- The *final* modifier for finalizing the implementations of classes, methods, and variables.
- The *abstract* modifier for creating abstract classes and methods.
- The *synchronized* and *volatile* modifiers, which are used for threads.

The Static Modifier

Static Variables

The *static* keyword is used to create variables that will exist independently of any instances created for the class. Only one copy of the static variable exists regardless of the number of instances of the class.

Static variables are also known as class variables. Local variables cannot be declared static.

Static Methods

The *static* keyword is used to create methods that will exist independently of any instances created for the class.

Static methods do not use any instance variables of any object of the class they are defined in. Static methods take all the data from parameters and compute something from those parameters, with no reference to variables.

Class variables and methods can be accessed using the class name followed by a dot and the name of the variable or method.

Example

The static modifier is used to create class methods and variables, as in the following example:

```java
public class InstanceCounter {
private static int numInstances = 0;
protected static int getCount() {
return numInstances;
}
private static void addInstance() {
numInstances++;
}
InstanceCounter() { InstanceCounter.addInstance();
}
public static void main(String[] arguments) {
System.out.println("Starting with " +
InstanceCounter.getCount() + "instances"); for
(int i = 0; i < 500; ++i){
new InstanceCounter();
}
```

```
System.out.println("Created " +
InstanceCounter.getCount() + "instances");
}
}
```

This will produce the following result:

Started with 0 instances

Created 500 instances

The Final Modifier

Final Variables

A final variable can be explicitly initialized only once. A reference variable declared final can never be reassigned to refer to an different object.

However, the data within the object can be changed. So, the state of the object can be changed but not the reference.

With variables, the *final* modifier often is used with *static* to make the constant a class variable.

Example

```
public class Test{
final int value = 10;
// The following are examples of declaring
constants:
public static final int BOXWIDTH = 6;
```

```
static final String TITLE = "Manager";
public void changeValue(){
value = 12; //will give an error
}
}
```

Final Methods

A final method cannot be overridden by any subclasses. As mentioned previously, the final modifier prevents a method from being modified in a subclass.

The main intention of making a method final would be that the content of the method should not be changed by any outsider.

Example

You declare methods using the *final* modifier in the class declaration, as in the following example:

```
public class Test{
public final void changeName(){
// body of method
}
}
```

Final Classes

The main purpose of using a class being declared as *final* is to prevent the class from being subclassed. If a class is marked as final then no class can inherit any feature from the final class.

Example

```
public final class Test {
// body of class
 }
```

The Abstract Modifier

Abstract Class

An abstract class can never be instantiated. If a class is declared as abstract then the sole purpose is for the class to be extended.

A class cannot be both abstract and final (since a final class cannot be extended). If a class contains abstract methods then the class should be declared abstract. Otherwise, a compile error will be thrown.

An abstract class may contain both abstract methods as well normal methods.

Example

abstract class Caravan{ private double price; private String model; private String year;

```
public abstract void goFast();
//an abstract method
public abstract void changeColor();
}
```

Abstract Methods

An abstract method is a method declared without any implementation. The methods body (implementation) is provided by the subclass. Abstract methods can never be final or strict.

Any class that extends an abstract class must implement all the abstract methods of the super class, unless the subclass is also an abstract class.

If a class contains one or more abstract methods, then the class must be declared abstract. An abstract class does not need to contain abstract methods.

The abstract method ends with a semicolon. Example: public abstract sample();

Example

```
public abstract class SuperClass{
abstract void m(); //abstract method
}
class SubClass extends SuperClass{
// implements the abstract method void m(){
. . . . . . . .
```

```
}
}
```

The Synchronized Modifier

The synchronized keyword used to indicate that a method can be accessed by only one thread at a time. The synchronized modifier can be applied with any of the four access level modifiers.

Example

```
public synchronized void showDetails(){
.......
}
```

The Transient Modifier

An instance variable is marked transient to indicate the JVM to skip the particular variable when serializing the object containing it.

This modifier is included in the statement that creates the variable, preceding the class or data type of the variable.

Example

```
public transient int limit = 55;  // will not
persist public int b; // will persist
```

The Volatile Modifier

The volatile modifier is used to let the JVM know that a thread accessing the variable must always merge its own private copy of the variable with the master copy in the memory.

Accessing a volatile variable synchronizes all the cached copied of the variables in the main memory. Volatile can only be applied to instance variables, which are of type object or private. A volatile object reference can be null.

Example

```
public class MyRunnable implements Runnable{
private volatile boolean active;
public void run(){
active = true;
while (active){ // line 1
// some code here
}
}
public void stop(){
active = false; // line 2
}
}
```

Usually, run() is called in one thread (the one you start using the Runnable), and stop() is called from another thread. If in line 1, the cached value of active is used, the loop may not stop when you set active to false in line 2. That's when you want to use *volatile*.

To use a modifier, you include its keyword in the definition of a class, method, or variable. The modifier precedes the rest of the statement, as in the following example.

```
public class className {
// ...
}
private boolean myFlag;
static final double weeks = 9.5;
protected static final int BOXWIDTH = 42;
public static void main(String[] arguments) {
// body of method
}
```

Access Control Modifiers

Java provides a number of access modifiers to set access levels for classes, variables, methods and constructors. The four access levels are:

- Visible to the package, the default. No modifiers are needed.
- Visible to the class only (private).
- Visible to the world (public).
- Visible to the package and all subclasses (protected).

Non-Access Modifiers

Java provides a number of non-access modifiers to achieve many other functionality.

- The *static* modifier for creating class methods and

variables.
- The *final* modifier for finalizing the implementations of classes, methods, and variables.
- The *abstract* modifier for creating abstract classes and methods.
- The *synchronized* and *volatile* modifiers, which are used for threads.

Basic Operators

Java provides a rich set of operators to manipulate variables. We can divide all the Java operators into the following groups:

- Arithmetic Operators
- Relational Operators
- Bitwise Operators
- Logical Operators
- Assignment Operators
- Misc Operators

The Arithmetic Operators

Arithmetic operators are used in mathematical expressions in the same way that they are used in algebra. The following table lists the arithmetic operators:

Assume integer variable A holds 10 and variable B holds 20, then:

Operator and Example

- **+ (Addition)** Adds values on either side of the operator
- **- (Subtraction)** Subtracts right-hand operand from left-hand operand
- *** (Multiplication)** Multiplies values on either side of the operator
- **/ (Division)** Divides left-hand operand byright-hand operand
- **% (Modulus)** Divides left-hand operand by right-hand operand and returns remainder
- **++ (Increment)** Increases the value of operand by 1
- **— (Decrement)** Decreases the value of operand by 1

Example

The following program is a simple example which demonstrates the arithmetic operators. Copy and paste the following Java program in Test.java file, and compile and run this program:

```java
public class Test {
public static void main(String args[]) {
int a = 10;
intb = 20;
int c = 25;
int d = 25;
System.out.println("a + b = "+ (a + b) );
System.out.println("a - b = " + (a - b) );
System.out.println("a * b = " + (a * b) );
System.out.println("b / a = " + (b / a) );
System.out.println("b % a = " + (b % a) );
System.out.println("c % a = " + (c % a) );
System.out.println("a++  = "+  (a++) );
System.out.println("b--  = " +  (a--) );
```

```
// Check the difference in d++ and ++d
 System.out.println("d++  = " +  (d++) );
 System.out.println("++d  = " +  (++d) );
 }
 }
```

This will produce the following result:

a + b = 30

a - b = -10

a * b = 200

b / a = 2

b % a = 0

c % a = 5

a++= 10

b- -= 11

d++= 25

++d= 27

The Relational Operators

There are following relational operators supported by Java language. Assume variable A holds 10 and variable B holds 20, then:

Operator and Description

- **==** **(equal to)** Checks if the values of two operands are equal or not, if yes then condition becomes true.
- **!=** **(not equal to)** Checks if the values of two operands

are equal or not, if values are not equal then condition becomes true.

- **>(greater than)** Checks if the value of left operand is greater than the value of right operand, if yes then condition becomes true.
- **< (less than)** Checks if the value of left operand is less than the value of right operand, if yes then condition becomes true.
- **>=(greater than or equal to)** Checks if the value of left operand is greater than or equal to the value of right operand, if yes then condition becomes true.
- **<= (less than or equal to)** Checks if the value of left operand is less than or equal to the value of right operand, if yes then condition becomes true.

Example

The following program is a simple example that demonstrates the relational operators. Copy and paste the following Java program in Test.java file and compile and run this program.

```java
public class Test {
public static void main(String args[]) {
int a = 10;
int b = 20;
System.out.println("a == b = " + (a== b) );
System.out.println("a!= b = " + (a != b) );
System.out.println("a >b = " + (a > b) );
System.out.println("a< b = " + (a < b) );
System.out.println("b >= a = " + (b >= a) );
System.out.println("b <= a = " + (b<= a) );
```

```
}
}
```

This will produce the following result:

```
a == b = false a !=b = true
   a > b = false
   a < b = true
   b >= a = true
   b <= a = false
```

The Bitwise Operators

Java defines several bitwise operators, which can be applied to the integer types, long, int, short, char, and byte.

Bitwise operator works on bits and performs bit-by-bit operation. Assume if a = 60 and b = 13; now in binary format they will be as follows:

```
a = 0011 1100 b =0000 1101
————————-
a&b = 0000 1100
a|b= 0011 1101
a^b = 0011 0001
~a = 1100 0011
```

The following table lists the bitwise operators:

Assume integer variable A holds 60 and variable B holds 13 then:

Operator and Description

- **& (bitwise and)** Binary AND Operator copies a bit to the result if it exists in both operands.
- **| (bitwise or)** Binary OR Operator copies a bit if it exists in either operand.
- **∧ (bitwise XOR)** Binary XOR Operator copies the bit if it is set in one operand but not both.
- **~ (bitwise compliment)** Binary Ones Complement Operator is unary and has the effect of 'flipping' bits.
- **« (left shift)** Binary Left Shift Operator. The left operands value is moved left by the number of bits specified by the right operand.
- **» (right shift)** Binary Right Shift Operator. The left operands value is moved right by the number of bits specified by the right operand.
- **»> (zero fill right shift)** Shift right zero fill operator. The left operands value is moved right by the number of bits specified by the right operand and shifted values are filled up with zeros.

Example

The following program is a simple example that demonstrates the bitwise operators. Copy and paste the following Java program in Test.java file and compile and run this program:

```java
public class Test {
public static void main(String args[]) {
```

```
int a = 60;    /* 60 = 0011 1100 */
int b = 13;    /* 13 =0000 1101 */
int c = 0;

c = a & b;        /* 12 =0000 1100 */
System.out.println("a& b = " + c );

c = a | b;        /* 61 =0011 1101 */
System.out.println("a| b = " + c );

c = a ^ b;        /* 49= 0011 0001 */
System.out.println("a^ b = " + c );

c = ~a; /*-61 = 1100 0011 */
System.out.println("~a= " + c );

c = a <<2;      /* 240 = 1111 0000 */
System.out.println("a<< 2 = " + c );

c = a >>2;      /* 15 = 1111 */
System.out.println("a>> 2 = " + c );

c = a >>> 2;    /* 15 =0000 1111 */
System.out.println("a>>> 2 = " + c );
}
}
```

This will produce the following result:

```
a & b = 12
   a | b =61
   a ^ b = 49
   ~a = -61
   a « 2 = 240
   a » 15
```

a »> 15

The Logical Operators

The following table lists the logical operators:

Assume Boolean variables A holds true and variable B holds false, then:

Description

- **&& (logical and)** Called Logical AND operator. If both the operands are non-zero, then the condition becomes true.
- **|| (logical or)** Called Logical OR Operator. If any of the two operands are non-zero, then the condition becomes true.
- **! (logical not)** Called Logical NOT Operator. Use to reverses the logical state of its operand. If a condition is true then Logical NOT operator will make false.

Example

The following simple example program demonstrates the logical operators. Copy and paste the following Java program in Test.java file and compile and run this program:

```
public class Test {
public static void main(String args[]) {
boolean a = true;
boolean b = false;
```

```
System.out.println("a && b = " + (a&&b));
System.out.println("a|| b = " + (a||b) );
System.out.println("!(a && b) = " + !(a && b));
}
}
```

This will produce the following result

a && b = false

a ||b = true

!(a && b)= true

The Assignment Operators

Following are the assignment operators supported by Java language:

Operator and Description

- = Simple assignment operator. Assigns values from right side operands to left side operand.
- += Add AND assignment operator. It adds right operand to the left operand and assign the result to left operand.
- -= Subtract AND assignment operator. It subtracts right operand from the left operand and assign the result to left operand.
- *= Multiply AND assignment operator. It multiplies right operand with the left operand and assign the result to left operand.
- /= Divide AND assignment operator. It divides left operand with the right operand and assign the result to

left operand.

- **%=** Modulus AND assignment operator. It takes modulus using two operands and assign the result to left operand.
- **«=** Left shift AND assignment operator.
- **»=** Right shift AND assignment operator
- **&=** Bitwise AND assignment operator.
- **^=** bitwise exclusive OR and assignment operator.
- **|=** bitwise inclusive OR and assignment operator.

Example

The following program is a simple example that demonstrates the assignment operators. Copy and paste the following Java program in Test.java file. Compile and run this program:

```java
public class Test {
public static void main(String args[]) {
int a = 10; intb = 20; int c = 0;
c = a + b;
System.out.println("c = a + b = "+ c );
c += a ;
System.out.println("c += a = " + c );
c -= a ;
System.out.println("c -= a = " + c );
c *= a ;
System.out.println("c *= a = " + c );
a = 10;
c = 15;
c /= a ;
System.out.println("c /= a = " + c );
a = 10;
```

```
c = 15;
c %= a ;
System.out.println("c %= a = " + c );
c <<= 2 ;
System.out.println("c <<= 2 = " + c );
c >>= 2 ;
System.out.println("c >>= 2 = " + c );
c >>= 2 ;
System.out.println("c >>= a = " + c );
c &= a ;
System.out.println("c &= 2 = " + c );
c ^= a ;
System.out.println("c ^= a   = " + c );
c |= a ;
System.out.println("c |= a   = " + c );
}
}
```

This will produce the following result:

```
c = a + b = 30 c += a = 40

c -= a = 30

c *= a = 300

c /= a = 1

c %= a = 5

c «= 2 = 20 c »= 2 = 5

c »= 2 = 1

c &= a = 0

c ^= a = 10 c |= a = 10
```

Miscellaneous Operators

There are few other operators supported by Java Language.

Conditional Operator (? :)

Conditional operator is also known as the **ternary operator**. This operator consists of three operands and is used to evaluate Boolean expressions. The goal of the operator is to decide, which value should be assigned to the variable. The operator is written as:

```
variable x = (expression) ? value if true: value
if false
```

Following is an example:

```
public class Test {
public static void main(String args[]){
int a, b;
a = 10;
b = (a == 1)? 20: 30;
System.out.println( "Value of b is : " +  b );
b = (a == 10)? 20: 30;
System.out.println( "Value of b is : " + b );
}
```

This will produce the following result:

Value of b is: 30

Value of b is : 20

instance of Operator

This operator is used only for object reference variables. The operator checks whether the object is of a particular type (class type or interface type). instanceof operator is written as:

```
( Object reference variable ) instanceof
(class/interface type)
```

If the object referred by the variable on the left side of the operator passes the IS-A check for the class/interface type on the right side, then the result will be true. Following is an example:

```
public class Test {
public static void main(String args[]){
String name = "James";
// following will return true since name is type
of String
boolean result = name instanceof String;
System.out.println( result );
}
}
```

This will produce the following result:

true

This operator will still return true, if the object being compared is the assignment compatible with the type on the right. Following is one more example:

```
class Vehicle {}
public class Car extends Vehicle {
public static void main(String args[]){
Vehicle a = new Car();
```

```
boolean result = a instanceof Car;
System.out.println( result );
}
}
```

This will produce the following result:

true

Precedence of Java Operators

Operator precedence determines the grouping of terms in an expression. This affects how an expression is evaluated. Certain operators have higher precedence than others; for example, the multiplication operator has higher precedence than the addition operator:

For example, x = 7 + 3 * 2; here x is assigned 13, not 20 because operator * has higher precedence than +, so it first gets multiplied with 3*2 and then adds into 7.

Here, operators with the highest precedence appear at the top of the table, those with the lowest appear at the bottom. Within an expression, higher precedence operators will be evaluated first.

Category	Operator	Associativity
Postfix	() [] . (dot operator)	Left to right
Unary	++ -- ! ~	Right to left
Multiplicative	* / %	Left to right
Additive	+ -	Left to right
Shift	>> >>> <<	Left to right
Relational	> >= < <=	Left to right
Equality	== !=	Left to right
Bitwise AND	&	Left to right
Bitwise XOR	^	Left to right
Bitwise OR	|	Left to right
Logical AND	&&	Left to right
Logical OR	||	Left to right
Conditional	?:	Right to left
Assignment	= += -= *= /= %= >>= <<= &= ^= |=	Right to left

Loop Control

There may be a situation when you need to execute a block of code several number of times. In general, statements are executed sequentially: The first statement in a function is executed first, followed by the second, and so on.

Programming languages provide various control structures that allow for more complicated execution paths.

A **loop** statement allows us to execute a statement or group of statements multiple times and following is the general form of a loop statement in most of the programming languages:

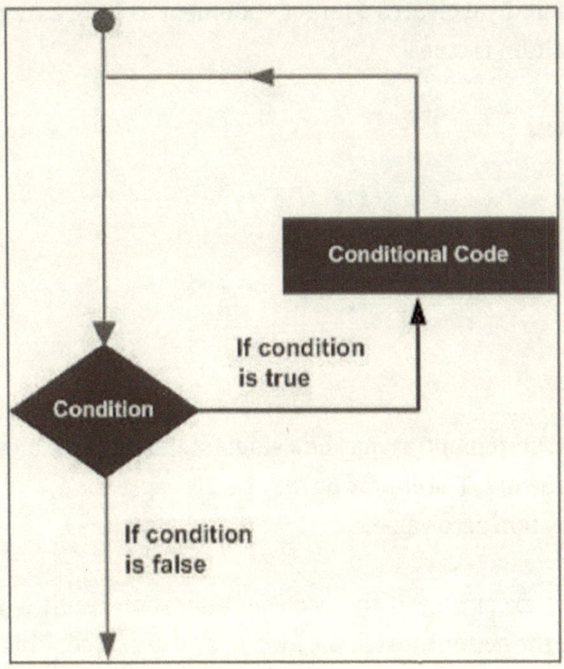

Java programming language provides the following types of loop to handle looping requirements. Click the following links to check their detail.

Loop Type	Description
while loop	Repeats a statement or group of statements while a given condition is true. It tests the condition before executing the loop body.
for loop	Execute a sequence of statements multiple times and abbreviates the code that manages the loop variable.
do...while loop	Like a while statement, except that it tests the condition at the end of the loop body.

While Loop in Java

A **while** loop statement in Java programming language repeatedly executes a target statement as long as a given condition is true.

Syntax

```
The syntax of a while loop is:
while(Boolean_expression)
{
//Statements
}
```

Here, **statement(s)** may be a single statement or a block of statements. The **condition** may be any expression, and true is any non zero value.

When executing, if the *boolean_expression* result is true, then the actions inside the loop will be executed. This will continue as long as the expression result is true.

When the condition becomes false, program control passes to the line immediately following the loop.

Flow Diagram

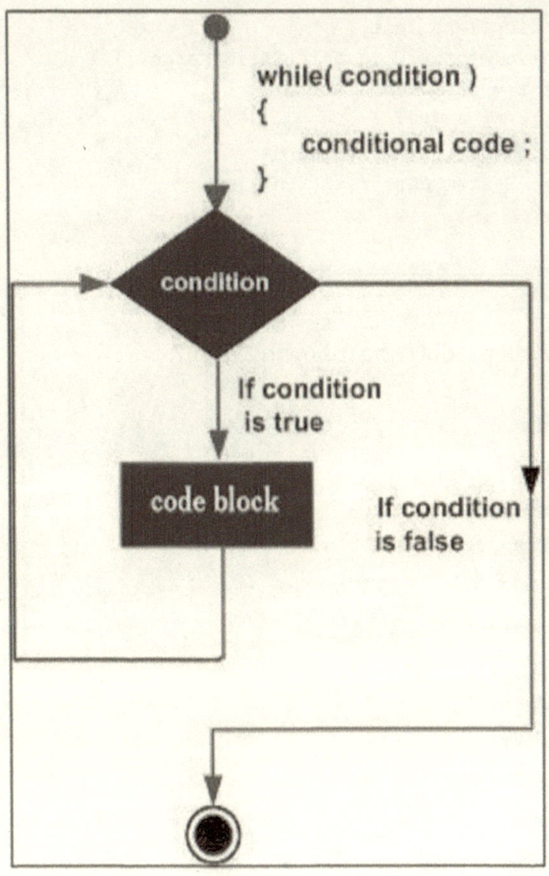

Here, key point of the *while* loop is that the loop might not ever run. When the expression is tested and the result is false, the loop body will be skipped and the first statement after the while loop will be executed.

Example

```java
public class Test {
public static void main(String args[]) {
int x = 10;
while( x < 20 ) {
System.out.print("value of x : "+ x );
x++; System.out.print("\n");
}
}
}
```

This will produce the following result:

value of x : 10

value of x : 11

value of x : 12

value of x : 13

value of x : 14

value of x : 15

value of x : 16

value of x : 17

value of x : 18

value of x : 19

for Loop in Java

A **for** loop is a repetition control structure that allows you to efficiently write a loop that needs to be executed a specific number of times. A **for** loop is useful when you know how many times a task is to be repeated.

Syntax

The syntax of a for loop is:

```
for(initialization; Boolean_expression; update)
{
//Statements
}
```

Here is the flow of control in a **for** loop:

- The **initialization** step is executed first, and only once. This step allows you to declare and initialize any loop control variables and this step ends with a semi colon (;).
- Next, the **Boolean expression** is evaluated. If it is true, the body of the loop is executed. If it is false, the body of the loop will not be executed and control jumps to the next statement past the for loop.
- After the **body** of the for loop gets executed, the control jumps back up to the update statement. This statement allows you to update any loop control variables. This statement can be left blank with a semicolon at the end.
- The Boolean expression is now evaluated again. If it is true, the loop executes and the process repeats (body of loop, then update step, then Boolean expression). After the Boolean expression is false, the for loop terminates.

Flow Diagram

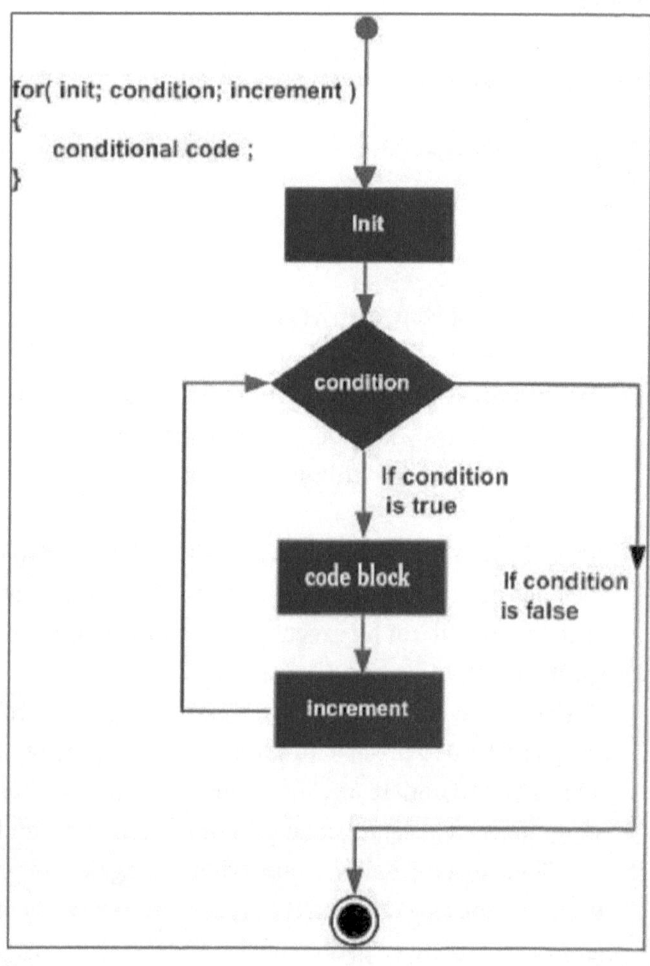

Example

Following is an example code of the for loop in Java.

```java
public class Test {
public static void main(String args[]) {
for(int x = 10; x < 20; x = x+1) {
System.out.print("value of x : " + x );
System.out.print("\n");
}
}
}
```

This will produce the following result:

value of x : 10

value of x : 11

value of x : 12

value of x : 13

value of x : 14

value of x : 15

value of x : 16

value of x : 17

value of x : 18

value of x : 19

Do While Loop in Java

A **do...while** loop is similar to a while loop, except that a do...while loop is guaranteed to execute at least one time.

Syntax

Following is the syntax of a do...while loop:

```
do
{
//Statements
}while(Boolean_expression);
```

Notice that the Boolean expression appears at the end of the loop, so the statements in the loop execute once before the Boolean is tested.

If the Boolean expression is true, the control jumps back up to do statement, and the statements in the loop execute again. This process repeats until the Boolean expression is false.

Flow Diagram

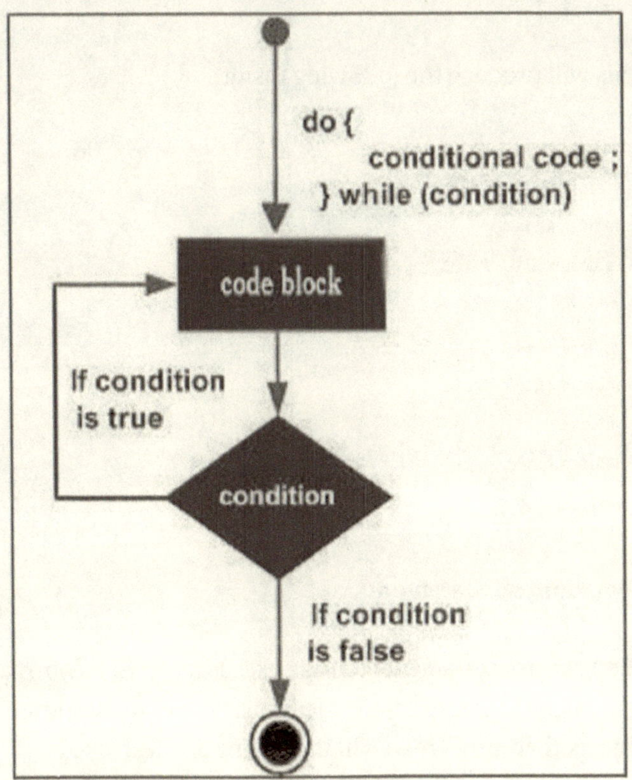

Example

```java
public class Test {
public static void main(String args[]){
int x = 10;
do{
System.out.print("value of x : "+ x );
x++; System.out.print("\n");
}while( x < 20 );
}
```

```
   }
```

This will produce the following result:

```
value of x : 10
    value of x : 11
    value of x : 12
    value of x : 13
    value of x : 14
    value of x : 15
    value of x : 16
    value of x : 17
    value of x : 18
    value of x : 19
```

Loop Control Statements

Loop control statements change execution from its normal sequence. When execution leaves a scope, all automatic objects that were created in that scope are destroyed.

Java supports the following control statements. Click the following links to check their detail.

Control Statement	Description
break statement	Terminates the loop or switch statement and transfers execution to the statement immediately following the loop or switch.
continue statement	Causes the loop to skip the remainder of its body and immediately retest its condition prior to reiterating.

Break Statement in Java

The **break** statement in Java programming language has the following two usages:

- When the **break** statement is encountered inside a loop, the loop is immediately terminated and the program control resumes at the next statement following the loop.
- It can be used to terminate a case in the **switch** statement (covered in the next chapter).

Syntax

The syntax of a break is a single statement inside any loop:

```
break;
```

Flow Diagram

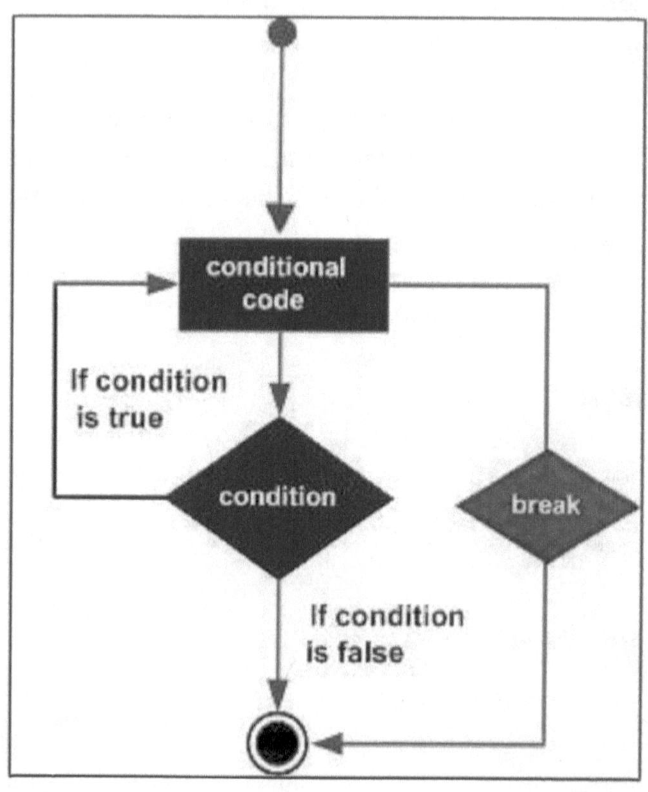

Example

```
public class Test {
public static void main(String args[]) {
int [] numbers = {10, 20, 30, 40, 50};
for(int x : numbers ) {
if( x == 30 ) {
break;
}
System.out.print( x ); System.out.print("\n");
```

```
    }
  }
}
```

This will produce the following result:

```
10

20
```

Continue Statement in Java

The **continue** keyword can be used in any of the loop control structures. It causes the loop to immediately jump to the next iteration of the loop.

- In a for loop, the continue keyword causes control to immediately jump to the update statement.
- In a while loop or do/while loop, control immediately jumps to the Boolean expression.

Syntax

The syntax of a continue is a single statement inside any loop:

```
continue;
```

Flow Diagram

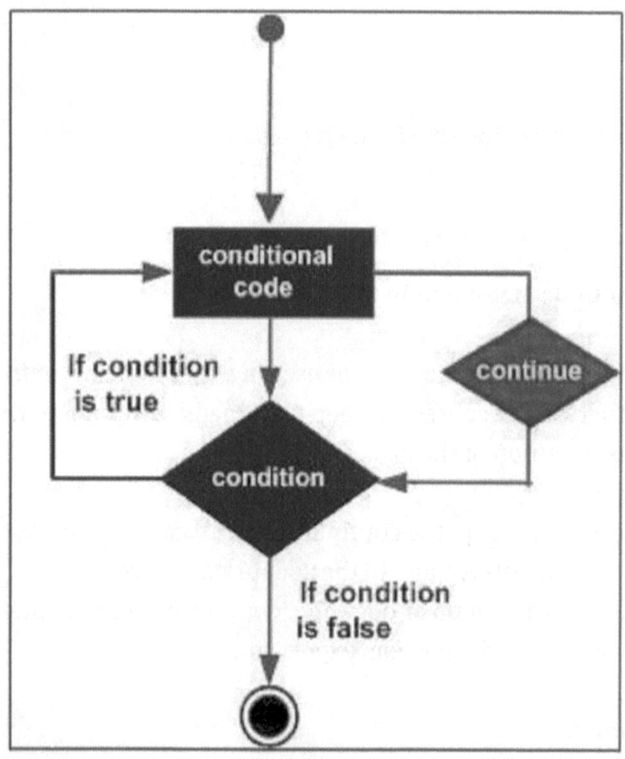

Example

```java
public class Test {
public static void main(String args[]) {
int [] numbers = {10, 20, 30, 40, 50};
for(int x : numbers ) {
if( x == 30 ){
continue;
}
System.out.print( x ); System.out.print("\n");
}
```

```
}
}
```

This will produce the following result:

```
10

20

40

50
```

Enhanced for loop in Java

As of Java 5, the enhanced for loop was introduced. This is mainly used to traverse collection of elements including arrays.

Syntax

Following is the syntax of enhanced for loop:

```
for(declaration : expression)
{
//Statements
}
```

- **Declaration:** The newly declared block variable, is of a type compatible with the elements of the array you are accessing. The variable will be available within the for block and its value would be the same as the current array element.
- **Expression:** This evaluates to the array you need to

loop through. The expression can be an array variable or method call that returns an array.

Example

```
public class Test {
public static void main(String args[]){
int [] numbers = {10, 20, 30, 40, 50};
for(int x : numbers ){ System.out.print( x );
System.out.print(",");
} System.out.print("\n");
String [] names ={"James", "Larry", "Tom",
"Lacy"};
for( String name : names ) { System.out.print(
name );
System.out.print(",");
}
}
}
```

This will produce the following result:

10,20,30,40,50,

James,Larry,Tom,Lacy,

What is Next?

In the following chapter, we will be learning about decision making statements in Java programming.

Decision Making

Decision making structures have one or more conditions to be evaluated or tested by the program, along with a statement or statements that are to be executed if the condition is determined to be true, and optionally, other statements to be executed if the condition is determined to be false.

Following is the general form of a typical decision making structure found in most of the programming languages:

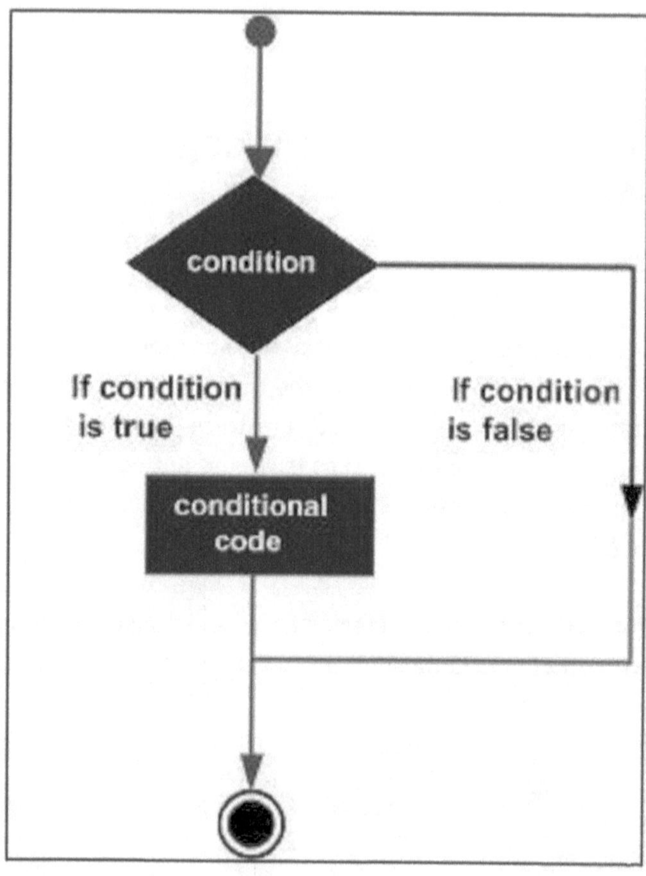

Java programming language provides following types of decision making statements. Click the following links to check their detail.

Statement	Description
if statement	An if statement consists of a Boolean expression followed by one or more statements.
if...else statement	An if statement can be followed by an optional else statement, which executes when the Boolean expression is false.

nested if statements	You can use one if or else if statement inside another if or else if statement(s).
switch statement	A switch statement allows a variable to be tested for equality against a list of values.

If Statement in Java

An **if** statement consists of a Boolean expression followed by one or more statements.

Syntax

Following is the syntax of an if statement:

```
if(Boolean_expression)
{
//Statements will execute if the Boolean
expression is true
}
```

If the Boolean expression evaluates to true then the block of code inside the if statement will be executed. If not, the first set of code after the end of the if statement (after the closing curly brace) will be executed

Flow Diagram

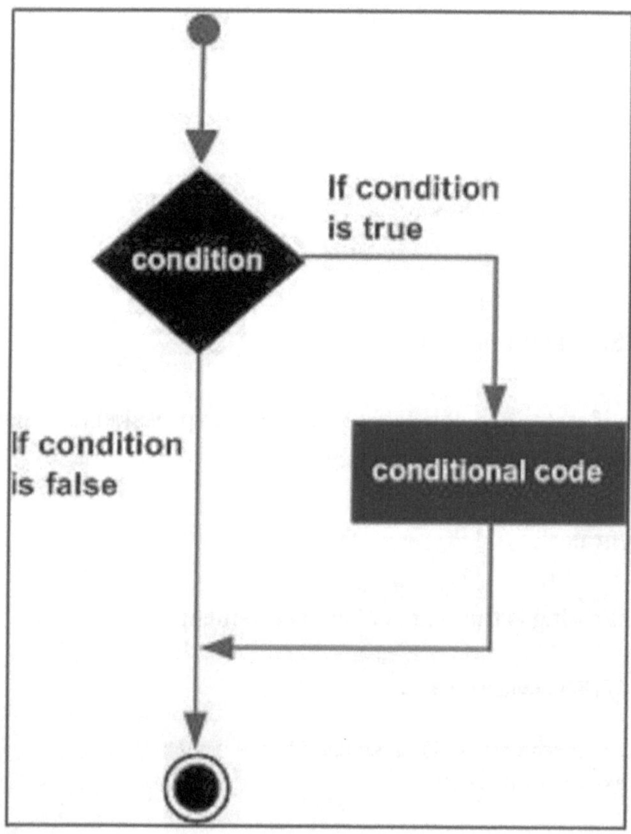

Example

```
public class Test {
public static void main(String args[]){
int x = 10;
if( x < 20 ){
System.out.print("This is if statement");
}
}
}
```

This will produce the following result:

This is if statement.

If-else Statement in Java

An **if** statement can be followed by an optional **else** statement, which executes when the Boolean expression is false.

Syntax

Following is the syntax of an if...else statement:

```
if(Boolean_expression){
//Executes when the Boolean expression is true
}else{
//Executes when the Boolean expression is false
}
```

If the boolean expression evaluates to true, then the if block
of code will be executed, otherwise else block of code will
be executed.

Flow Diagram

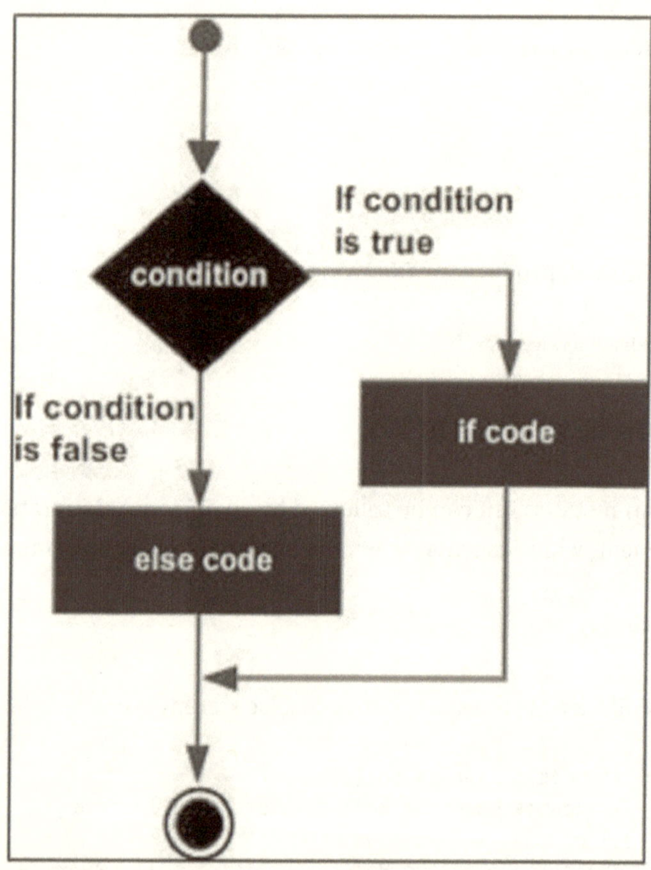

Example

```
public class Test {
public static void main(String args[]){
int x = 30;
if( x < 20 ){
```

```
System.out.print("This is if statement");
}else{
System.out.print("This is else statement");
}
}
}
```

This will produce the following result:

This is else statement

The if...else if...else Statement

An if statement can be followed by an optional *else if...else* statement, which is very useful to test various conditions using single if...else if statement.

When using if, else if, else statements there are a few points to keep in mind.

- An if can have zero or one else's and it must come after any else if's.
- An if can have zero to many else if's and they must come before the else.
- Once an else if succeeds, none of the remaining else if's or else's will be tested.

Syntax

Following is the syntax of an if...else statement:

```
if(Boolean_expression 1){
//Executes when the Boolean expression 1 is true
}else if(Boolean_expression 2){
//Executes when the Boolean expression 2 is true
}else if(Boolean_expression 3){
//Executes when the Boolean expression 3 is true
}else {
//Executes when the none of the above condition
is true.
}
```

Example

```
public class Test {
public static void main(String args[]){
int x = 30;
if( x == 10 ){
System.out.print("Value of X is 10");
}else if( x == 20 ){ System.out.print("Value of X
is 20");
}else if( x == 30 ){ System.out.print("Value of X
is 30");
}else{
System.out.print("This is else statement");
}
}
}
```

This will produce the following result:

Value of X is 30

Nested if Statement in Java

It is always legal to nest if-else statements which means you can use one if or else if statement inside another if or else if statement.

Syntax

The syntax for a nested if...else is as follows:

```
if(Boolean_expression 1){
//Executes when the Booleanexpression 1 is true
if(Boolean_expression 2){
//Executes when the Boolean expression 2 is true
}
}
```

You can nest **else if...else** in the similar way as we have nested *if* statement.

Example

```
public class Test {
public static void main(String args[]){
int x = 30;
int y = 10;
if( x == 30 ){
if( y == 10 ){
System.out.print("X = 30 and Y = 10");
}
}
}
}
```

This will produce the following result:

X = 30 and Y = 10

Switch Statement in Java

A **switch** statement allows a variable to be tested for equality against a list of values. Each value is called a case, and the variable being switched on is checked for each case.

Syntax

The syntax of enhanced for loop is:

```
switch(expression){
case value :
//Statements break; //optional
case value :
//Statements break; //optional
//You can have any number of case statements.
default : //Optional
//Statements
}
```

The following rules apply to a **switch** statement:

- The variable used in a switch statement can only be in-tegers, convertable integers (byte, short, char), strings and enums.
- You can have any number of case statements within a switch. Each case is followed by the value to be compared to and a colon.
- The value for a case must be the same data type as the

variable in the switch and it must be a constant or a literal.

- When the variable being switched on is equal to a case, the statements following that case will execute until a *break* statement is reached.
- When a *break* statement is reached, the switch terminates, and the flow of control jumps to the next line following the switch statement.
- Not every case needs to contain a break. If no break appears, the flow of control will *fall through* to subsequent cases until a break is reached.
- A *switch* statement can have an optional default case, which must appear at the end of the switch. The default case can be used for performing a task when none of the cases is true. No break is needed in the default case.

Flow Diagram

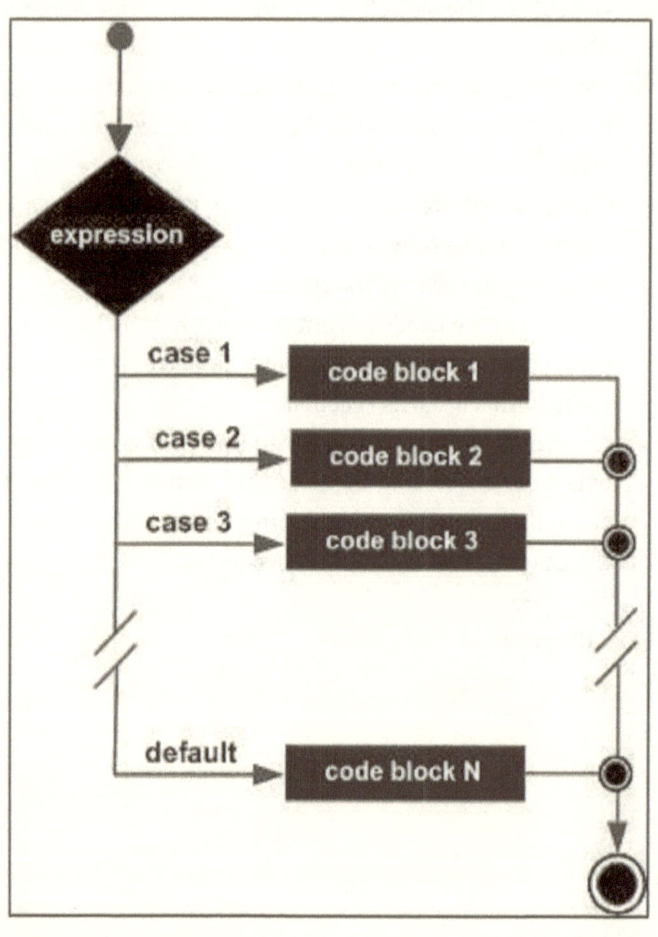

Example

```java
public class Test {
public static void main(String args[]){
//char grade = args[0].charAt(0);
char grade = 'C';
```

```
switch(grade)
{
case 'A' : System.out.println("Excellent!");
break;
case 'B' :
case 'C' :
System.out.println("Well done");
break;
case 'D' :
System.out.println("You passed");
case 'F' :
System.out.println("Better try again");
break;
default :
System.out.println("Invalid grade");
}
System.out.println("Your grade is " + grade);
}
}
```

Compile and run the above program using various command line arguments. This will produce the following result:

```
$ java Test
    Well done
    Your grade is a C
    $
```

The ? : Operator:

We have covered **conditional operator ? :** in the previous chapter which can be used to replace **if...else** statements. It has the following general form:

```
Exp1 ? Exp2 : Exp3;
```

Where Exp1, Exp2, and Exp3 are expressions. Notice the use and placement of the colon. To determine the value of the whole expression, initially exp1 is evaluated.

- If the value of exp1 is true, then the value of Exp2 will be the value of the whole expression.
- If the value of exp1 is false, then Exp3 is evaluated and its value becomes the value of the entire expression.

What is Next?

In the next chapter, we will discuss about Number class (in the java.lang package) and its subclasses in Java Language. We will be looking into some of the situations where you will use instantiations of these classes rather than the primitive data types, as well as classes such as formatting, mathematical functions that you need to know about when working with Numbers.

Numbers Class

Normally, when we work with Numbers, we use primitive data types such as byte, int, long, double, etc.

Example

```
int i = 5000;
float gpa = 13.65;
byte mask = 0xaf;
```

However, in development, we come across situations where we need to use objects instead of primitive data types. In order to achieve this, Java provides **wrapper classes**.

All the wrapper classes (Integer, Long, Byte, Double, Float, Short) are subclasses of the abstract class Number.

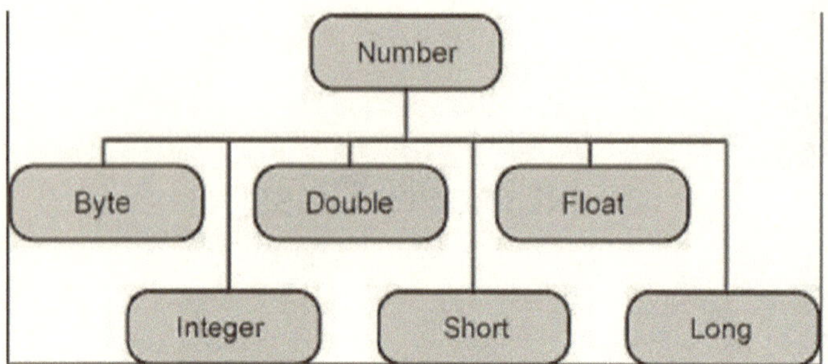

The object of the wrapper class contains or wraps its respective primitive data type. Converting primitive data types into object is called **boxing**, and this is taken care by the compiler. Therefore, while using a wrapper class you just need to pass the value of the primitive data type to the constructor of the Wrapper class.

And the Wrapper object will be converted back to a primitive data type, and this process is called unboxing. The **Number** class is part of the java.lang package.

Following is an example of boxing and unboxing:

```
public class Test{
public static void main(String args[]){
Integer x = 5; // boxes int to an Integer object
x =  x + 10;  // unboxes the Integer to a int
System.out.println(x);
}
}
```

This will produce the following result:

When x is assigned an integer value, the compiler boxes the integer because x is integer object. Later, x is unboxed so that they can be added as an integer.

Number Methods

Following is the list of the instance methods that all the subclasses of the Number class implements:

Methods with Description

- **xxxValue()** Converts the value of *this* Number object to the xxx data type and returns it.
- **compareTo()** Compares *this* Number object to the argument.
- **equals()** Determines whether *this* number object is equal to the argument.
- **valueOf()** Returns an Integer object holding the value of the specified primitive.
- **toString()** Returns a String object representing the value of a specified int or Integer.
- **parseInt()** This method is used to get the primitive data type of a certain String.
- **abs()** Returns the absolute value of the argument.
- **ceil()** Returns the smallest integer that is greater than or equal to the argument. Returned as a double.
- **floor()** Returns the largest integer that is less than or equal to the argument. Returned as a double.
- **rint()** Returns the integer that is closest in value to the

argument. Returned as a double.

- **round()** Returns the closest long or int, as indicated by the method's return type to the argument.
- **min()** Returns the smaller of the two arguments.
- **max()** Returns the larger of the two arguments.
- **exp()** Returns the base of the natural logarithms, e, to the power of the argument.
- **log()** Returns the natural logarithm of the argument.
- **pow()** Returns the value of the first argument raised to the power of the second argument.
- **sqrt()** Returns the square root of the argument.
- **sin()** Returns the sine of the specified double value.
- **cos()** Returns the cosine of the specified double value.
- **tan()** Returns the tangent of the specified double value.
- **asin()** Returns the arcsine of the specified double value.
- **acos()** Returns the arccosine of the specified double value.
- **atan()** Returns the arctangent of the specified double value.
- **atan2()** Converts rectangular coordinates (x, y) to polar coordinate (r, theta) and returns theta.
- **toDegrees()** Converts the argument to degrees.
- **toRadians()** Converts the argument to radians.
- **random()** Returns a random number.

Java XXX Value Method

Description

The method converts the value of the Number Object that invokes the method to the primitive data type that is returned from the method.

Syntax

Here is a separate method for each primitive data type:

```
byte byteValue() shortshortValue() int intValue()
long longValue()
float floatValue()
double doubleValue()
```

Parameters

Here is the detail of parameters:

- All these are default methods and accepts no parameter.

Return Value

- This method returns the primitive data type that is given in the signature.

Example

```
public class Test{
public static void main(String args[]){ Integer x
= 5;
// Returns byte primitive data type
System.out.println( x.byteValue() );
// Returns double primitive data type
System.out.println(x.doubleValue());
// Returns long primitive data type
System.out.println( x.longValue() );
```

```
  }
}
```

This will produce the following result:

```
5
5.0
5
```

Java – compareTo() Method

Description

The method compares the Number object that invoked the method to the argument. It is possible to compare Byte, Long, Integer, etc.

However, two different types cannot be compared, both the argument and the Number object invoking the method should be of the same type.

Syntax

```
public int compareTo( NumberSubClass
referenceName )
```

Parameters

Here is the detail of parameters:

- **referenceName** — This could be a Byte, Double, Integer, Float, Long, or Short.

Return Value

- If the Integer is equal to the argument then 0 is returned.
- If the Integer is less than the argument then -1 is returned.
- If the Integer is greater than the argument then 1 is returned.

Example

```java
public class Test{
public static void main(String args[]){ Integer x
= 5; System.out.println(x.compareTo(3));
System.out.println(x.compareTo(5));
System.out.println(x.compareTo(8));
}
}
```

This will produce the following result:

```
1

0

-1
```

Java – equals() Method

Description

The method determines whether the Number object that

invokes the method is equal to the object that is passed as an argument.

Syntax

```
public boolean equals(Object o)
```

Parameters

Here is the detail of parameters:
— Any object

Return Value

- The method returns True if the argument is not null and is an object of the same type and with the same numeric value. There are some extra requirements for Double and Float objects that are described in the Java API documentation.

Example

```
public class Test{
public static void main(String args[]){ Integer x
= 5;
Integer y = 10;
Integer z =5; Short a = 5;
System.out.println(x.equals(y));
System.out.println(x.equals(z));
System.out.println(x.equals(a));
}
}
```

This will produce the following result:

```
false true

  false
```

Java – valueOf() Method

Description

The valueOf method returns the relevant Number Object holding the value of the argument passed. The argument can be a primitive data type, String, etc.

This method is a static method. The method can take two arguments, where one is a String and the other is a radix.

Syntax

Following are all the variants of this method:

```
static Integer valueOf(int i)
static Integer valueOf(Strings)
static Integer valueOf(String s, int radix)
```

Parameters

Here is the detail of parameters:

i — An int for which Integer representation would be returned.

s — A String for which Integer representation would be

returned.

radix — This would be used to decide the value of returned Integer based on the passed String.

Return Value

- **valueOf(int i):** This returns an Integer object holding the value of the specified primitive.
- **valueOf(String s):** This returns an Integer object holding the value of the specified string representation.
- **valueOf(String s, int radix):** This returns an Integer object holding the integer value of the specified string representation, parsed with the value of radix.

```
public class Test{
public static void main(String args[]){
Integer x =Integer.valueOf(9); Double c =
Double.valueOf(5); Float a = Float.valueOf("80");
Integer b = Integer.valueOf("444",16);
System.out.println(x); System.out.println(c);
System.out.println(a); System.out.println(b);
}
}
```

This will produce the following result:

9

5.0

80.0

1092

Java – toString() Method

Description

The method is used to get a String object representing the value of the Number Object.

If the method takes a primitive data type as an argument, then the String object representing the primitive data type value is returned.

If the method takes two arguments, then a String representation of the first argument in the radix specified by the second argument will be returned.

Syntax

Following are all the variants of this method:

```
String toString()
static String toString(inti)
```

Parameters

Here is the detail of parameters:

i — An int for which string representation would be returned.

Return Value

- **toString():** This returns a String object representing the value of **this** Integer.
- **toString(int i):** This returns a String object representing the specified integer.

Example

```
public class Test{
public static void main(String args[]){
Integer x = 5;
System.out.println(x.toString());
System.out.println(Integer.toString(12));
}
}
```

This will produce the following result:

5

12

Java – parseInt() Method

Description

This method is used to get the primitive data type of a certain String. parseXxx() is a static method and can have one argument or two.

Syntax

Following are all the variants of this method:

```
static int parseInt(String s)
static int parseInt(String s, int radix)
```

Parameters

Here is the detail of parameters:

- **s** — This is a string representation of decimal.
- **radix** — This would be used to convert String **s** into integer.

Return Value

- **parseInt(String s):** This returns an integer (decimal only).
- **parseInt(int i):** This returns an integer, given a string representation of decimal, binary, octal, or hexadecimal (radix equals 10, 2, 8, or 16 respectively) numbers as input.

Example

```java
public class Test{
public static void main(String args[]){
int x =Integer.parseInt("9");
double c = Double.parseDouble("5");
int b = Integer.parseInt("444",16);
System.out.println(x); System.out.println(c);
System.out.println(b);
}
}
```

This will produce the following result:

```
9

5.0

1092
```

Java – abs() Method

Description

The method gives the absolute value of the argument. The argument can be int, float, long, double, short, byte.

Syntax

Following are all the variants of this method:

```
double abs(double d) float abs(float f)
intabs(int i)
long abs(long lng)
```

Parameters

Here is the detail of parameters:

- Any primitive data type

Return Value

- This method Returns the absolute value of the argument.

Example

```
public class Test{
public static void main(String args[]){ Integer a
= -8;
double d = -100;
float f = -90;
System.out.println(Math.abs(a));
System.out.println(Math.abs(d));
System.out.println(Math.abs(f));
}
}
```

This will produce the following result:

```
8
100.0
90.0
```

Java – ceil() Method

Description

The method ceil gives the smallest integer that is greater than or equal to the argument.

Syntax

This method has the following variants:

```
double ceil(double d)
double ceil(float f)
```

Parameters

Here is the detail of parameters:

- A double or float primitive data type

Return Value

- This method returns the smallest integer that is greater than or equal to the argument. Returned as a double

Example

```java
public class Test{
public static void main(String args[]){
double d = -100.675;
float f = -90;
System.out.println(Math.ceil(d));
System.out.println(Math.ceil(f));
System.out.println(Math.floor(d));
System.out.println(Math.floor(f));
}
}
```

This will produce the following result:

```
-100.0
-90.0
-101.0
-90.0
```

Java – floor() Method

Description

The method floor gives the largest integer that is less than or equal to the argument.

Syntax

This method has the following variants:

```
double floor(double d)
double floor(float f)
```

Parameters

Here is the detail of parameters:

- A double or float primitive data type.

Return Value

This method returns the largest integer that is less than or equal to the argument. Returned as a double.

Example

```
public class Test{
public static void main(String args[]){
double d = -100.675;
float f = -90;
System.out.println(Math.floor(d));
System.out.println(Math.floor(f));
```

```
System.out.println(Math.ceil(d));
System.out.println(Math.ceil(f));
}
}
```

This will produce the following result:

```
-101.0

-90.0

-100.0

-90.0
```

Java – rint() Method

Description

The method rint returns the integer that is closest in value to the argument.

Syntax

```
double rint(double d)
```

Parameters

Here is the detail of parameters:

- **d** — it accepts a double value as parameter.

Return Value

- This method returns the integer that is closest in value to the argument. Returned as a double.

Example

```java
public class Test{
public static void main(String args[]){
double d = 100.675;
double e = 100.500;
double f = 100.200;
System.out.println(Math.rint(d));
System.out.println(Math.rint(e));
System.out.println(Math.rint(f));
}
}
```

This will produce the following result:

```
101.0

100.0

100.0
```

Java – round() Method

Description

The method round returns the closest long or int, as given by the methods return type.

Syntax

This method has the following variants:

```
long round(double d)
int round(float f)
```

Parameters

Here is the detail of parameters:

- **d** — A double or float primitive data type
- **f** — A float primitive data type

Return Value

- This method returns the closest long or int, as indicated by the method's return type, to the argument.

Example

```
public class Test{
public static void main(String args[]){
double d = 100.675;
double e = 100.500;
float f = 100;
float g = 90f;
System.out.println(Math.round(d));
System.out.println(Math.round(e));
System.out.println(Math.round(f));
System.out.println(Math.round(g));
}
}
```

This will produce the following result:

```
101
```

101

100

90

Java – min() Method

Description

The method gives the smaller of the two arguments. The argument can be int, float, long, double.

Syntax

This method has the following variants:

```
double min(double arg1, double arg2)
float min(float arg1, float arg2)
int min(int arg1, int arg2)
long min(long arg1, long arg2)
```

Parameters

Here is the detail of parameters:

- This method accepts any primitive data type as a parameter

Return Value

- This method returns the smaller of the two arguments.

Example

```
public class Test{
public static void main(String args[]){
System.out.println(Math.min(12.123, 12.456));
System.out.println(Math.min(23.12, 23.0));
}
}
```

This will produce the following result:

```
12.123

23.0
```

Java – max() Method

Description

This method gives the maximum of the two arguments. The argument can be int, float, long, double.

Syntax

This method has the following variants:

```
double max(double arg1, double arg2)
float max(float arg1, float arg2)
int max(int arg1, int arg2)
long max(long arg1, long arg2)
```

Parameters

Here is the detail of parameters:

- This method accepts any primitive data type as a parameter.

Return Value

- This method returns the maximum of the two arguments

Example

```
public class Test{
public static void main(String args[]){
System.out.println(Math.max(12.123, 12.456));
System.out.println(Math.max(23.12, 23.0));
}
}
```

This will produce the following result:

    12.456

    23.12

Java – exp() Method

Description

The method returns the base of the natural logarithms, e, to the power of the argument.

Syntax

```
double exp(double d)
```

Parameters

Here is the detail of parameters:

- **d** —Any primitive data type.

Return Value

- This method returns the base of the natural logarithms, e, to the power of the argument.

Example

```
public class Test{
public static void main(String args[]){
double x = 11.635;
double y = 2.76;
System.out.printf("The value of e is %.4f%n",
Math.E); System.out.printf("exp(%.3f) is %.3f%n",
x, Math.exp(x));
}
}
```

This will produce the following result:

The value of e is 2.7183 exp(11.635) is 112983.831

Java – log() Method

Description

The method returns the natural logarithm of the argument.

Syntax

```
double log(double d)
```

Parameters

Here is the detail of parameters:

- **d** — Any primitive data type.

Return Value

- This method returns the natural logarithm of the argument.

Example

```java
public class Test{
public static void main(String args[]){
double x = 11.635;
double y = 2.76;
System.out.printf("The value of e is %.4f%n",
Math.E); System.out.printf("log(%.3f) is %.3f%n",
x, Math.log(x));
}
}
```

This will produce the following result:

The value of e is 2.7183 log(11.635) is 2.454

Java – pow() Method

Description

The method returns the value of the first argument raised to the power of the second argument.

Syntax

```
double pow(double base, double exponent)
```

Parameters

Here is the detail of parameters −

- **base** — Any primitive data type.
- **exponenet** — Any primitive data type.

Return Value

This method returns the value of the first argument raised to the power of the second argument.

Example

```
public class Test{
public static void main(String args[]){
double x = 11.635;
double y = 2.76;
System.out.printf("The value of e is %.4f%n",
Math.E); System.out.printf("pow(%.3f, %.3f) is
%.3f%n",x, y, Math.pow(x, y));
```

```
   }
 }
```

This will produce the following result –

The value of e is 2.7183 pow(11.635, 2.760) is 874.008

Java – sqrt() Method

Description

The method returns the square root of the argument.

Syntax

```
double sqrt(double d)
```

Parameters

Here is the detail of parameters:

d — Any primitive data type.

Return Value

This method returns the square root of the argument.

Example

```java
public class Test{
public static void main(String args[]){
double x = 11.635;
double y = 2.76;
System.out.printf("The value of e is %.4f%n",
Math.E); System.out.printf("sqrt(%.3f) is
%.3f%n", x, Math.sqrt(x));
}
}
```

This will produce the following result:

The value of e is 2.7183 sqrt(11.635) is 3.411

Java – sin() Method

Description

The method returns the sine of the specified double value.

Syntax

```java
double sin(double d)
```

Parameters

Here is the detail of parameters:

d — A double data type.

Return Value

This method returns the sine of the specified double value.

Example

```java
public class Test{
public static void main(String args[]){
double degrees = 45.0;
double radians = Math.toRadians(degrees);
System.out.format("The value of pi is %.4f%n",
Math.PI); System.out.format("Thesine of %.1f
degrees is %.4f%n", degrees,
Math.sin(radians));
}
}
```

This will produce the following result:

The value of pi is3.1416

The sine of 45.0 degrees is 0.7071

Java – cos() Method

Description

The method returns the cosine of the specified double value.

Syntax

```java
double cos(double d)
```

Parameters

Here is the detail of parameters:

d — This method accepts a value of double data type.

Return Value

This method returns the cosine of the specified double value.

Example

```
public class Test{
public static void main(String args[]){
double degrees = 45.0;
double radians = Math.toRadians(degrees);
System.out.format("The value of pi is %.4f%n",
Math.PI); System.out.format("Thecosine of %.1f
degrees is %.4f%n",degrees,
Math.cos(radians));
}
}
```

This will produce the following result:

The value of pi is3.1416

The cosine of 45.0 degrees is 0.7071

Java – tan() Method

Description

The method returns the tangent of the specified double value.

Syntax

```
double tan(double d)
```

Parameters

Here is the detail of parameters:

- **d** — A double data type.

Return Value

- This method returns the tangent of the specified double value.

Example

```
public class Test{
public static void main(String args[]){
double degrees = 45.0;
double radians = Math.toRadians(degrees);
System.out.format("The value of pi is %.4f%n",
Math.PI); System.out.format("Thetangent of %.1f
degrees is %.4f%n",degrees,
Math.tan(radians));
}
}
```

This will produce the following result:

The value of pi is3.1416

The tangent of 45.0 degrees is 1.0000

Java – asin() Method

Description

The method returns the arcsine of the specified double value.

Syntax

```
double asin(double d)
```

Parameters

Here is the detail of parameters:

d — A double data types.

Return Value

This method returns the arcsine of the specified double value.

Example

```
public class Test{
public static void main(String args[]){
double degrees = 45.0;
double radians = Math.toRadians(degrees);
System.out.format("The value of pi is %.4f%n",
Math.PI); System.out.format("Thearcsine of %.4f
is %.4f degrees %n",
```

```
Math.sin(radians),
Math.toDegrees(Math.asin(Math.sin(radians))));
}
}
```

This will produce the following result:

The value of pi is 3.1416

The arcsine of 0.7071 is 45.0000 degrees

Java – acos() Method

Description

The method returns the arccosine of the specified double value.

Syntax

```
double acos(double d)
```

Parameters

Here is the detail of parameters:

- **d** — A double data type.

Return Value

- This method returns the arccosine of the specified

double value.

Example

```
public class Test{
public static void main(String args[]){
double degrees = 45.0;
double radians = Math.toRadians(degrees);
System.out.format("The value of pi is %.4f%n",
Math.PI); System.out.format("Thearccosine of %.4f
is %.4f degrees %n",
Math.cos(radians),
Math.toDegrees(Math.acos(Math.sin(radians))));
}
}
```

This will produce the following result:

The value of pi is3.1416

The arccosine of 0.7071 is 45.0000 degrees

Java – atan() Method

Description

The method returns the arctangent of the specified double value.

Syntax

```
double atan(double d)
```

Parameters

Here is the detail of parameters:

- **d** — A double data type.

Return Value

This method returns the arctangent of the specified double value.

Example

```java
public class Test{
public static void main(String args[]){
double degrees = 45.0;
double radians = Math.toRadians(degrees);
System.out.format("The value of pi is %.4f%n",
Math.PI); System.out.format("Thearctangent of
%.4f is %.4f degrees %n",
Math.cos(radians),
Math.toDegrees(Math.atan(Math.sin(radians))));
}
}
```

This will produce the following result:

The value of pi is3.1416

The arctangent of 1.0000 is 45.0000 degrees

Java – atan2() Method

Description

The method converts rectangular coordinates (x, y) to polar coordinate (r, theta) and returns theta.

Syntax

double atan2(double y, double x)

Parameters

Here is the detail of parameters:

- **X** — X co-ordinate in double data type.
- **Y** — Y co-ordinate in double data type.

Return Value

This method returns theta from polar coordinate (r, theta).

Example

```
public class Test{
public static void main(String args[]){
double x = 45.0;
double y = 30.0;
System.out.println( Math.atan2(x, y) );
}
}
```

This will produce the following result:

0.982793723247329

Java – toDegrees() Method

Description

The method converts the argument value to degrees.

Syntax

```
double toDegrees(double d)
```

Parameters

Here is the detail of parameters:

- **d** — A double data type

Return Value

- This method returns a double value.

Example

```java
public class Test{
public static void main(String args[]){
double x = 45.0;
double y = 30.0;
System.out.println( Math.toDegrees(x) );
System.out.println( Math.toDegrees(y) );
}
```

```
}
```

This will produce the following result:

```
2578.3100780887044
  1718.8733853924698
```

Java – toRadians() Method

Description

The method converts the argument value to radians.

Syntax

```
double toRadians(double d)
```

Parameters

Here is the detail of parameters:

- **d** — A double data type.

Return Value

- This method returns a double value.

Example

```
public class Test{
public static void main(String args[]){
double x = 45.0;
double y = 30.0;
System.out.println( Math.toRadians(x) );
System.out.println( Math.toRadians(y) );
}
}
```

This will produce the following result:

0.7853981633974483

0.5235987755982988

Java – random() Method

Description

The method is used to generate a random number between 0.0 and 1.0. The range is: 0.0=< Math.random < 1.0. Different ranges can be achieved by using arithmetic operations.

Syntax

```
static double random()
```

Parameters

Here is the detail of parameters:

This is a default method and accepts no parameter.

Return Value

This method returns a double.

Example

```
public class Test{
public static void main(String args[]){
System.out.println( Math.random() );
System.out.println( Math.random() );
}
}
```

This will produce the following result:

0.16763945061451657

0.4005512537623.43

Note: The above result will vary every time you call random() method.

What is Next?

In the next chapter, we will be going through the Character class in Java. You will be learning how to use object Characters and primitive data type char in Java.

Character Class

Normally, when we work with characters, we use primitive data types char.

Example

```
char ch = 'a';
// Unicode for uppercase Greek omega character
char uniChar = '\u039A';
// an array of chars
char[] charArray ={ 'a', 'b', 'c', 'd', 'e' };
```

However in development, we come across situations where we need to use objects instead of primitive data types. In order to achieve this, Java provides wrapper class **Character** for primitive data type char.

The Character class offers a number of useful class (i.e., static) methods for manipulating characters. You can create a Character object with the Character constructor:

```
Character ch = newCharacter('a');
```

The Java compiler will also create a Character object for you under some circumstances. For example, if you pass a primitive char into a method that expects an object, the compiler automatically converts the char to a Character for you. This feature is called auto boxing or unboxing, if the conversion goes the other way.

Example

```
// Here following primitive char 'a'
// is boxed into the Characterobject ch
Character ch = 'a';
// Here primitive 'x' is boxed for method test,
// return is unboxed to char 'c' char c =
test('x');
```

Escape Sequences

A character preceded by a backslash (\) is an escape sequence and has a special meaning to the compiler.

The newline character (\n) has been used frequently in this book in System.out.println() statements to advance to the next line after the string is printed.

Following table shows the Java escape sequences:

Escape Sequence	Description
\t	Inserts a tab in the text at this point.
\b	Inserts a backspace in the text at this point.
\n	Inserts a newline in the text at this point.
\r	Inserts a carriage return in the text at this point.
\f	Inserts a form feed in the text at this point.
\'	Inserts a single quote character in the text at this point.
\"	Inserts a double quote character in the text at this point.
\\	Inserts a backslash character in the text at this point.

When an escape sequence is encountered in a print statement, the compiler interprets it accordingly.

Example

If you want to put quotes within quotes, you must use the escape sequence, \", on the interior quotes:

```
public class Test {
public static void main(String args[]) {
System.out.println("She said \"Hello!\"to me.");
}
}
```

This will produce the following result:

She said "Hello!" to me.

Character Methods

Following is the list of the important instance methods that all the subclasses of the Character class implement:

Methods with Description

- **isLetter()** Determines whether the specified char value is a letter.
- **isDigit()** Determines whether the specified char value is a digit.
- **isWhitespace()** Determines whether the specified char value is white space.
- **isUpperCase()** Determines whether the specified char value is uppercase.
- **isLowerCase()** Determines whether the specified char value is lowercase.
- **toUpperCase()** Returns the uppercase form of the specified char value.
- **toLowerCase()** Returns the lowercase form of the specified char value.
- **toString()** Returns a String object representing the specified character value that is, a one-character string.

Java – isLetter() Method

Description

The method determines whether the specified char value is a letter.

Syntax

```
boolean isLetter(char ch)
```

Parameters

Here is the detail of parameters:

ch — Primitive character type.

Return Value

This method returns true if the passed character is really a character.

Example

```
public class Test {
public static void main(String args[]) {
System.out.println(Character.isLetter('c'));
System.out.println(Character.isLetter('5'));
}
}
```

This will produce the following result:

true false

Java – isDigit() Method

Description

The method determines whether the specified char value is a digit.

Syntax

```
boolean isDigit(char ch)
```

Parameters

Here is the detail of parameters:

ch — Primitive character type.

Return Value

This method returns true, if the passed character is really a digit.

Example

```
public class Test {
public static void main(String args[]) {
System.out.println(Character.isDigit('c'));
System.out.println(Character.isDigit('5'));
}
}
```

This will produce the following result:

false true

Java – isWhitespace() Method

Description

The method determines whether the specified char value is a white space, which includes space, tab, or new line.

Syntax

```
boolean isWhitespace(char ch)
```

Parameters

Here is the detail of parameters:

ch — Primitive character type.

Return Value

This method returns true, if the passed character is really a white space.

Example

```
public class Test{
public static void main(String args[]){
System.out.println(Character.isWhitespace('c'));
System.out.println(Character.isWhitespace(' '));
System.out.println(Character.isWhitespace('\n'));
System.out.println(Character.isWhitespace('\t'));
```

```
    }
}
```

This will produce the following result:

```
false true true
   true
```

Java – isUpperCase( ) Method

Description

This method determines whether the specified char value is uppercase.

Syntax

boolean isUpperCase(char ch)

Parameters

Here is the detail of parameters:

- **ch** — Primitive character type.

Return Value

- This method returns true, if the passed character is really an uppercase.

Example

```java
public class Test{
public static void main(String args[]){
System.out.println( Character.isUpperCase('c'));
System.out.println( Character.isUpperCase('C'));
System.out.println( Character.isUpperCase('\n'));
System.out.println( Character.isUpperCase('\t'));
}
}
```

This will produce the following result:

false true false

false

Java – isLowerCase() Method

Description

The method determines whether the specified char value is lowercase.

Syntax

```java
boolean isLowerCase(char ch)
```

Parameters

Here is the detail of parameters:

- **ch** — Primitive character type.

Return Value

- This method returns true, if the passed character is really in lowercase.

Example

```
public class Test{
public static void main(String args[]){
System.out.println(Character.isLowerCase('c'));
System.out.println(Character.isLowerCase('C'));
System.out.println(Character.isLowerCase('\n'));
System.out.println(Character.isLowerCase('\t'));
}
}
```

This will produce the following result:

```
true false false
  false
```

Java – toUpperCase() Method

Description

The method returns the uppercase form of the specified char value.

Syntax

```
char toUpperCase(char ch)
```

Parameters

Here is the detail of parameters:

- **ch** — Primitive character type.

Return Value

- This method returns the uppercase form of the specified char value.

Example

```
public class Test{
public static void main(String args[]){
System.out.println(Character.toUpperCase('c'));
System.out.println(Character.toUpperCase('C'));
}
}
```

This will produce the following result:

C C

Java – toLowerCase() Method

Description

The method returns the lowercase form of the specified char

value.

Syntax

```
char toLowerCase(char ch)
```

Parameters

Here is the detail of parameters:

- **ch** — Primitive character type.

Return Value

- This method returns the lowercase form of the specified char value.

Example

```
public class Test{
public static void main(String args[]){
System.out.println(Character.toLowerCase('c'));
System.out.println(Character.toLowerCase('C'));
}
}
```

This will produce the following result:

c c

Java – toString() Method

Description

This method returns a String object representing the specified character value, that is, a one-character string.

Syntax

```
String toString(char ch)
```

Parameters

Here is the detail of parameters:

- **ch** — Primitive character type.

Return Value

- This method returns String object.

Example

```
public class Test{
public static void main(String args[]){
System.out.println(Character.toString('c'));
System.out.println(Character.toString('C'));
}
}
```

This will produce the following result:
c

C

For a complete list of methods, please refer to the java.lang.Character API specification.

What is Next?

In the next chapter, we will be going through the String class in Java. You will be learning how to declare and use Strings efficiently as well as some of the important methods in the String class.

Strings Class

Strings, which are widely used in Java programming, are a sequence of characters. In Java programming language, strings are treated as objects.

The Java platform provides the String class to create and manipulate strings.

Creating Strings

The most direct way to create a string is to write:

```
String greeting = "Hello world!";
```

Whenever it encounters a string literal in your code, the compiler creates a String object with its value in this case, "Hello world!".

As with any other object, you can create String objects by using the new keyword and a constructor. The String class has 11 constructors that allow you to provide the initial value of the string using different sources, such as an array of characters.

```
public class StringDemo{
public static void main(String args[]){
char[] helloArray = { 'h', 'e', 'l', 'l', 'o',
'.'}; String helloString = newString(helloArray);
System.out.println( helloString );
}
}
```

This will produce the following result:

hello.

Note: The String class is immutable, so that once it is created a String object cannot be changed. If there is a necessity to make a lot of modifications to Strings of characters, then you should use String Buffer & String Builder Classes.

Java – String Buffer & String Builder Classes

The **StringBuffer** and **StringBuilder** classes are used when there is a necessity to make a lot of modifications to Strings of characters.

Unlike Strings, objects of type StringBuffer and String builder can be modified over and over again without leaving behind a lot of new unused objects.

The StringBuilder class was introduced as of Java 5 and the

main difference between the StringBuffer and StringBuilder is that StringBuilders methods are not thread safe (not synchronized).

It is recommended to use **StringBuilder** whenever possible because it is faster than StringBuffer. However, if the thread safety is necessary, the best option is StringBuffer objects.

Example

```
public class Test{
public static void main(String args[]){
StringBuffer sBuffer = new StringBuffer(" test");
sBuffer.append("String Buffer");
System.out.println(sBuffer);
}
}
```

This will produce the following result:

test String Buffer

StringBuffer Methods

Here is the list of important methods supported by String-Buffer class:

Methods with Description

- **public StringBuffer append(String s)** Updates the value of the object that invoked the method. The method takes boolean, char, int, long, Strings, etc.

- **public StringBuffer reverse()** The method reverses the value of the StringBuffer object that invoked the method.
- **public delete(int start, int end)** Deletes the string starting from the start index until the end index.
- **public insert(int offset, int i)** This method inserts a string **s** at the position mentioned by the offset.
- **replace(int start, int end, String str)** This method replaces the characters in a substring of this StringBuffer with characters in the specified String.

Java – String Buffer append() Method

Description

This method updates the value of the object that invoked the method. The method takes boolean, char, int, long, Strings, etc.

Syntax

Here is a separate method for each primitive data type:

```
public StringBuffer append(boolean b)
public StringBuffer append(char c)
public StringBuffer append(char[] str)
public StringBuffer append(char[] str, int
offset, int len)
public StringBuffer append(double d)
```

```
public StringBuffer append(float f)
public StringBuffer append(int i)
public StringBuffer append(long l)
public StringBuffer append(Object obj)
public StringBuffer append(StringBuffer sb)
public StringBuffer append(String str)
```

Parameters

Here is the detail of parameters:

- Here the parameter depends on what you are trying to append in the String Buffer.

Return Value

- These methods return the updated StringBuffer objects.

Example

```
public class Test {
public static void main(String args[]) {
StringBuffer sb = newStringBuffer("Test");
sb.append(" String Buffer");
System.out.println(sb);
}
}
```

This will produce the following result:

Test String Buffer

Java – String Buffer reverse() Method

Description

This method reverses the value of the StringBuffer object that invoked the method. Let n be the length of the old character sequence, the one contained in the string buffer just prior to the execution of the reverse method. Then, the character at index k in the new character sequence is equal to the character at index n-k-1 in the old character sequence.

Syntax

Here is the syntax for this method:

```
public StringBuffer reverse()
```

Parameters

Here is the detail of parameters:

- NA

Return Value

- This method returns StringBuffer object with the re-versed sequence.

Example

```
public class Test {
public static void main(String args[]) {
StringBuffer buffer = new StringBuffer("Game
Plan");
buffer.reverse(); System.out.println(buffer);
}
}
```

This will produce the following result:

nalP emaG

Java – String Buffer delete() Method

Description

This method removes the characters in a substring of this StringBuffer. The substring begins at the specified start and extends to the character at index end - 1 or to the end of the StringBuffer if no such character exists. If start is equal to end, no changes are made.

Syntax

Here is the syntax of this method:

```
public StringBuffer delete(int start, int end)
```

Parameters

Here is the detail of parameters:

- **start** — The beginning index, inclusive.
- **end** — The ending index, exclusive

Return Value

- This method returns the StringBuffer object.

Example

```
public class Test {
public static void main(String args[]) {
StringBuffer sb = newStringBuffer("abcdefghijk");
sb.delete(3,7); System.out.println(sb);
}
}
```

This will produce the following result:

abchijk

Java – String Buffer insert() Method

Description

This method removes the characters in a substring of this

StringBuffer. The substring begins at the specified start and extends to the character at index end – 1 or to the end of the StringBuffer, if no such character exists. If start is equal to end, no changes are made.

Syntax

Here is a separate method for each primitive data type:

```
public StringBuffer insert(int offset, boolean b)
public StringBuffer insert(int offset, char c)
public insert(int offset, char[] str)
public StringBuffer insert(int index, char[] str,
int offset, int len)
public StringBuffer insert(int offset, float f)
public StringBuffer insert(int offset, int i)
public StringBuffer insert(int offset, long l)
public StringBuffer insert(int offset, Object obj)
public StringBuffer insert(int offset, String str)
```

Parameters

Here is the detail of parameters:

- Parameter depends on what you are trying to insert.

Return Value

- This method returns the modified StringBuffer object.

Example

```
public class Test {
public static void main(String args[]) {
StringBuffer sb = newStringBuffer("abcdefghijk");
sb.insert(3,"123"); System.out.println(sb);
}
}
```

This will produce the following result:

abc123defghijk

Java – String Buffer replace() Method

Description

This method replaces the characters in a substring of this StringBuffer with characters in the specified String. The substring begins at the specified start and extends to the character at index end - 1 or to the end of the StringBuffer, if no such character exists. First the characters in the substring are removed and then the specified String is inserted at start.

Syntax

Here is the syntax of this method:

```
public StringBuffer replace(int start, int end,
String str)
```

Parameters

Here is the detail of parameters:

- **start** — The beginning index, inclusive.
- **end** — The ending index, exclusive.
- **str** — String that will replace previous contents.

Return Value

This method returns the modified StringBuffer object.

Example

```
public class Test {
public static void main(String args[]) {
StringBuffer sb = newStringBuffer("abcdefghijk");
sb.replace(3, 8, "ZARA"); System.out.println(sb);
}
}
```

This will produce the following result:

abcZARAijk

Here is the list of other methods (except set methods) which are very similar to String class:

Methods with Description

- **int capacity()** Returns the current capacity of the String buffer.
- **char charAt(int index)** The specified character of the sequence currently represented by the string buffer, as indicated by the index argument, is returned.
- **void ensureCapacity(int minimumCapacity)** Ensures that the capacity of the buffer is at least equal to the specified minimum.
- **void getChars(int srcBegin, int srcEnd, char[] dst,int dstBegin)** Characters are copied from this string buffer into the destination character array dst.
- **int indexOf(String str)** Returns the index within this string of the first occurrence of the specified substring.
- **int indexOf(String str, int fromIndex)** Returns the index within this string of the first occurrence of the specified substring, starting at the specified index.
- **int lastIndexOf(String str)** Returns the index within this string of the rightmost occurrence of the specified substring.
- **int lastIndexOf(String str, int fromIndex)** Returns the index within this string of the last occurrence of the specified substring.
- **int length()** Returns the length (character count) of this string buffer.
- **void setCharAt(int index, char ch)** The character at the specified index of this string buffer is set toch.
- **void setLength(int newLength)** Sets the length of this String buffer.
- **CharSequence subSequence(int start, int end)** Returns

a new character sequence that is a subsequence of this sequence.

- **String substring(int start)** Returns a new String that contains a subsequence of characters currently contained in this StringBuffer.The substring begins at the specified index and extends to the end of the String-Buffer.
- **String substring(int start, int end)** Returns a new String that contains a subsequence of characters currently contained in this StringBuffer.
- **String toString()** Converts to a string representing the data in this string buffer.

String Length

Methods used to obtain information about an object are known as **accessor methods**. One accessor method that you can use with strings is the length() method, which returns the number of characters contained in the string object.

The following program is an example of **length()**, method String class.

```java
public class StringDemo {
public static void main(String args[]) { String
palindrome = "Dot saw I was Tod"; int len =
palindrome.length();
System.out.println( "String Length is : " + len );
}
}
```

This will produce the following result:

String Length is : 17

Concatenating Strings

The String class includes a method for concatenating two strings:

```
string1.concat(string2);
```

This returns a new string that is string1 with string2 added to it at the end. You can also use the concat() method with string literals, as in:

```
"My name is ".concat("Zara");
```

Strings are more commonly concatenated with the + operator, as in:

```
"Hello," + "world" + "!"
```

which results in:

"Hello, world!"

Let us look at the following example:

```
public class StringDemo {
public static void main(String args[]) { String
```

```
string1 = "sawI was ";
System.out.println("Dot " + string1 + "Tod");
   }
}
```

This will produce the following result:

Dot saw I was Tod

Creating Format Strings

You have printf() and format() methods to print output with formatted numbers. The String class has an equivalent class method, format(), that returns a String object rather than a PrintStream object.

Using String's static format() method allows you to create a formatted string that you can reuse, as opposed to a one-time print statement. For example, instead of:

```
System.out.printf("The value of the float
variable is " +
                  "%f, while the value of the
                  integer " +
                  "variable is %d, and the string
                  " +
                  "is %s", floatVar, intVar,
                  stringVar);
```

You can write:

```
String fs;
fs = String.format("The value of the float
variable is " +
"%f, while the value of the integer " +
"variable is %d, and the string " +
"is %s",floatVar, intVar, stringVar);
System.out.println(fs);
```

String Methods

Here is the list of methods supported by String class:

Methods with Description

- **char charAt(int index)** Returns the character at the specified index.
- **int compareTo(Object o)** Compares this String to another Object.
- **int compareTo(String anotherString)** Compares two strings lexicographically.
- **int compareToIgnoreCase(String str)** Compares two strings lexicographically, ignoring case differences.
- **String concat(String str)** Concatenates the specified string to the end of this string.
- **boolean contentEquals(StringBuffer sb)** Returns true if and only if this String represents the same sequence of characters as the specified StringBuffer.
- **static String copyValueOf(char[] data)** Returns a String that represents the character sequence in the array specified.
- **static String copyValueOf(char[] data, int offset,int**

count)

- Returns a String that represents the character sequence in the array specified.
- **boolean endsWith(String suffix)** Tests if this string ends with the specified suffix.
- **boolean equals(Object anObject)** Compares this string to the specified object.
- **boolean equalsIgnoreCase(String anotherString)** Compares this String to another String, ignoring case considerations.
- **byte getBytes()** Encodes this String into a sequence of bytes using the platform's default charset, storing the result into a new byte array.
- **byte[] getBytes(String charsetName)** Encodes this String into a sequence of bytes using the named charset, storing the result into a new byte array.
- **void getChars(int srcBegin, int srcEnd, char[] dst,int dstBegin)** Copies characters from this string into the destination character array.
- **int hashCode()** Returns a hash code for this string.
- **int indexOf(int ch)** Returns the index within this string of the first occurrence of the specified character.
- **int indexOf(int ch, int fromIndex)** Returns the index within this string of the first occurrence of the specified character, starting the search at the specified index.
- **int indexOf(String str)** Returns the index within this string of the first occurrence of the specified substring.
- **int indexOf(String str, int fromIndex)** Returns the index within this string of the first occurrence of the specified substring, starting at the specified index.
- **String intern()** Returns a canonical representation for

the string object.

- **int lastIndexOf(int ch)** Returns the index within this string of the last occurrence of the specified character.
- **int lastIndexOf(int ch, int fromIndex)** Returns the index within this string of the last occurrence of the specified character, searching backward starting at the specified index.
- **int lastIndexOf(String str)** Returns the index within this string of the rightmost occurrence of the specified substring.
- **int lastIndexOf(String str, int fromIndex)** Returns the index within this string of the last occurrence of the specified substring, searching backward starting at the specified index.
- **int length()** Returns the length of this string.
- **boolean matches(String regex)** Tells whether or not this string matches the given regular expression.
- **boolean regionMatches(boolean ignoreCase, int toffset, String other, int ooffset, int len)** Tests if two string regions are equal.
- **boolean regionMatches(int toffset, String other, int ooffset, int len)** Tests if two string regions are equal.
- **String replace(char oldChar, char newChar)** Returns a new string resulting from replacing all occurrences of oldChar in this string with newChar.
- **String replaceAll(String regex, String replacement)** Replaces each substring of this string that matches the given regular expression with the given replacement.
- **String replaceFirst(String regex, String replacement)** Replaces the first substring of this string that matches the given regular expression with the given replace-

ment.

- **String[] split(String regex)** Splits this string around matches of the given regular expression.
- **String[] split(String regex, int limit)** Splits this string around matches of the given regular expression.
- **boolean startsWith(String prefix)** Tests if this string starts with the specified prefix.
- **boolean startsWith(String prefix, int toffset)** Tests if this string starts with the specified prefix beginning a specified index.
- **CharSequence subSequence(int beginIndex, int endIndex)** Returns a new character sequence that is a subsequence of this sequence.
- **String substring(int beginIndex)** Returns a new string that is a substring of this string.
- **String substring(int beginIndex, int endIndex)** Returns a new string that is a substring of this string.
- **char[] toCharArray()** Converts this string to a new character array.
- **String toLowerCase()** Converts all of the characters in this String to lower case using the rules of the default locale.
- **String toLowerCase(Locale locale)** Converts all of the characters in this String to lower case using the rules of the given Locale.
- **String toString()** This object (which is already a string!) is itself returned.
- **String toUpperCase()** Converts all of the characters in this String to upper case using the rules of the default locale.
- **String toUpperCase(Locale locale)** Converts all of the

characters in this String to upper case using the rules of the given Locale.
- **String trim()** Returns a copy of the string, with leading and trailing whitespace omitted.
- **static String valueOf(primitive data type x)** Returns the string representation of the passed data type argument.

Java – String chartAt() Method

Description

This method returns the character located at the String's indexes start from zero.

Syntax

Here is the syntax of this method:

```
public char charAt(int index)
```

Parameters

Here is the detail of parameters:

- **index** — Index of the character to be returned.

Return Value

- This method returns a char at the specified index.

Example

```
public class Test {
public static void main(String args[]) { String s
= "Strings are immutable"; char result =
s.charAt(8);
System.out.println(result);
}
}
```

This will produce the following result:

a

Java – String compareTo(Object o) Method

Description

This method compares this String to another Object.

Syntax

Here is the syntax of this method:

```
int compareTo(Object o)
```

Parameters

Here is the detail of parameters:

- **O**— the Object to be compared.

Return Value

The value 0 if the argument is a string lexicographically equal to this string; a value less than 0 if the argument is a string lexicographically greater than this string; and a value greater than 0 if the argument is a string lexicographically less than this string.

Example

```
public class Test {
public static void main(String args[]) { String
str1 = "Strings are immutable";
String str2 = new String("Strings are immutable");
String str3 = new String("Integers are not
immutable");
int result = str1.compareTo( str2 );
System.out.println(result);
result = str2.compareTo( str3 );
System.out.println(result);
}
}
```

This will produce the following result:

0

10

Java – String compareTo(String anotherString) Method

Description

This method compares two strings lexicographically.

Syntax

Here is the syntax of this method:

```
int compareTo(String anotherString)
```

Parameters

Here is the detail of parameters:

- **anotherString** — the String to be compared.

Return Value

The value 0 if the argument is a string lexicographically equal to this string; a value less than 0 if the argument is a string lexicographically greater than this string; and a value greater than 0 if the argument is a string lexicographically less than this string.

Example

```
public class Test {
public static void main(String args[]) { String
str1= "Strings are immutable"; String str2 =
"Strings are immutable"; String str3 =
"Integersare not immutable";
```

```
int result = str1.compareTo( str2 );
System.out.println(result);
 result = str2.compareTo( str3 );
System.out.println(result);
 result = str3.compareTo( str1 );
System.out.println(result);
 }
 }
```

This will produce the following result:

```
0

10

-10
```

Java – String compareToIgnoreCase() Method

Description

This method compares two strings lexicographically, ignoring case differences.

Syntax

Here is the syntax of this method:

```
int compareToIgnoreCase(Stringstr)
```

Parameters

Here is the detail of parameters:

- **str** — the String to be compared.

Return Value

This method returns a negative integer, zero, or a positive integer as the specified String is greater than, equal to, or less than this String, ignoring case considerations.

Example

```
public class Test {
public static void main(String args[]) { String
str1 = "Strings are immutable"; String str2 =
"Strings are immutable"; String str3 = "Integers
are not immutable";
int result = str1.compareToIgnoreCase( str2 );
System.out.println(result);
result = str2.compareToIgnoreCase( str3 );
System.out.println(result);
result = str3.compareToIgnoreCase( str1 );
System.out.println(result);
}
}
```

This will produce the following result:
```
0

10

-10
```

Java – String concat() Method

Description

This method appends one String to the end of another. The method returns a String with the value of the String passed into the method, appended to the end of the String, used to invoke this method.

Syntax

Here is the syntax of this method:

```
public String concat(String s)
```

Parameters

Here is the detail of parameters:

- **s** — the String that is concatenated to the end of this String.

Return Value

This methods returns a string that represents the concatenation of this object's characters followed by the string argument's characters.

Example

```
public class Test {
public static void main(String args[]) { String s
= "Strings are immutable";
s = s.concat("all the time");
System.out.println(s);
}
}
```

This will produce the following result:

Strings are immutable all the time

Java – String contentEquals() Method

Description

This method returns true if and only if this String represents the same sequence of characters as specified in StringBuffer.

Syntax

Here is the syntax of this method:

```
public boolean contentEquals(StringBuffer sb)
```

Parameters

Here is the detail of parameters:

- **sb** — the StringBuffer to compare.

Return Value

- This method returns true if and only if this String represents the same sequence of characters as the specified in StringBuffer, otherwise false.

Example

```
public class Test {
public static void main(String args[]) { String
str1 = "Not immutable";
String str2 = "Strings are immutable";
StringBuffer str3 = new StringBuffer( "Not
immutable");
boolean result = str1.contentEquals( str3 );
System.out.println(result);
result = str2.contentEquals( str3 );
System.out.println(result);
}
}
```

This will produce the following result:

true false

Java – String copyValueOf(char[] data) Method

Description

This method returns a String that represents the character sequence in the array specified.

Syntax

Here is the syntax of this method:

```
public static String copyValueOf(char[] data)
```

Parameters

Here is the detail of parameters:

- **data** — the character array.

Return Value

This method returns a String that contains the characters of the character array.

Example

```
public class Test {
public static void main(String args[]) {
char[] Str1 = {'h', 'e', 'l', 'l', 'o', ' ', 'w',
'o', 'r', 'l', 'd'}; String Str2 = "";
Str2 = Str2.copyValueOf( Str1 );
System.out.println("Returned String: " + Str2);
}
}
```

This will produce the following result:

Returned String: hello world

Java – String copyValueOf(char[] data, int offset, int count) Method

Description

This returns a String that represents the character sequence in the array specified.

Syntax

Here is the syntax of this method:

```
public static String copyValueOf(char[] data, int offset, int count)
```

Parameters

Here is the detail of parameters:

- **data** — the character array.
- **offset** — initial offset of the subarray.
- **count** — length of the subarray.

Return Value

This method returns a String that contains the characters of the character array.

Example

```
public class Test {
public static void main(String args[]) {
char[] Str1 = {'h', 'e', 'l', 'l', 'o', ' ', 'w',
'o', 'r', 'l', 'd'}; String Str2 = "";
Str2 = Str2.copyValueOf( Str1, 2, 6 );
System.out.println("Returned String: " + Str2);
}
}
```

This will produce the following result:

Returned String: llo wo

Java – String endsWith() Method

Description

This method tests if this string ends with the specified suffix.

Syntax

Here is the syntax of this method:

```
public boolean endsWith(String suffix)
```

Parameters

Here is the detail of parameters:

suffix — the suffix.

Return Value

This method returns true if the character sequence represented by the argument is a suffix of the character sequence represented by this object; false otherwise. Note that the result will be true if the argument is the empty string or is equal to this String object as determined by the equals(Object) method.

Example

```
public class Test{
public static void main(String args[]){
String Str = new String("Thisis really not
immutable!!");
boolean retVal;
retVal = Str.endsWith( "immutable!!" );
System.out.println("Returned Value = " + retVal );
retVal = Str.endsWith( "immu");
System.out.println("Returned Value = " + retVal );
}
}
```

This will produce the following result:

Returned Value = true

Returned Value = false

Java – String equals() Method

Description

This method compares this string to the specified object. The result is true if and only if the argument is not null and is a String object that represents the same sequence of characters as this object.

Syntax

Here is the syntax of this method:

```
public boolean equals(Object anObject)
```

Parameters

Here is the detail of parameters:

anObject — the object to compare this String against.

Return Value

This method returns true if the String are equal; false otherwise.

Example

```
public class Test {
public static void main(String args[]) {
String Str1 = new String("This is really not
immutable!!"); String Str2 = Str1;
String Str3 = new String("This is really not
immutable!!");
```

```
boolean retVal;
retVal = Str1.equals( Str2 );
System.out.println("Returned Value = " + retVal );
retVal = Str1.equals( Str3 );
System.out.println("Returned Value = " + retVal );
}
}
```

This will produce the following result:

Returned Value = true

Returned Value = true

Java – String equalsIgnoreCase() Method

Description

This method compares this String to another String, ignoring case considerations. Two strings are considered equal ignoring case, if they are of the same length, and corresponding characters in the two strings are equal ignoring case.

Syntax

Here is the syntax of this method:

```
public boolean equalsIgnoreCase(String
anotherString)
```

Parameters

Here is the detail of parameters:

- **anotherString** — the String to compare this String against

Return Value

This method returns true if the argument is not null and the Strings are equal, ignoring case; false otherwise.

Example

```
public class Test {
public static void main(String args[]) {
String Str1 = new String("This is really not
immutable!!"); String Str2 = Str1;
String Str3 = new String("This is really not
immutable!!");
String Str4 = new String("This IS REALLY NOT
IMMUTABLE!!");
boolean retVal;
retVal = Str1.equals( Str2 );
System.out.println("Returned Value = " + retVal );
retVal = Str1.equals( Str3 );
System.out.println("Returned Value = " + retVal );
retVal = Str1.equalsIgnoreCase( Str4 );
System.out.println("Returned Value = " + retVal );
}
}
```

This will produce the following result:

Returned Value = true Returned Value = true Returned Value = true

Java – String getBytes(String charsetName) Method

This method encodes this String into a sequence of bytes using the named charset, storing the result into a new byte array.

Syntax

Here is the syntax of this method:

```
public byte[] getBytes(StringcharsetName) throws
UnsupportedEncodingException
```

Parameters

Here is the detail of parameters:

- **charsetName** — the name of a supported charset.

Return Value

This method returns the resultant byte array.

Example

```
import java.io.*;
public class Test{
public static void main(String args[]){
String Str1 = new String("Welcome to java.com");
try{
Str2 = Str1.getBytes( "UTF-8");
```

```
System.out.println("Returned Value " + Str2 );
Str2 = Str1.getBytes( "ISO-8859-1");
System.out.println("Returned Value " + Str2 );
}catch( UnsupportedEncodingException e){
System.out.println("Unsupported character set");
}
}
}
```

This will produce the following result:

Returned Value [B@15ff48b

Returned Value [B@1b90b39

Java – String getBytes() Method

Description

This method encodes this String into a sequence of bytes using the platform's default charset, storing the result into a new byte array.

Syntax

Here is the syntax of this method:

```
public byte[] getBytes()
```

Return Value

This method returns the resultant byte array.

Example

```java
import java.io.*;
public class Test{
public static void main(String args[]){
String Str1 = new String("Welcome to java.com");
try{
byte[] Str2 = Str1.getBytes();
System.out.println("Returned Value "+ Str2 );
}catch( UnsupportedEncodingException e){
System.out.println("Unsupported character set");
}
}
}
```

This will produce the following result:

Returned Value [B@192d342

Java – String getChars() Method

Description

This method copies characters from this string into the destination character array.

Syntax

Here is the syntax of this method:

```
public void getChars(int srcBegin, int srcEnd,
char[] dst, int dstBegin)
```

Parameters

Here is the detail of parameters:

- **srcBegin** — index of the first character in the string to copy.
- **srcEnd** — index after the last character in the string to copy.
- **dst** — the destination array.
- **dstBegin** — the start offset in the destination array.

Return Value

It does not return any value but throws IndexOutOfBoundsException.

Example

```
import java.io.*;
public class Test{
public static void main(String args[]){
String Str1 = new String("Welcome to java.com");
char[] Str2 = new char[7];
try{
Str1.getChars(2, 9, Str2, 0);
System.out.print("Copied Value = " );
System.out.println(Str2 );
}catch( Exception ex){
System.out.println("Raised exception...");
}
```

```
    }
}
```

This will produce the following result:

Copied Value = lcome t

Java – String hashCode() Method

Description

This method returns a hash code for this string. The hash code for a String object is computed as:

```
s[0]*31^(n-1) + s[1]*31^(n-2) + ... + s[n-1]
```

Using int arithmetic, where s[i] is the character of the string, n is the length of the string, and ∧ indicates exponentiation. (The hash value of the empty string is zero.)

Syntax

Here is the syntax of this method:

```
public int hashCode()
```

Parameters

Here is the detail of parameters:

- This is a default method and this will not accept any parameters.

Return Value

- This method returns a hash code value for this object.

Example

```
import java.io.*;
public class Test{
public static void main(String args[]){
String Str = new String("Welcome to java.com");
System.out.println("Hashcode for Str :" +
Str.hashCode() );
}
}
```

This will produce the following result:

Hashcode for Str :1186874997

Java – String indexOf(int ch) Method

Description

This method returns the index within this string of the first occurrence of the specified character or -1, if the character does not occur.

Syntax

Here is the syntax of this method:

```
public int indexOf(int ch )
```

Parameters

Here is the detail of parameters:

- **ch** — a character.

Return Value

See the description.

Example

```
import java.io.*;
public class Test {
public static void main(String args[]) {
String Str = new String("Welcome to java.com");
System.out.print("Found Index :" );
System.out.println(Str.indexOf( 'o' ));
}
}
```

This will produce the following result:

Found Index :4

Java – String indexOf(int ch, int fromIndex) Method

Description

This method returns the index within this string of the first occurrence of the specified character, starting the search at the specified index or -1, if the character does not occur.

Syntax

Here is the syntax of this method:

```
public int indexOf(int ch, int fromIndex)
```

Parameters

Here is the detail of parameters:

- **ch** — a character.
- **fromIndex** — the index to start the search from.

Return Value

- See the description.

Example

```
import java.io.*;
public class Test {
public static void main(String args[]) {
String Str = new String("Welcome to java.com");
System.out.print("Found Index :" );
System.out.println(Str.indexOf( 'o', 5 ));
```

```
    }
}
```

This will produce the following result:

Found Index :9

Java – String indexOf(String str) Method

Description

This method returns the index within this string of the first occurrence of the specified substring. If it does not occur as a substring, -1 is returned.

Syntax

Here is the syntax of this method:

```
int indexOf(String str)
```

Parameters

Here is the detail of parameters:

- **str** — a string.

Return Value

- See the description.

Example

```
import java.io.*;
public class Test {
public static void main(String args[]) {
String Str = new String("Welcome to java.com");
String SubStr1 = new String("book");
System.out.println( Str.indexOf( SubStr1 ));
}
}
```

This will produce the following result:

Found Index :11

Java – String indexOf(String str, int fromIndex) Method

This method returns the index within this string of the first occurrence of the specified substring, starting at the specified index. If it does not occur, -1 is returned.

Syntax

Here is the syntax of this method:

```
int indexOf(String str, int fromIndex)
```

Parameters

Here is the detail of parameters:

- **fromIndex** — the index to start the search from.
- **str** — a string.

Return Value

- See the description.

Example

```java
import java.io.*;
public class Test {
public static void main(String args[]) {
String Str = new String("Welcome to java.com");
String SubStr1 = new String("java" );
System.out.print("Found Index :" );
System.out.println( Str.indexOf( SubStr1, 15 ));
}
}
```

This will produce the following result:

```
Found Index :-1
```

Java – String Intern() Method

Description

This method returns a canonical representation for the string object. It follows that for any two strings **s** and **t**, s.intern() == t.intern() is true if and only if s.equals(t) is true.

Syntax

Here is the syntax of this method:

```
public String intern()
```

Parameters

Here is the detail of parameters:

- This is a default method and this do not accept any parameters.

Return Value

- This method returns a canonical representation for the string object.

Example

```
import java.io.*;
public class Test{
public static void main(String args[]){
String Str1 = new String("Welcome to java.com");
String Str2 = new String("WELCOME TO JAVA.COM");
System.out.print("Canonical representation:" );
System.out.println(Str1.intern());
System.out.print("Canonical representation:" );
System.out.println(Str2.intern());
}
}
```

This will produce the following result:

Canonical representation: Welcome to java.com

Canonical representation: WELCOME TO JAVA.COM

Java – String lastIndexOf(int ch) Method

Description

This method returns the index of the last occurrence of the character in the character sequence represented by this object that is less than or equal to from Index, or -1 if the character does not occur before that point.

Syntax

Here is the syntax of this method:

```
int lastIndexOf(int ch)
```

Parameters

Here is the detail of parameters:

- **ch** — a character.

Return Value

- This method returns the index.

Example

```java
import java.io.*;
public class Test {
public static void main(String args[]) {
String Str = new String("Welcome to java.com");
System.out.print("Found Last Index :" );
System.out.println(Str.lastIndexOf( 'o' ));
}
}
```

This will produce the following result:

Found Last Index :27

Java – String lastIndexOf(int ch, int fromIndex) Method

Description

This method returns the index of the last occurrence of the character in the character sequence represented by this object that is less than or equal to from Index, or -1 if the character does not occur before that point.

Syntax

Here is the syntax of this method:

```java
public int lastIndexOf(int ch, int fromIndex)
```

Parameters

Here is the detail of parameters:

- **ch** — a character.
- **fromIndex** — the index to start the search from.

Return Value

- This method returns the index.

Example

```java
import java.io.*;
public class Test {
public static void main(String args[]) {
String Str = new String("Welcome to java.com");
System.out.print("Found Last Index :" );
System.out.println(Str.lastIndexOf( 'o', 5 ));
}
}
```

This will produce the following result:

Found Last Index :4

Java – String lastIndexOf(String str) Method

Description

This method accepts a String as an argument, if the string

argument occurs one or more times as a substring within this object, then it returns the index of the first character of the last such substring is returned. If it does not occur as a substring, -1 is returned.

Syntax

Here is the syntax of this method:

```
public int lastIndexOf(Stringstr)
```

Parameters

Here is the detail of parameters:

- **str** — a string

Return Value

- This method returns the index.

Example

```
import java.io.*;
public class Test {
public static void main(String args[]) {
String Str = new String("Welcome to java.com");
String SubStr1 = new String("java" );
System.out.print("Found Last Index :" );
System.out.println( Str.lastIndexOf(SubStr1 ));
}
}
```

This will produce the following result:

Found Last Index :11

Java – String lastIndexOf(String str, int fromIndex) Method

Description

This method returns the index within this string of the last occurrence of the specified substring, searching backward starting at the specified index.

Syntax

Here is the syntax of this method:

```
public int lastIndexOf(Stringstr, int fromIndex)
```

Parameters

Here is the detail of parameters:

- **fromIndex** — the index to start the search from.
- **str** — a string.

Return Value

- This method returns the index.

Example

```java
import java.io.*;
public class Test {
public static void main(String args[]) {
String Str = new String("Welcome to java.com");
String SubStr1 = new String("java" );
System.out.print("Found Last Index :" );
System.out.println( Str.lastIndexOf(SubStr1, 15
));
}
}
```

This will produce the following result:

Found Last Index :11

Java – String length() Method

Description

This method returns the length of this string. The length is equal to the number of 16-bit Unicode characters in the string.

Syntax

Here is the syntax of this method:

```java
public int length()
```

Parameters

Here is the detail of parameters:

- NA

Return Value

This method returns the the length of the sequence of characters represented by this object.

Example

```java
import java.io.*;
public class Test{
public static void main(String args[]){
String Str1 = new String("Welcome to java.com");
String Str2 = new String("java");
System.out.print("String Length :" );
System.out.println(Str1.length());
System.out.print("String Length :" );
System.out.println(Str2.length());
}
}
```

This will produce the following result:

String Length :29

String Length :9

Java – String matches() Method

Description

This method tells whether or not this string matches the given regular expression. An invocation of this method of the form str.matches(regex) yields exactly the same result as the expression Pattern.matches(regex, str).

Syntax

Here is the syntax of this method:

```
public boolean matches(Stringregex)
```

Parameters

Here is the detail of parameters:

- **regex** — the regular expression to which this string is to be matched.

Return Value

- This method returns true if, and only if, this string matches the given regular expression.

Example

```java
import java.io.*;
public class Test{
public static void main(String args[]){
String Str = new String("Welcome to java.com");
System.out.print("Return Value :" );
System.out.println(Str.matches("(.*)java(.*)"));
```

```
System.out.print("Return Value :" );
System.out.println(Str.matches("java"));
System.out.print("Return Value :" );
System.out.println(Str.matches("Welcome(.*)"));
   }
}
```

This will produce the following result:

```
Return Value :true

Return Value :false

Return Value :true
```

Java – String regionMatches() Method

Description

This method has two variants which can be used to test if two string regions are equal.

Syntax

Here is the syntax of this method:

```
public boolean regionMatches(int toffset, String other, int ooffset,
int len)
```

or

```
public boolean regionMatches(boolean ignoreCase, int toffset,
```

```
String other, int ooffset,
int len)
```

Parameters

Here is the detail of parameters:

- **toffset** — the starting offset of the subregion in this string.
- **other** — the string argument.
- **ooffset** — the starting offset of the subregion in the string argument.
- **len** — the number of characters to compare.
- **ignoreCase** — if true, ignore case when comparing characters.

Return Value

It returns true if the specified subregion of this string matches the specified subregion of the string argument; false otherwise. Whether the matching is exact or case insensitive depends on the ignore Case argument.

Example

```
import java.io.*;
public class Test{
public static void main(String args[]){
String Str1 = new String("Welcome to java.com");
String Str2 = new String("java");
String Str3 = new String("JAVA");
```

```
System.out.print("Return Value :" );
System.out.println(Str1.regionMatches(11, Str2,
0, 9));
System.out.print("Return Value :" );
System.out.println(Str1.regionMatches(11, Str3,
0, 9));
System.out.print("Return Value :" );
System.out.println(Str1.regionMatches(true, 11,
Str3, 0, 9));
   }
}
```

This will produce the following result:

Return Value :true

Return Value :false

Return Value :true

Java – String regionMatches() Method

Description

This method has two variants which can be used to test if two string regions are equal.

Syntax

Here is the syntax of this method:

```
public boolean regionMatches(int toffset, String
other, int ooffset, int len)
```

or

```
public boolean regionMatches(boolean ignoreCase,
int toffset,
String other, int ooffset, int len)
```

Parameters

Here is the detail of parameters:

- **toffset** — the starting offset of the subregion in this string.
- **other** — the string argument.
- **ooffset** — the starting offset of the subregion in the string argument.
- **len** — the number of characters to compare.
- **ignoreCase** — if true, ignore case when comparing characters.

Return Value

It returns true if the specified subregion of this string matches the specified subregion of the string argument; false otherwise. Whether the matching is exact or case insensitive depends on the ignoreCase argument.

Example

```
import java.io.*;
public class Test{
```

```
public static void main(String args[]){
String Str1 = new String("Welcome to java.com");
String Str2 = new String("java");
String Str3 = new String("JAVA");
System.out.print("Return Value :" );
System.out.println(Str1.regionMatches(11, Str2,
0, 9));
System.out.print("Return Value :" );
System.out.println(Str1.regionMatches(11, Str3,
0, 9));
System.out.print("Return Value :" );
System.out.println(Str1.regionMatches(true, 11,
Str3, 0, 9));
}
}
```

This will produce the following result:

Return Value :true Return Value :false Return Value :true

Java – String replace() Method

Description

This method returns a new string resulting from replacing all occurrences of oldChar in this string with newChar.

Syntax

Here is the syntax of this method:

```
public String replace(char oldChar, char newChar)
```

Parameters

Here is the detail of parameters:

- **oldChar** — the old character.
- **newChar** — the new character.

Return Value

It returns a string derived from this string by replacing every occurrence of oldChar with newChar.

Example

```java
import java.io.*;
public class Test{
public static void main(String args[]){
String Str = new String("Welcome to java.com");
System.out.print("Return Value :" );
System.out.println(Str.replace('o', 'T'));
System.out.print("Return Value :" );
System.out.println(Str.replace('l', 'D'));
}
}
```

This will produce the following result:

Return Value :WelcTme tT TutTrialspTint.cTm

Return Value :WeDcome to TutoriaDspoint.com

Java – String replaceAll() Method

Description

This method replaces each substring of this string that matches the given regular expression with the given replacement.

Syntax

Here is the syntax of this method:

```
public String replaceAll(String regex, String
replacement)
```

Parameters

Here is the detail of parameters:

- **regex** — the regular expression to which this string is to be matched.
- **replacement** — the string which would replace found expression.

Return Value

This method returns the resulting String.

Example

```java
import java.io.*;
public class Test{
public static void main(String args[]){
String Str = new String("Welcome to java.com");
System.out.print("Return Value :" );
System.out.println(Str.replaceAll("(.*)java(.*)",
"AMROOD" ));
}
}
```

This will produce the following result:

Return Value :AMROOD

Java – String replaceFirst() Method

Description

This method replaces the first substring of this string that matches the given regular expression with the given replacement.

Syntax

Here is the syntax of this method:

```java
public String replaceFirst(String regex, String
replacement)
```

Parameters

Here is the detail of parameters:

- **regex** — the regular expression to which this string is to be matched.
- **replacement** — the string which would replace found expression.

Return Value

This method returns a resulting String.

Example

```java
import java.io.*;
public class Test{
public static void main(String args[]){
String Str = new String("Welcome to java.com");
System.out.print("Return Value :" );
System.out.println(Str.replaceFirst("(.*)java(.*)",
"AMROOD" ));
System.out.print("Return Value :" );
System.out.println(Str.replaceFirst("java",
"AMROOD" ));
}
}
```

This will produce the following result:

Return Value :AMROOD

Return Value :Welcome to AMROODpoint.com

Java – String split() Method

Description

This method has two variants and splits this string around matches of the given regular expression.

Syntax

Here is the syntax of this method:

```
public String[] split(String regex, int limit)
```

or

```
public String[] split(String regex)
```

Parameters

Here is the detail of parameters:

- **regex** — the delimiting regular expression.
- **limit** — the result threshold, which means how many strings to be returned

Return Value

It returns the array of strings computed by splitting this string around matches of the given regular expression.

Example

```java
import java.io.*;
public class Test{
public static void main(String args[]){
String Str = new String("Welcome-to-java.com");
System.out.println("Return Value :" );
for (String retval: Str.split("-", 2)){
System.out.println(retval);
} System.out.println("");
System.out.println("Return Value :" ); for
(String retval: Str.split("-", 3)){
System.out.println(retval);
}
System.out.println("");
System.out.println("Return Value :" ); for
(String retval: Str.split("-", 0)){
System.out.println(retval);
} System.out.println("");
System.out.println("Return Value :" ); for
(String retval: Str.split("-")){
System.out.println(retval);
}
}
}
```

This will produce the following result:

```
Return Value : Welcome to-java.com

Return Value : Welcome to java.com

Return Value: Welcome to java.com

Return Value : Welcome to java.com
```

Java – String split() Method

Description

This method has two variants and splits this string around matches of the given regular expression.

Syntax

Here is the syntax of this method:

```
public String[] split(String regex, int limit)
```

or

```
public String[] split(String regex)
```

Parameters

Here is the detail of parameters:

- **regex** — the delimiting regular expression.
- **limit** — the result threshold which means how many strings to be returned.

Return Value

It returns the array of strings computed by splitting this string around matches of the given regular expression.

Example

```
import java.io.*;
public class Test{
```

```
public static void main(String args[]){
String Str = new String("Welcome-to-java.com");
System.out.println("Return Value :" );
for (String retval: Str.split("-", 2)){
System.out.println(retval);
} System.out.println("");
System.out.println("Return Value :" ); for
(String retval: Str.split("-", 3)){
System.out.println(retval);
}
System.out.println("");
System.out.println("Return Value :" ); for
(String retval: Str.split("-", 0)){
System.out.println(retval);
} System.out.println("");
System.out.println("Return Value :" ); for
(String retval: Str.split("-")){
System.out.println(retval);
}
}
}
```

This will produce the following result:

```
Return Value : Welcome to-java.com
Return Value : Welcome to java.com
Return Value: Welcome to java.com
Return Value : Welcome to java.com
```

Java – String startsWith() Method

Description

This method has two variants and tests if a string starts with the specified prefix beginning a specified index or by default at the beginning.

Syntax

Here is the syntax of this method:

```
public boolean startsWith(String prefix, int
toffset)
```

or

```
public boolean startsWith(String prefix)
```

Parameters

Here is the detail of parameters:

- **prefix** — the prefix to be matched.
- **toffset** — where to begin looking in the string.

Return Value

It returns true if the character sequence represented by the argument is a prefix of the character sequence represented by this string; false otherwise.

Example

```java
import java.io.*;
public class Test{
public static void main(String args[]){
String Str = new String("Welcome to java.com");
System.out.print("Return Value :" );
System.out.println(Str.startsWith("Welcome") );
System.out.print("Return Value :" );
System.out.println(Str.startsWith("java") )
System.out.print("Return Value :" );
System.out.println(Str.startsWith("java", 11) );
}
}
```

This will produce the following result:

```
Return Value :true
   Return Value :false
   Return Value :true
```

Java – String startsWith() Method

Description

This method has two variants and tests if a string starts with the specified prefix beginning a specified index or by default at the beginning.

Syntax

Here is the syntax of this method:

```
public boolean startsWith(String prefix, int
toffset)
```

or

```
public boolean startsWith(String prefix)
```

Parameters

Here is the detail of parameters:

- **prefix** — the prefix to be matched.
- **toffset** — where to begin looking in the string.

Return Value

It returns true if the character sequence represented by the argument is a prefix of the character sequence represented by this string; false otherwise.

Example

```
import java.io.*;
public class Test{
public static void main(String args[]){
String Str = new String("Welcome to java.com");
System.out.print("Return Value :" );
System.out.println(Str.startsWith("Welcome") );
System.out.print("Return Value :" );
System.out.println(Str.startsWith("java") );
System.out.print("Return Value :" );
System.out.println(Str.startsWith("java", 11) );
```

```
    }
}
```

This will produce the following result:

```
Return Value :true
    Return Value :false
    Return Value :true
```

Java – String subsequence() Method

Description

This method returns a new character sequence that is a subsequence of this sequence.

Syntax

Here is the syntax of this method:

```
public CharSequence subSequence(int beginIndex,
int endIndex)
```

Parameters

Here is the detail of parameters:

- **beginIndex** — the begin index, inclusive.
- **endIndex** — the end index, exclusive.

Return Value

This method returns the specified subsequence.

Example

```java
import java.io.*;
public class Test{
public static void main(String args[]){
String Str = new String("Welcome to java.com");
System.out.print("Return Value :" );
System.out.println(Str.subSequence(0, 10) );
System.out.print("Return Value :" );
System.out.println(Str.subSequence(10, 15) );
}
}
```

This will produce the following result:

Return Value :Welcome to

Return Value : Tuto

Java – String substring() Method

Description

This method has two variants and returns a new string that is a substring of this string. The substring begins with the character at the specified index and extends to the end of this string or up to endIndex − 1, if the second argument is given.

Syntax

Here is the syntax of this method:

```
public String substring(int beginIndex)
```

or

```
public String substring(int beginIndex, int
endIndex)
```

Parameters

Here is the detail of parameters:

- beginIndex — the begin index, inclusive.
- **endIndex** — the end index, exclusive.

Return Value

The specified substring.

Example

```
import java.io.*;
public class Test{
public static void main(String args[]){
String Str = new String("Welcome to java.com");
System.out.print("Return Value :" );
System.out.println(Str.substring(10) );
System.out.print("Return Value :" );
```

```
System.out.println(Str.substring(10, 15) );
   }
}
```

This will produce the following result:

Return Value : java.com

Return Value : Tuto

Java – String substring() Method

Description

This method has two variants and returns a new string that is a substring of this string. The substring begins with the character at the specified index and extends to the end of this string or up to endIndex – 1, if the second argument is given.

Syntax

Here is the syntax of this method:

```
public String substring(int beginIndex)
```

or

```
public String substring(int beginIndex, int
endIndex)
```

Parameters

Here is the detail of parameters:

- **beginIndex** — the begin index, inclusive.
- **endIndex** — the end index, exclusive.

Return Value

The specified substring.

Example

```java
import java.io.*;
public class Test{
public static void main(String args[]){
String Str = new String("Welcome to java.com");
System.out.print("Return Value :" );
System.out.println(Str.substring(10) );
System.out.print("Return Value :" );
System.out.println(Str.substring(10, 15) );
}
}
```

This will produce the following result:

Return Value : java.com

Return Value : Tuto

Java – String toCharArray() Method

Description

This method converts this string to a new character array.

Syntax

Here is the syntax of this method:

```
public char[] toCharArray()
```

Parameters

Here is the detail of parameters:

- NA

Return Value

It returns a newly allocated character array, whose length is the length of this string and whose contents are initialized to contain the character sequence represented by this string.

Example

```
import java.io.*;
public class Test{
public static void main(String args[]){
String Str = new String("Welcome to java.com");
System.out.print("Return Value :" );
System.out.println(Str.toCharArray() );
}
}
```

This will produce the following result:

Return Value :Welcome to java.com

Description

This method has two variants. The first variant converts all of the characters in this String to lower case using the rules of the given Locale. This is equivalent to calling toLowerCase(Locale.getDefault()). The second variant takes locale as an argument to be used while converting into lower case.

Syntax

Here is the syntax of this method:

```
public String toLowerCase()
```

or

```
public String toLowerCase(Locale locale)
```

Parameters

Here is the detail of parameters:

- NA

Return Value

It returns the String, converted to lowercase.

Example

```java
import java.io.*;
public class Test{
public static void main(String args[]){
String Str = new String("Welcome to java.com");
System.out.print("Return Value :");
System.out.println(Str.toLowerCase());
}
}
```

This will produce the following result:

Return Value :welcome to java.com

Description

This method has two variants. The first variant converts all of the characters in this String to lower case using the rules of the given Locale. This is equivalent to calling toLowerCase(Locale.getDefault()).

The second variant takes locale as an argument to be used while converting into lower case.

Syntax

Here is the syntax of this method:

```
public String toLowerCase()
```

or

```
public String toLowerCase(Locale locale)
```

Parameters

Here is the detail of parameters:

- NA

Return Value

It returns the String, converted to lowercase.

Example

```java
import java.io.*;
public class Test{
public static void main(String args[]){
String Str = new String("Welcome to java.com");
System.out.print("Return Value :");
System.out.println(Str.toLowerCase());
}
}
```

This will produce the following result:

Return Value :welcome to java.com

Java – String toString() Method

Description

This method returns itself a string.

Syntax

Here is the syntax of this method:

```
public String toString()
```

Parameters

Here is the detail of parameters:

- NA

Return Value

This method returns the string itself.

Example

```
import java.io.*;
public class Test {
public static void main(String args[]) {
String Str = new String("Welcome to java.com");
System.out.print("Return Value :");
System.out.println(Str.toString());
}
```

```
  }
```

This will produce the following result:

Return Value :Welcome to java.com

Java – String toUpperCase() Method

This method has two variants. The first variant converts all of the characters in this String to upper case using the rules of the given Locale. This is equivalent to calling toUpperCase(Locale.getDefault()).

The second variant takes locale as an argument to be used while converting into upper case.

Syntax

Here is the syntax of this method:

```
public String toUpperCase()
```

or

```
public String toUpperCase(Locale locale)
```

Parameters

Here is the detail of parameters:

- NA

Return Value

- It returns the String, converted to uppercase.

Example

```
import java.io.*;
public class Test{
public static void main(String args[]){
String Str = new String("Welcome to java.com");
System.out.print("Return Value :" );
System.out.println(Str.toUpperCase() );
}
}
```

This will produce the following result:

Return Value :WELCOME TO JAVA.COM

Java – String toUpperCase() Method

This method has two variants. The first variant converts all of the characters in this String to upper case using the rules of the given Locale. This is equivalent to calling toUpperCase(Locale.getDefault()).

The second variant takes locale as an argument to be used while converting into upper case.

Syntax

Here is the syntax of this method:

```
public String toUpperCase()
```

or

```
public String toUpperCase(Locale locale)
```

Parameters

Here is the detail of parameters:

- NA

Return Value

- It returns the String, converted to uppercase.

Example

```
import java.io.*;
public class Test{
public static void main(String args[]){
String Str = new String("Welcome to java.com");
System.out.print("Return Value :" );
System.out.println(Str.toUpperCase() );
}
}
```

This produces the following result:

Return Value :WELCOME TO JAVA.COM

Java – String trim() Method

Description

This method returns a copy of the string, with leading and trailing whitespace omitted.

Syntax

Here is the syntax of this method:

```
public String trim()
```

Parameters

Here is the detail of parameters:

- NA

Return Value

It returns a copy of this string with leading and trailing white space removed, or this string if it has no leading or trailing white space.

Example

```
import java.io.*;
public class Test{
public static void main(String args[]){
String Str = new String("  Welcome to java.com
");
System.out.print("Return Value :" );
System.out.println(Str.trim() );
}
}
```

This produces the following result:

Return Value :Welcome to java.com

Java – String valueOf( ) Method

Description

This method has the following variants, which depend on the passed parameters. This method returns the string representation of the passed argument.

- **valueOf(boolean b):** Returns the string representation of the boolean argument.
- **valueOf(char c):** Returns the string representation of the char argument.
- **valueOf(char[] data):** Returns the string representation of the char array argument.
- **valueOf(char[] data, int offset, int count):** Returns the string representation of a specific subarray of thechar array argument.

- **valueOf(double d):** Returns the string representation of the double argument.
- **valueOf(float f):** Returns the string representation of the float argument.
- **valueOf(int i):** Returns the string representation of the int argument.
- **valueOf(long l):** Returns the string representation of the long argument.
- **valueOf(Object obj):** Returns the string representation of the Object argument.

Syntax

Here is the syntax of this method:

```
static String valueOf(boolean b)
```

or

```
static String valueOf(char c)
```

or

```
static String valueOf(char[] data)
```

or

```
static String valueOf(char[] data, int offset,
int count)
```

or

```
  static String valueOf(double d)
```

or

```
  static String valueOf(float f)
```

or

```
  static String valueOf(int i)
```

or

```
  static String valueOf(long l)
```

or

```
  static String valueOf(Object obj)
```

Parameters

Here is the detail of parameters:

See the description.

Return Value

This method returns the string representation.

Example

```java
import java.io.*;
public class Test{
public static void main(String args[]){
double d = 102939939.939;
boolean b = true;
long l = 1232874;
char[] arr = {'a', 'b', 'c', 'd', 'e', 'f','g' };
System.out.println("Return Value : " +
String.valueOf(d) ); System.out.println("Return
Value : " + String.valueOf(b) );
System.out.println("Return Value : " +
String.valueOf(l) ); System.out.println("Return
Value : " + String.valueOf(arr) );
}
}
```

This will produce the following result:

Return Value : 1.02939939939E8

Return Value : true

Return Value : 1232874

Return Value : abcdefg

Arrays

Java provides a data structure, the **array**, which stores a fixed-size sequential collection of elements of the same type. An array is used to store a collection of data, but it is often more useful to think of an array as a collection of variables of the same type.

Instead of declaring individual variables, such as number0, number1, ..., and number99, you declare one array variable such as numbers and use numbers[0], numbers[1], and ..., numbers[99] to represent individual variables.

This chapter introduces how to declare array variables, create arrays, and process arrays using indexed variables.

Declaring Array Variables

To use an array in a program, you must declare a variable to reference the array, and you must specify the type of array the variable can reference. Here is the syntax for declaring an array variable:

```
dataType[] arrayRefVar;  // preferred way.
```

or

```
dataType arrayRefVar[]; // works but not
preferredway.
```

Note: The style **dataType[] arrayRefVar** is preferred. The style **dataType arrayRefVar[]** comes from the C/C++ language and was adopted in Java to accommodate C/C++ programmers.

Example

The following code snippets are examples of this syntax:

```
double[] myList;        // preferred way.
```

or

```
double myList[];        // works but not
preferredway.
```

Creating Arrays

You can create an array by using the new operator with the following syntax:

```
arrayRefVar = new dataType[arraySize];
```

The above statement does two things:

- It creates an array using new dataType[arraySize].
- It assigns the reference of the newly created array to the variable arrayRefVar. Declaring an array variable, creating an array, and assigning the reference of the array to the variable can be combined in one statement, as shown below:

```
dataType[] arrayRefVar = newdataType[arraySize];
```

Alternatively you can create arrays as follows:

```
dataType[] arrayRefVar = {value0, value1, ...,
valuek};
```

The array elements are accessed through the **index**. Array indices are 0-based; that is, they start from 0 to **arrayRef-Var.length-1**.

Example

Following statement declares an array variable, myList, creates an array of 10 elements of double type and assigns its reference to myList:

```
double[] myList = new double[10];
```

Following picture represents array myList. Here, myList holds ten double values and the indices are from 0 to 9.

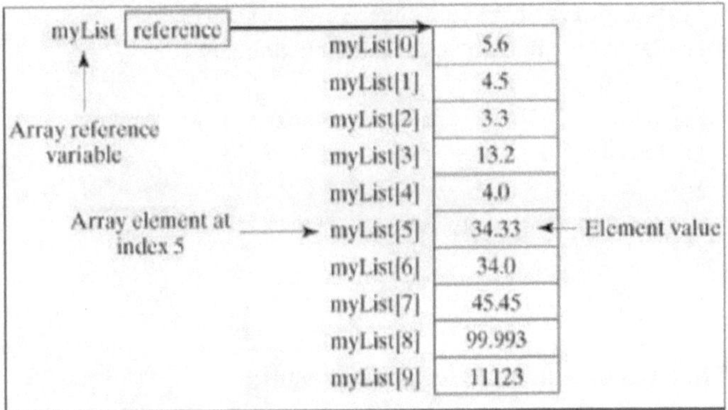

Processing Arrays

When processing array elements, we often use either **for** loop or **foreach** loop because all of the elements in an array are of the same type and the size of the array is known.

Example

Here is a complete example showing how to create, initialize, and process arrays:

```
public class TestArray {
public static void main(String[] args) {
double[] myList = {1.9, 2.9, 3.4, 3.5};
// Print all the array elements
```

```java
for (int i = 0; i < myList.length; i++) {
System.out.println(myList[i] + " ");
}
// Summing all elements double total = 0;
for (int i = 0; i < myList.length; i++) {
total += myList[i];
}
System.out.println("Total is " + total);
// Finding the largest element double max =
myList[0];
for (int i = 1; i < myList.length; i++) {
if (myList[i] > max)max = myList[i];
}
System.out.println("Max is "+ max);
}
}
```

This will produce the following result:

1.9

2.9

3.4

3.5

Total is 11.7

Max is 3.5

The foreach Loops

JDK 1.5 introduced a new for loop known as foreach loop or enhanced for loop, which enables you to traverse the complete array sequentially without using an index variable.

Example

```
The following code displays all the elements in
the array myList:
public class TestArray {
public static void main(String[] args) {
double[] myList = {1.9, 2.9, 3.4, 3.5};
// Print all the array elements for (double
element: myList) {
System.out.println(element);
}
}
}
```

This will produce the following result:

1.9

2.9

3.4

3.5

Passing Arrays to Methods

Just as you can pass primitive type values to methods, you can also pass arrays to methods. For example, the following method displays the elements in an **int** array:

```
public static void printArray(int[] array) {
for (int i = 0; i < array.length; i++) {
System.out.print(array[i] + " ");
}
}
```

You can invoke it by passing an array. For example, the following statement invokes the printArray method to display 3, 1, 2, 6, 4, and 2:

    printArray(new int[]{3, 1, 2, 6, 4, 2});

Returning an Array from a Method

A method may also return an array. For example, the following method returns an array that is the reversal of another array:

```java
public static int[] reverse(int[] list) {
int[] result = new int[list.length];
for (int i = 0, j = result.length - 1; i
<list.length; i++, j--) {
result[j] = list[i];
}
return result;
}
```

The Arrays Class

The java.util.Arrays class contains various static methods for sorting and searching arrays, comparing arrays, and filling array elements. These methods are overloaded for all primitive types.

Methods with Description

- **public static int binarySearch(Object[]a, Object key)**
  Searches the specified array of Object (Byte, Int , double, etc.) for the specified value using the binary search

algorithm. The array must be sorted prior to making this call. This returns index of the search key, if it is contained in the list; otherwise, it returns (− (insertion point + 1)).

- **public static boolean equals(long[] a, long[] a2)** Returns true if the two specified arrays of longs are equal to one another. Two arrays are considered equal if both arrays contain the same number of elements, and all corresponding pairs of elements in the two arrays are equal. This returns true if the two arrays are equal. Same method could be used by all other primitive data types (Byte, short, Int, etc.)
- **public static void fill(int[] a, int val)** Assigns the specified int value to each element of the specified array of ints. The same method could be used by all other primitive data types (Byte, short, Int, etc.)
- **public static void sort(Object[] a)** Sorts the specified array of objects into an ascending order, according to the natural ordering of its elements. The same method could be used by all other primitive data types (Byte, short, Int, etc.)

Date & Time

Java provides the **Date** class available in **java.util** package, this class encapsulates the current date and time.

The Date class supports two constructors as shown in the following table.

Sr. No	Constructor and Description
1	Date( ) This constructor initializes the object with the current date and time.
2	Date(long millisec) This constructor accepts an argument that equals the number of milliseconds that have elapsed since midnight, January 1, 1970.

Following are the methods of the date class.

Methods with Description

- **boolean after(Date date)** Returns true if the invoking Date object contains a date that is later than the one specified by date, otherwise, it returns false.

- **boolean before(Date date)** Returns true if the invoking Date object contains a date that is earlier than the one specified by date, otherwise, it returns false.
- **Objectclone( )** Duplicates the invoking Date object.
- **int compareTo(Date date)** Compares the value of the invoking object with that of date. Returns 0 if the values are equal. Returns a negative value if the invoking object is earlier than date. Returns a positive value if the invoking object is later than date.
- **int compareTo(Object obj)** Operates identically to compareTo(Date) if obj is of class Date. Otherwise, it throws a ClassCastException.
- **boolean equals(Object date)** Returns true if the invoking Date object contains the same time and date as the one specified by date, otherwise, it returns false.
- **long getTime( )** Returns the number of milliseconds that have elapsed since January 1, 1970.
- **int hashCode( )** Returns a hash code for the invoking object.
- **void setTime(long time)** Sets the time and date as specified by time, which represents an elapsed time in milliseconds from midnight, January 1, 1970
- **String toString( )** Converts the invoking Date object into a string and returns the result.

Getting Current Date & Time

This is a very easy method to get current date and time in Java. You can use a simple

Date object with *toString()* method to print the current date and time as follows:

```java
import java.util.Date;
public class DateDemo {
public static void main(String args[]) {
// Instantiate a Date object
Date date = new Date();
// display time and date using toString()
System.out.println(date.toString());
}
}
```

This will produce the following result:

on May 04 09:51:52 CDT 2009

Date Comparison

Following are the three ways to compare two dates:

- You can use getTime( ) to obtain the number of millisec-onds that have elapsed since midnight, January 1, 1970, for both objects and then compare these two values.
- You can use the methods before( ), after( ), and equals( ). Because the 12th of the month comes before the 18th, for example, new Date(99, 2, 12).before(new Date (99, 2, 18)) returns true.
- You can use the compareTo( ) method, which is defined by the Comparable interface and implemented by Date.

Date Formatting Using SimpleDateFormat

SimpleDateFormat is a concrete class for formatting and parsing dates in a locale-sensitive manner. SimpleDateFormat allows you to start by choosing any user-defined patterns for date-time formatting. For example:

```java
import java.util.*;
import java.text.*;
public class DateDemo {
public static void main(String args[]) {
Date dNow = new Date( ); SimpleDateFormat ft =
new SimpleDateFormat ("Eyyyy.MM.dd 'at' hh:mm:ss
a zzz");
System.out.println("Current Date: "+
ft.format(dNow));
}
}
```

This will produce the following result:

Current Date: Sun 2004.07.18 at 04:14:09 PM PDT

Date Formatting Using printf

Date and time formatting can be done very easily using **printf** method. You use a two- letter format, starting with **t** and ending in one of the letters of the table as shown in the following code. For example:

```java
import java.util.Date;
public class DateDemo {
public static void main(String args[]) {
// Instantiate a Date object
Date date = new Date();
```

```
// display time and date using toString()
String str = String.format("Current Date/Time :
%tc",date );
System.out.printf(str);
}
}
```

This will produce the following result:

Current Date/Time : Sat Dec 15 16:37:57 MST 2012

It would be a bit silly if you had to supply the date multiple times to format each part. For that reason, a format string can indicate the index of the argument to be formatted.

The index must immediately follow the % and it must be terminated by a $. For example:

```
import java.util.Date;
public class DateDemo {
public static void main(String args[]) {
// Instantiate a Date object
Date date = new Date();
// display time and date using toString()
System.out.printf("%1$s %2$tB %2$td, %2$tY",
"Due date:", date);
}
}
```

This will produce the following result:

Due date: February 09, 2004

Alternatively, you can use the < flag. It indicates that the same argument as in the preceding format specification should be used again. For example:

```java
import java.util.Date;
public class DateDemo {
public static void main(String args[]) {
// Instantiate a Date object
Date date = new Date();
// display formatted date
System.out.printf("%s %tB %<te, %<tY", "Due
date:", date);
}
}
```

This will produce the following result:

Due date: February 09, 2004

Date and Time Conversion Characters

Character	Description	Example
c	Complete date and time	Mon May 04 09:51:52 CDT 2009
F	ISO 8601 date	2004-02-09
D	U.S. formatted date (month/day/year)	02/09/2004
T	24-hour time	18:05:19
r	12-hour time	06:05:19 pm
R	24-hour time, no seconds	18:05
Y	Four-digit year (with leading zeroes)	2004
y	Last two digits of the year (with leading zeroes)	04
C	First two digits of the year (with leading zeroes)	20
B	Full month name	February
b	Abbreviated month name	Feb
m	Two-digit month (with leading zeroes)	02
d	Two-digit day (with leading zeroes)	03
e	Two-digit day (without leading zeroes)	9
A	Full weekday name	Monday
a	Abbreviated weekday name	Mon
j	Three-digit day of year (with leading zeroes)	069
H	Two-digit hour (with leading zeroes), between 00 and 23	18
k	Two-digit hour (without leading zeroes), between 0 and 23	18

I	Two-digit hour (with leading zeroes), between 01 and 12	06
l	Two-digit hour (without leading zeroes), between 1 and 12	6
M	Two-digit minutes (with leading zeroes)	05
S	Two-digit seconds (with leading zeroes)	19
L	Three-digit milliseconds (with leading zeroes)	047
N	Nine-digit nanoseconds (with leading zeroes)	047000000
P	Uppercase morning or afternoon marker	PM
p	Lowercase morning or afternoon marker	pm
z	RFC 822 numeric offset from GMT	-0800
Z	Time zone	PST
s	Seconds since 1970-01-01 00:00:00 GMT	1078884319
Q	Milliseconds since 1970-01-01 00:00:00 GMT	1078884319047

There are other useful classes related to Date and time. For more details, you can refer to Java Standard documentation.

Parsing Strings into Dates

The SimpleDateFormat class has some additional methods, notably parse( ), which tries to parse a string according to the format stored in the given SimpleDateFormat object. For example:

```java
import java.util.*;
import java.text.*;
public class DateDemo {
public static void main(String args[]) {
```

```
SimpleDateFormat ft = new SimpleDateFormat
("yyyy-MM-dd");
String input = args.length == 0 ? "1818-11-11" :
args[0]; System.out.print(input + "Parses as ");
Date t;
try {
t = ft.parse(input); System.out.println(t);
} catch (ParseException e) {
System.out.println("Unparseable using "+ ft);
}
}
}
```

A sample run of the above program would produce the following result:

```
$ java DateDemo

  1818-11-11 Parses as Wed Nov 11 00:00:00 GMT 1818

  $ java DateDemo 2007-12-01

  2007-12-01 Parses as Sat Dec 01 00:00:00 GMT 2007
```

Sleeping for a While

You can sleep for any period of time from one millisecond up to the lifetime of your computer. For example, the following program would sleep for 10 seconds:

```
import java.util.*;
public class SleepDemo {
public static void main(String args[]) {
try {
System.out.println(new Date( ) + "\n");
Thread.sleep(5*60*10); System.out.println(new
```

```
Date( ) + "\n");
} catch (Exception e) {
System.out.println("Got an exception!");
}
}
}
```

This will produce the following result:

Sun May 03 18:04:41 GMT 2009

Sun May 03 18:04:51 GMT 2009

Measuring Elapsed Time

Sometimes, you may need to measure point in time in milliseconds. So let's re-write the above example once again:

```
import java.util.*;
public class DiffDemo {
public static void main(String args[]) {
try {
long start = System.currentTimeMillis( );
System.out.println(new Date( ) + "\n");
Thread.sleep(5*60*10); System.out.println(new
Date( ) + "\n"); long end =
System.currentTimeMillis( ); long diff = end -
start;
System.out.println("Difference is : " + diff);
} catch (Exception e) { System.out.println("Got
an exception!");
}
}
}
```

This will produce the following result:

Sun May 03 18:16:51 GMT 2009

Sun May 03 18:16:57 GMT 2009

Difference is : 5993

GregorianCalendar Class

GregorianCalendar is a concrete implementation of a Calendar class that implements the normal Gregorian calendar with which you are familiar. We did not discuss Calendar class in this chapter, you can look up standard Java documentation for this.

The **getInstance( )** method of Calendar returns a GregorianCalendar initialized with the current date and time in the default locale and time zone. GregorianCalendar defines two fields: AD and BC. These represent the two eras defined by the Gregorian calendar.

There are also several constructors for GregorianCalendar objects:

Constructor with Description

- **GregorianCalendar()** Constructs a default GregorianCalendar using the current time in the default time zone with the default locale.
- **GregorianCalendar(int year, int month,int date)** Constructs a GregorianCalendar with the given date set in the default time zone with the default locale.

- **GregorianCalendar(int year, int month,int date, int hour, int minute)** Constructs a GregorianCalendar with the given date and time set for the default time zone with the default locale.
- **GregorianCalendar(int year, int month, int date, int hour, int minute, int second)** Constructs a Gregorian-Calendar with the given date and time set for the default time zone with the default locale.
- **GregorianCalendar(Locale aLocale)** Constructs a Gre-gorianCalendar based on the current time in the default time zone with the given locale.
- **GregorianCalendar(TimeZone zone)** Constructs a Gre-gorianCalendar based on the current time in the given time zone with the default locale.
- **GregorianCalendar(TimeZone zone, Locale aLocale)** Constructs a GregorianCalendar based on the current time in the given time zone with the given locale.

Here is the list of few useful support methods provided by GregorianCalendar class:

Methods with Description

- **void add(int field, int amount)** Adds the specified (signed) amount of time to the given time field, based on the calendar's rules.
- **protected void computeFields()** Converts UTC as mil-liseconds to time field values.
- **protected void computeTime()** Overrides Calendar Converts time field values to UTC as milliseconds.
- **boolean equals(Object obj)** Compares this Gregorian-

Calendar to an object reference.

- **int get(int field)** Gets the value for a given time field.
- **int getActualMaximum(intfield)** Returns the maximum value that this field could have, given the current date.
- **int getActualMinimum(int field)** Returns the minimum value that this field could have, given the current date.
- **int getGreatestMinimum(int field)** Returns highest minimum value for the given field if varies.
- **Date getGregorianChange()** Gets the Gregorian Calendar change date.
- **int getLeastMaximum(int field)** Returns lowest maximum value for the given field if varies.
- **int getMaximum(int field)** Returns maximum value for the given field.
- **Date getTime()** Gets this Calendar's current time.
- **long getTimeInMillis()** Gets this Calendar's current time as a long.
- **TimeZone getTimeZone()** Gets the time zone.
- **int getMinimum(int field)** Returns minimum value for the given field.
- **int hashCode()** Overrides hashCode.
- **boolean isLeapYear(int year)** Determines if the given year is a leap year.
- **void roll(int field, boolean up)** Adds or subtracts(up-/down) a single unit of time on the given time field without changing larger fields.
- **void set(int field, int value)** Sets the time field with the given value.
- **void set(int year, int month, int date)** Sets the values

for the fields year, month, and date.

- **void set(int year, int month, int date,int hour, int minute)** Sets the values for the fields year, month, date, hour, and minute.
- **void set(int year, int month, int date,int hour, int minute, int second)** Sets the values for the fields year, month, date, hour, minute, and second.
- **void setGregorianChange(Date date)** Sets the GregorianCalendar change date.
- **void setTime(Date date)** Sets this Calendar's current time with the given Date.
- **void setTimeInMillis(long millis)** Sets this Calendar's current time from the given long value.
- **void setTimeZone(TimeZone value)** Sets the time zone with the given time zone value.
- **String toString()** Returns a string representation of this calendar.

Example

```java
import java.util.*;
public class GregorianCalendarDemo {
public static void main(String args[]) { String
months[] = {
"Jan", "Feb", "Mar", "Apr", "May", "Jun", "Jul",
"Aug", "Sep", "Oct", "Nov", "Dec"};
int year;
// Create a Gregorian calendar initialized
// with the current date and time in the
// default locale and timezone.
GregorianCalendar gcalendar = new
GregorianCalendar();
```

```java
// Display current time and date information.
System.out.print("Date: ");
System.out.print(months[gcalendar.get(Calendar.MONTH)]);
System.out.print(" " +
gcalendar.get(Calendar.DATE) + " ");
System.out.println(year =
gcalendar.get(Calendar.YEAR));
System.out.print("Time: ");
System.out.print(gcalendar.get(Calendar.HOUR) +
":");
System.out.print(gcalendar.get(Calendar.MINUTE) +
":");
System.out.println(gcalendar.get(Calendar.SECOND));
// Test if the current year is a leap year
if(gcalendar.isLeapYear(year)) {
System.out.println("The current year is a leap
year");
}
else {
System.out.println("The current year is not a
leap year");
}
}
}
```

This will produce the following result:

Date: Apr 22 2009

Time: 11:25:27

The current year is not a leap year

For a complete list of constant available in Calendar class, you can refer the standard Java documentation.

Regular Expressions

Java provides the java.util.regex package for pattern matching with regular expressions. Java regular expressions are very similar to the Perl programming language and very easy to learn.

A regular expression is a special sequence of characters that helps you match or find other strings or sets of strings, using a specialized syntax held in a pattern. They can be used to search, edit, or manipulate text and data.

The java.util.regex package primarily consists of the following three classes:

- **Pattern Class:** A Pattern object is a compiled representation of a regular expression. The Pattern class provides no public constructors. To create a pattern, you must first invoke one of its public static **compile()** methods, which will then return a Pattern object. These methods accept a regular expression as the first argument.
- **Matcher Class:** A Matcher object is the engine that interprets the pattern and performs match operations against an input string. Like the Pattern class, Matcher

defines no public constructors. You obtain a Matcher object by invoking the **matcher()** method on a Pattern object.

- **PatternSyntaxException:** A PatternSyntaxException object is an unchecked exception that indicates a syntax error in a regular expression pattern.

Capturing Groups

Capturing groups are a way to treat multiple characters as a single unit. They are created by placing the characters to be grouped inside a set of parentheses. For example, the regular expression (dog) creates a single group containing the letters "d", "o",and "g".

Capturing groups are numbered by counting their opening parentheses from the left to the right. In the expression ((A)(B(C))), for example, there are four such groups:

- ((A)(B(C)))
- (A)
- (B(C))
- (C)

To find out how many groups are present in the expression, call the groupCount method on a matcher object. The groupCount method returns an **int** showing the number of capturing groups present in the matcher's pattern.

There is also a special group, group 0, which always represents the entire expression. This group is not included in the total reported by groupCount.

Example

Following example illustrates how to find a digit string from the given alphanumeric string:

```java
import java.util.regex.Matcher;
import java.util.regex.Pattern;
public class RegexMatches
{
public static void main( String args[] ){
// String to be scannedto find the pattern.
String line = "This order was placed for QT3000!
OK?"; String pattern = "(.*)(\\d+)(.*)";
// Create a Pattern object
Pattern r = Pattern.compile(pattern);
// Now create matcher object. Matcher m =
r.matcher(line); if (m.find( )) {
System.out.println("Found value: " + m.group(0) );
System.out.println("Found value: " + m.group(1)
); System.out.println("Found value: " +
m.group(2) );
} else {
System.out.println("NO MATCH");
}
}
}
```

This will produce the following result:

Found value: This order was placed for QT3000! OK?

Found value: This order was placed for QT300

Found value: 0

Regular Expression Syntax

Here is the table listing down all the regular expression metacharacter syntax available in Java:

Subexpression	Matches
^	Matches the beginning of the line.
$	Matches the end of the line.
.	Matches any single character except newline. Using m option allows it to match the newline as well.
[...]	Matches any single character in brackets.
[^...]	Matches any single character not in brackets.
\A	Beginning of the entire string.
\z	End of the entire string.
\Z	End of the entire string except allowable final line terminator.
re*	Matches 0 or more occurrences of the preceding expression.
re+	Matches 1 or more of the previous thing.

re?	Matches 0 or 1 occurrence of the preceding expression.
re{ n}	Matches exactly n number of occurrences of the preceding expression.
re{ n,}	Matches n or more occurrences of the preceding expression.
re{ n, m}	Matches at least n and at most m occurrences of the preceding expression.
a| b	Matches either a or b.
(re)	Groups regular expressions and remembers the matched text.
(?: re)	Groups regular expressions without remembering the matched text.

(?> re)	Matches the independent pattern without backtracking.
\w	Matches the word characters.
\W	Matches the nonword characters.
\s	Matches the whitespace. Equivalent to [\t\n\r\f].
\S	Matches the nonwhitespace.

\d	Matches the digits. Equivalent to [0-9].
\D	Matches the nondigits.
\A	Matches the beginning of the string.
\Z	Matches the end of the string. If a newline exists, it matches just before newline.
\z	Matches the end of the string.
\G	Matches the point where the last match finished.
\n	Back-reference to capture group number "n".

\b	Matches the word boundaries when outside the brackets. Matches the backspace (0x08) when inside the brackets.
\B	Matches the nonword boundaries.
\n, \t, etc.	Matches newlines, carriage returns, tabs, etc.
\Q	Escape (quote) all characters up to \E.
\E	Ends quoting begun with \Q.

Methods of the Matcher Class

Here is a list of useful instance methods:

Index Methods

Index methods provide useful index values that show precisely where the match was found in the input string:

Sr. No.	Methods with Description
1	**public int start()** Returns the start index of the previous match.
2	**public int start(int group)** Returns the start index of the subsequence captured by the given group during the previous match operation.
3	**public int end()** Returns the offset after the last character matched.
4	**public int end(int group)** Returns the offset after the last character of the subsequence captured by the given group during the previous match operation.

Study Methods

Study methods review the input string and return a Boolean indicating whether or not the pattern is found:

Sr. No.	Methods with Description
1	**public boolean lookingAt()** Attempts to match the input sequence, starting at the beginning of the region, against the pattern.
2	**public boolean find()** Attempts to find the next subsequence of the input sequence that matches the pattern.

3	**public boolean find(int start)** Resets this matcher and then attempts to find the next subsequence of the input sequence that matches the pattern, starting at the specified index.
4	**public boolean matches()** Attempts to match the entire region against the pattern.

Replacement Methods

Replacement methods are useful methods for replacing text in an input string:

Sr. No.	Methods with Description
1	**public Matcher appendReplacement(StringBuffer sb, String replacement)** Implements a non-terminal append-and-replace step.
2	**public StringBuffer appendTail(StringBuffer sb)** Implements a terminal append-and-replace step.
3	**public String replaceAll(String replacement)** Replaces every subsequence of the input sequence that matches the pattern with the given replacement string.
4	**public String replaceFirst(String replacement)** Replaces the first subsequence of the input sequence that matches the pattern with the given replacement string.
5	**public static String quoteReplacement(String s)** Returns a literal replacement String for the specified String. This method produces a String that will work as a literal replacement s in the appendReplacement method of the Matcher class.

The *start* and *end* Methods

Following is the example that counts the number of times the word "cat" appears in the input string:

```java
import java.util.regex.Matcher;
import java.util.regex.Pattern;
public class RegexMatches
{
private static final String REGEX = "\\bcat\\b";
private static final String INPUT =
"cat cat cat cattie cat";
public static void main( String args[] ){ Pattern
p = Pattern.compile(REGEX);
Matcher m = p.matcher(INPUT); // get a matcher
object
int count = 0;
while(m.find()) {
count++;
System.out.println("Match number "+count);
System.out.println("start(): "+m.start());
System.out.println("end(): "+m.end());
}
}
}
```

This will produce the following result:

Match number 1 start(): 0 end(): 3

Match number 2 start(): 4 end(): 7

Match number 3 start(): 8 end(): 11

Match number 4 start(): 19

end(): 22

You can see that this example uses word boundaries to ensure that the letters "c" "a" "t" are not merely a substring in a longer word. It also gives some useful information about where in the input string the match has occurred.

The start method returns the start index of the subsequence captured by the given group during the previous match operation, and the end returns the index of the last character matched, plus one.

The *matches* and *lookingAt* Methods

The matches and lookingAt methods both attempt to match an input sequence against a pattern. The difference, however, is that matches requires the entire input sequence to be matched, while lookingAt does not.

Both methods always start at the beginning of the input string. Here is the example explaining the functionality:

```java
import java.util.regex.Matcher;
import java.util.regex.Pattern;
public class RegexMatches
{
private static final String REGEX = "foo";
private static final String INPUT =
"fooooooooooooooooooo";
private static Pattern pattern;
private static Matcher matcher;
public static void main( String args[] ){ pattern
= Pattern.compile(REGEX); matcher =
pattern.matcher(INPUT);
System.out.println("Current REGEX is: "+REGEX);
System.out.println("Current INPUT is: "+INPUT);
System.out.println("lookingAt():
```

```
"+matcher.lookingAt());
System.out.println("matches():
"+matcher.matches());
}
}
```

This will produce the following result:

Current REGEX is: foo

    Current INPUT is: fooooooooooooooooo lookingAt(): true

    matches(): false

The replaceFirst and replaceAll Methods

The replaceFirst and replaceAll methods replace the text that matches a given regular expression. As their names indicate, replaceFirst replaces the first occurrence, and replaceAll replaces all occurrences.

Here is the example explaining the functionality:

```
import java.util.regex.Matcher;
import java.util.regex.Pattern;
public class RegexMatches
{
private static String REGEX = "dog";
private static String INPUT = "The dog says meow.
"+ "All dogs say meow.";
private static String REPLACE = "cat";
public static void main(String[] args) { Pattern
p = Pattern.compile(REGEX);
// get a matcher object Matcherm =
```

```
p.matcher(INPUT); INPUT = m.replaceAll(REPLACE);
System.out.println(INPUT);
}
}
```

This will produce the following result:

The cat says meow. All cats say meow.

The appendReplacement and appendTail Methods

The Matcher class also provides appendReplacement and appendTail methods for text replacement.

Here is the example explaining the functionality:

```
import java.util.regex.Matcher;
import java.util.regex.Pattern;
public class RegexMatches
{
private static String REGEX = "a*b";
private static String INPUT =
"aabfooaabfooabfoob";
private static String REPLACE = "-";
public static void main(String[] args) { Pattern
p = Pattern.compile(REGEX);
// get a matcher object Matcher m =
p.matcher(INPUT); StringBuffer sb = new
StringBuffer(); while(m.find()){
m.appendReplacement(sb,REPLACE);
} m.appendTail(sb);
System.out.println(sb.toString());
}
```

```
}
```

This will produce the following result:

```
-foo-foo-foo-
```

PatternSyntaxException Class Methods

A PatternSyntaxException is an unchecked exception that indicates a syntax error in a regular expression pattern. The PatternSyntaxException class provides the following methods to help you determine what went wrong:

Sr. No.	Methods with Description
1	**public String getDescription()** Retrieves the description of the error.
2	**public int getIndex()** Retrieves the error index.
3	**public String getPattern()** Retrieves the erroneous regular expression pattern.
4	**public String getMessage()** Returns a multi-line string containing the description of the syntax error and its index, the erroneous regular expression pattern, and a visual indication of the error index within the pattern.

Methods

A Java method is a collection of statements that are grouped together to perform an operation. When you call the System.out.**println()** method, for example, the system actually executes several statements in order to display a message on the console.

Now you will learn how to create your own methods with or without return values, invoke a method with or without parameters, and apply method abstraction in the program design.

Creating Method

Considering the following example to explain the syntax of a method:

```
public static int methodName(int a, int b) {
// body
}
```

Here,

- **public static**: modifier
- **int**: return type
- **methodName**: name of the method
- **a, b**: formal parameters
- **int a, int b**: list of parameters

Method definition consists of a method header and a method body. The same is shown in the following syntax:

```
modifier returnType nameOfMethod (Parameter List)
{
// method body
}
```

The syntax shown above includes:

- **modifier:** It defines the access type of the method and it is optional to use.
- **returnType:** Method may return a value.
- **nameOfMethod:** This is the method name. The method signature consists of the method name and the parameter list.
- **Parameter List:** The list of parameters, it is the type, order, and number of parameters of a method. These are optional, method may contain zero parameters.
- **method body:** The method body defines what the method does with the statements.

Example

Here is the source code of the above defined method called

max(). This method takes two parameters num1 and num2 and returns the maximum between the two:

```
/** the snippet returns the minimum between two
numbers */
public static int minFunction(int n1, int n2) {
int min;
if (n1 > n2)
min = n2;
else
min = n1;
return min;
}
```

Method Calling

For using a method, it should be called. There are two ways in which a method is called i.e., method returns a value or returning nothing (no return value).

The process of method calling is simple. When a program invokes a method, the program control gets transferred to the called method. This called method then returns control to the caller in two conditions, when:

- the return statement is executed.
- it reaches the method ending closing brace.

The methods returning void is considered as call to a statement. Lets consider an example:

```
System.out.println("This is java.com!");
```

The method returning value can be understood by the following example:

int result = sum(6, 9);

Example

Following is the example to demonstrate how to define a method and how to call it:

```
public class ExampleMinNumber{
public static void main(String[] args) {
int a = 11;
int b = 6;
int c = minFunction(a, b);
System.out.println("Minimum Value = " + c);
}
/** returns the minimum of two numbers */
public static int minFunction(int n1, int n2) {
int min;
if (n1 > n2)
min = n2;
else
min = n1;
return min;
}
}
```

This will produce the following result:

Minimum value = 6

The void Keyword

The void keyword allows us to create methods which do not return a value. Here, in the following example we're considering a void method *methodRankPoints*.This method is a void method, which does not return any value. Call to a void method must be a statement i.e. *methodRankPoints(255.7);*. It is a Java statement which ends with a semicolon as shown in the following example.

Example

```
public class ExampleVoid {
public static void main(String[] args) {
methodRankPoints(255.7);
}
public static void methodRankPoints(double
points) {
if (points >= 202.5) {
System.out.println("Rank:A1");
}
else if (points >= 122.4) {
System.out.println("Rank:A2");
}
else { System.out.println("Rank:A3");
}
}
}
```

This will produce the following result:

Rank:A1

Passing Parameters by Value

While working under calling process, arguments is to be passed. These should be in the same order as their respective parameters in the method specification. Parameters can be passed by value or by reference.

Passing Parameters by Value means calling a method with a parameter. Through this, the argument value is passed to the parameter.

Example

The following program shows an example of passing parameter by value. The values of the arguments remains the same even after the method invocation.

```
public class swappingExample {
public static void main(String[] args) {
int a = 30;
int b = 45;
System.out.println("Before swapping, a = "+
a + " and b = " +b);
// Invoke the swap method swapFunction(a, b);
System.out.println("\n**Now, Before and After
swapping values will be same here**:");
System.out.println("After swapping, a = " +
a + " and b is " +b);
}
public static void swapFunction(int a, int b) {
System.out.println("Before swapping(Inside), a =
" + a
+ " b = " + b);
```

```
// Swap n1 with n2 int c = a;
a = b;
b = c;
System.out.println("After swapping(Inside), a = "
+ a
+ " b = " + b);
}
}
```

This will produce the following result:

Before swapping, a = 30 and b = 45

Before swapping(Inside), a = 30 b = 45

After swapping(Inside), a = 45b = 30

Now, Before and After swapping values will be same here: After swapping, a = 30 and b is 45

Method Overloading

When a class has two or more methods by the same name but different parameters, it is known as method overloading. It is different from overriding. In overriding, a method has the same method name, type, number of parameters, etc.

Let's consider the example discussed earlier for finding minimum numbers of integer type. If, let's say we want to find the minimum number of double type. Then the concept of overloading will be introduced to create two or more methods with the same name but different parameters.

The following example explains the same:

```java
public class ExampleOverloading{
public static void main(String[] args) {
int a = 11; int b = 6; double c = 7.3; double d =
9.4;
int result1 = minFunction(a, b);
// same function name with different parameters
double result2 = minFunction(c, d);
System.out.println("Minimum Value = " + result1);
System.out.println("Minimum Value = " + result2);
}
// for integer
public static int minFunction(int n1, int n2) {
int min;
if (n1 > n2)
min = n2;
else
min = n1;
return min;
}
// for double
public static double minFunction(double n1,
double n2) {
double min;
if (n1 > n2)
min = n2;
else
min = n1;
return min;
}
}
```

This will produce the following result:

Minimum Value = 6

Minimum Value = 7.3

Overloading methods makes program readable. Here, two methods are given by the same name but with different parameters. The minimum number from integer and double types is the result.

Using Command-Line Arguments

Sometimes you will want to pass some information into a program when you run it. This is accomplished by passing command-line arguments to main( ).

A command-line argument is the information that directly follows the program's name on the command line when it is executed. To access the command-line arguments inside a Java program is quite easy. They are stored as strings in the String array passed tomain( ).

Example

The following program displays all of the command-line arguments that it is called with:

```java
public class CommandLine {
public static void main(String args[]){
for(int i=0; i<args.length; i++){
System.out.println("args["+ i + "]: " +
args[i]);
}
}
}
```

Try executing this program as shown here:

```
$java CommandLine this is a command line 200 -100
```

This will produce the following result:

args[0]: this args[1]: is args[2]: a args[3]: command args[4]: line args[5]: 200 args[6]: -

The Constructors

A constructor initializes an object when it is created. It has the same name as its class and is syntactically similar to a method. However, constructors have no explicit return type.

Typically, you will use a constructor to give initial values to the instance variables defined by the class, or to perform any other startup procedures required to create a fully formed object.

All classes have constructors, whether you define one or not, because Java automatically provides a default constructor that initializes all member variables to zero. However, once you define your own constructor, the default constructor is no longer used.

Example

Here is a simple example that uses a constructor without parameters:

```
// A simple constructor. class MyClass {
int x;
// Following is the constructor
MyClass() {
x = 10;
}
}
```

You will have to call constructor to initialize objects as follows:

```
public class ConsDemo {
public static void main(String args[]) { MyClass
t1 = new MyClass();
MyClass t2 = new MyClass();
System.out.println(t1.x + " " + t2.x);
}
}
```

Parameterized Constructor

Most often, you will need a constructor that accepts one or more parameters. Parameters are added to a constructor in the same way that they are added to a method, just declare them inside the parentheses after the constructor's name.

Example

Here is a simple example that uses a constructor with a parameter:

```
// A simple constructor. class MyClass {
int x;
// Following is the constructor
MyClass(int i ) {
x = i;
}
}
```

You will need to call a constructor to initialize objects as follows:

```
public class ConsDemo {
public static void main(String args[]) { MyClass
t1 = new MyClass( 10 ); MyClass t2 = new MyClass(
20 );
System.out.println(t1.x + " " + t2.x);
}
}
```

This will produce the following result:

10 20

The this keyword

this is a keyword in Java which is used as a reference to the object of the current class, with in an instance method or a constructor. Using *this* you can refer the members of a class such as constructors, variables and methods.

Note: The keyword *this* is used only within instance methods or constructors

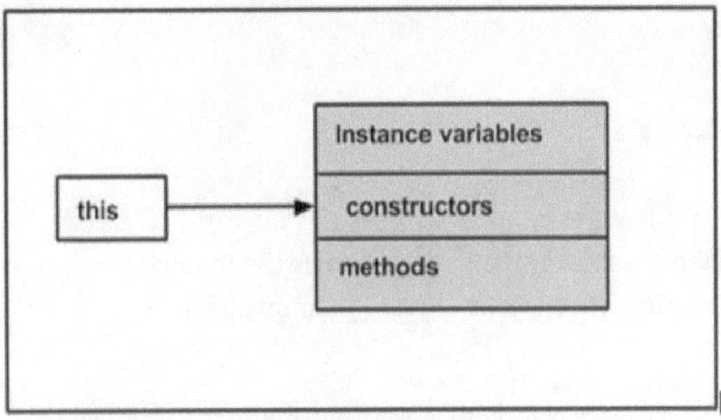

In general, the keyword *this* is used to :

Differentiate the instance variables from local variables if they have same names, within a constructor or a method.

```
class Student{
int age; Student(int age){ this.age=age;
}
}
```

Call one type of constructor (parametrized constructor or default) from other in a class. It is known as explicit constructor invocation.

```
class Student{
int age Student(){ this(20);
}
Student(int age){
this.age=age;
}
```

```
}
```

Example

Here is an example that uses *this* keyword to access the members of a class. Copy and paste the following program in a file with the name, **This_Example.java**.

```java
public class This_Example {
//Instance variable num intnum=10;
This_Example(){
System.out.println("This is an example program on
keyword this ");
}
This_Example(int num){
//Invoking the default constructor
this();
//Assigning the local variable num to theinstance
variable num
this.num=num;
}
public void greet(){
System.out.println("Hi Welcome to java");
}
public void print(){
//Local variable num intnum=20;
//Printing the instance variable
System.out.println("value of local variable num
is : "+num);
//Printing the local variable
System.out.println("value of instance variable
num is :"+this.num);
//Invoking the greet method of a class
this.greet();
```

```
}
public static void main(String[] args){
//Instantiating the class
This_Example obj1=new This_Example();
//Invoking the print method obj1.print();
//Passing a new value to the num variable through
parametrized constructor
This_Example obj2=new This_Example(30);
//Invoking the print method again obj2.print();
}
}
```

This will produce the following result:

This is an example program on keyword this value of local variable num is : 20

value of instance variable num is : 10

Hi Welcome to java

This is an example program on keyword this value of local variable num is : 20

value of instance variable num is : 30

Hi Welcome to java

Variable Arguments(var-args)

JDK 1.5 enables you to pass a variable number of arguments of the same type to a method. The parameter in the method is declared as follows:

```
typeName... parameterName
```

In the method declaration, you specify the type followed by an ellipsis (...). Only one variable-length parameter may be specified in a method, and this parameter must be the last parameter. Any regular parameters must precede it.

Example

```java
public class VarargsDemo {
public static void main(String args[]) {
// Call method with variable args printMax(34, 3,
3, 2, 56.5);
printMax(new double[]{1, 2, 3});
}
public static void printMax( double... numbers) {
if (numbers.length == 0){
System.out.println("Noargument passed");
return;
}
double result = numbers[0];
for (int i = 1; i < numbers.length; i++)
if (numbers[i] > result)
result = numbers[i];
System.out.println("The max value is " + result);
}
}
```

This will produce the following result:

The max value is 56.5

The max value is 3.0

The finalize( ) Method

It is possible to define a method that will be called just before
an object's final destruction by the garbage collector. This
method is called **finalize( )**, and it can be used to ensure

that an object terminates cleanly.

For example, you might use finalize( ) to make sure that an open file owned by that object is closed.

To add a finalizer to a class, you simply define the finalize( ) method. The Java runtime calls that method whenever it is about to recycle an object of that class.

Inside the finalize( ) method, you will specify those actions that must be performed before an object is destroyed.

The finalize( ) method has this general form:

```
protected void finalize( )
{
// finalization code here
}
```

Here, the keyword protected is a specifier that prevents access to finalize( ) by code defined outside its class.

This means that you cannot know when or even if finalize( ) will be executed. For example, if your program ends before garbage collection occurs, finalize( ) will not execute.

Files & I/O

The java.io package contains nearly every class you might ever need to perform input and output (I/O) in Java. All these streams represent an input source and an output destination. The stream in the java.io package supports many data such as primitives, object, localized characters, etc.

Stream

A stream can be defined as a sequence of data. There are two kinds of Streams:

- **InPutStream:** The InputStream is used to read data from a source.
- **OutPutStream:** The OutputStream is used for writing data to a destination.

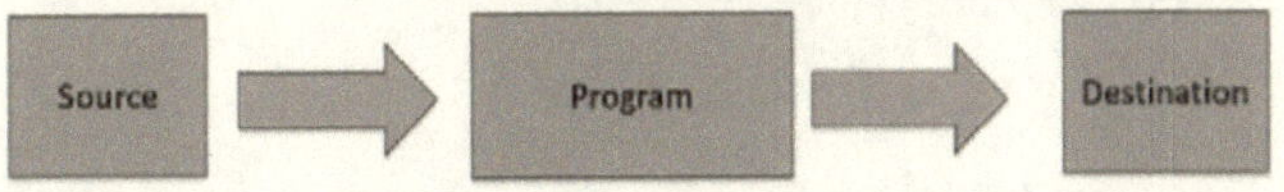

Java provides strong but flexible support for I/O related to files and networks butthis chapter covers very basic functionality related to streams and I/O. We will see the most commonly used examples one by one:

Byte Streams

Java byte streams are used to perform input and output of 8-bit bytes. Though there are many classes related to byte streams but the most frequently used classes are, **FileInputStream** and **FileOutputStream**. Following is an example which makes use of these two classes to copy an input file into an output file:

```java
import java.io.*;
public class CopyFile {
public static void main(String args[]) throws
IOException
{
FileInputStream in = null; FileOutputStream out =
null;
try {
in = new FileInputStream("input.txt");
out = new FileOutputStream("output.txt");
int c;
while ((c = in.read()) != -1) {
out.write(c);
}
```

```
}finally {
if (in != null) {
in.close();
}
if (out != null) {
out.close();
}
}
}
}
```

Now let's have a file **input.txt** with the following content:

This is test for copy file.

As a next step, compile the above program and execute it, which will result in creating output.txt file with the same content as we have in input.txt. So let's put the above code in CopyFile.java file and do the following:

```
$javac CopyFile.java
$java CopyFile
```

Character Streams

Java **Byte** streams are used to perform input and output of 8-bit bytes, whereas Java **Character** streams are used to perform input and output for 16-bit unicode. Though there are many classes related to character streams but the most frequently used classes are, **FileReader** and **FileWriter**. Though internally FileReader uses FileInputStream and

FileWriter uses FileOutputStream but here the major difference is that FileReader reads two bytes at a time and FileWriter writes two bytes at a time.

We can re-write the above example, which makes the use of these two classes to copy an input file (having unicode characters) into an output file:

```
import java.io.*;
public class CopyFile {
public static void main(String args[]) throws
IOException
{
FileReader in = null; FileWriter out = null;
try {
in = new FileReader("input.txt");
out = new FileWriter("output.txt");
int c;
while ((c = in.read()) != -1) {
out.write(c);
}
}finally {
if (in != null) {
in.close();
}
if (out != null) {
out.close();
}
}
}
}
```

Now let's have a file **input.txt** with the following content:

This is test for copy file.

As a next step, compile the above program and execute it, which will result in creating output.txtfile with the same content as we have in input.txt. So let's put the above code inCopyFile.java file and do the following:

```
$javac CopyFile.java
$java CopyFile
```

Standard Streams

All the programming languages provide support for standard I/O where the user's program can take input from a keyboard and then produce an output on the computer screen. If you are aware of C or C++ programming languages, then you must be aware of three standard devices STDIN, STDOUT and STDERR. Similarly, Java provides the following three standard streams:

- **Standard Input:** This is used to feed the data to user's program and usually a keyboard is used as standard input stream and represented as **System.in**.
- **Standard Output:** This is used to output the data produced by the user's program andusually a computer screen is used for standard output stream and represented as **System.out**.
- **Standard Error:** This is used to output the error data produced by the user's program and usually a computer screen is used for standard error stream and repre-

sented as **System.err**.

Following is a simple program, which creates **InputStream-Reader** to read standard input stream until the user types a "q":

```java
import java.io.*;
public class ReadConsole {
public static void main(String args[]) throws
IOException
{
InputStreamReader cin = null;
try {
cin = new InputStreamReader(System.in);
System.out.println("Enter characters, 'q' to
quit."); char c;
do {
c = (char) cin.read(); System.out.print(c);
} while(c != 'q');
}finally {
if (cin != null) {
cin.close();
}
}
}
}
```

Let's keep the above code in ReadConsole.java file and try to compile and execute it as shown in the following program. This program continues to read and output the same character until we press 'q':

$javac ReadConsole.java

$java ReadConsole

Enter characters, 'q' to quit.

1

1 e e q

q

Reading and Writing Files

As described earlier, a stream can be defined as a sequence of data. The **InputStream** is used to read data from a source and the **OutputStream** is used for writing data to a destination.

Here is a hierarchy of classes to deal with Input and Output streams.

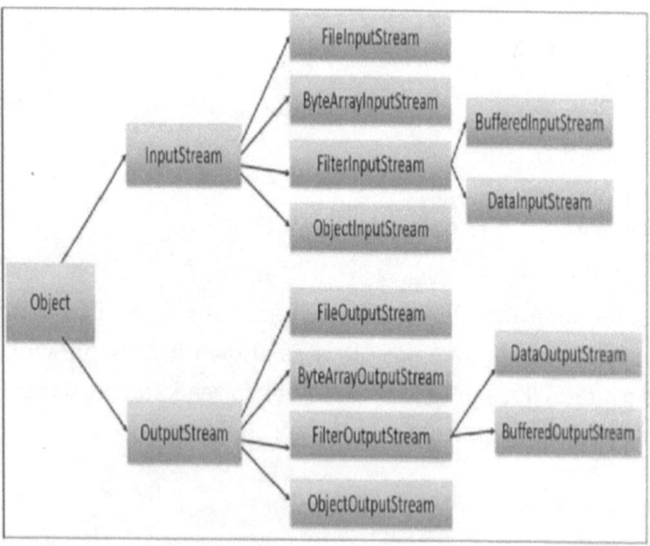

The two important streams are **FileInputStream** and **File-OutputStream**, which would be discussed in this chapter

FileInputStream

This stream is used for reading data from the files. Objects can be created using the keyword **new** and there are several types of constructors available.

Following constructor takes a file name as a string to create an input stream object to read the file:

```
InputStream f = new
FileInputStream("C:/java/hello");
```

Following constructor takes a file object to create an input stream object to read the file. First we create a file object using File() method as follows:

```
File f = new File("C:/java/hello"); InputStream f
= new FileInputStream(f);
```

Once you have *InputStream* object in hand, then there is a list of helper methods which can be used to read to stream or to do other operations on the stream.

Methods with Description

- **public void close() throws IOException{}** This method closes the file output stream. Releases any system resources associated with the file. Throws an IOException.

- **protected void finalize()throws IOException {}** This method cleans up the connection to the file. Ensures that the close method of this file output stream is called when there are no more references to this stream. Throws an IOException.
- **public int read(int r)throws IOException{}** This method reads the specified byte of data from the InputStream. Returns an int. Returns the next byte of data and –1will be returned if it's the end of the file.
- **public int read(byte[] r) throws IOException{}** This method reads r.length bytes from the input stream into an array.Returns the total number of bytes read. Ifit is the end of the file, –1 will be returned.
- **public int available() throws IOException{}** Gives the number of bytes that can be read from this file input stream. Returns an int.

There are other important input streams available, for more detail you can refer to the following links:

- ByteArrayInputStream
- DataInputStream

ByteArrayInputStream

The ByteArrayInputStream class allows a buffer in the memory to be used as an InputStream. The input source is a byte array. ByteArrayInputStream class provides the following constructors.

Sr.No	Constructor and Description
1	ByteArrayInputStream(byte [] a) This constructor accepts a byte array as a parameter.
2	ByteArrayInputStream(byte [] a, int off, int len) This constructor takes an array of bytes, and two integer values, where **off** is the first byte to be read and **len** is the number of bytes to be read.

Once you have *ByteArrayInputStream* object in hand then there is a list of helper methods which can be used to read the stream or to do other operations on the stream.

Methods with Description

- **public int read()** This method reads the next byte of data from the InputStream. Returns an int as the next byte of data. If it is the end of the file, then it returns -1.
- **public int read(byte[] r, int off, int len)** This method reads up to **len** number of bytes starting from **off** from the input stream into an array. Returns the total number of bytes read. If it is the end of the file, -1 will be returned.
- **public int available()** Gives the number of bytes that can be read from this file input stream. Returns an int that gives the number of bytes to be read.
- **public void mark(int read)** This sets the current marked position in the stream. The parameter gives the maximum limit of bytes that can be read before the marked position becomes invalid.

- **public long skip(long n)** Skips 'n' number of bytes from the stream. This returns the actual number of bytes skipped.

Example

Following is the example to demonstrate ByteArrayInput-Stream and ByteArrayOutputStream.

```java
import java.io.*;
public class ByteStreamTest {
public static void main(String args[])throws
IOException { ByteArrayOutputStream bOutput = new
ByteArrayOutputStream(12);
while( bOutput.size()!= 10 ) {
// Gets the inputs from the user
bOutput.write(System.in.read());
}
byte b [] = bOutput.toByteArray();
System.out.println("Print the content"); for(int
x= 0 ; x < b.length; x++) {
// printing the characters
System.out.print((char)b[x] + "   ");
}
System.out.println("   ");
int c;
ByteArrayInputStream bInput = new
ByteArrayInputStream(b);
System.out.println("Converting characters to
Upper case " );
for(int y = 0 ; y < 1; y++ ) {
while(( c= bInput.read())!= -1) {
System.out.println(Character.toUpperCase((char)c));
}
bInput.reset();
```

```
    }
  }
}
```

Following is the sample run of the above program:

asdfghjkly

Print the content

a s d f g h j k l y

Converting characters to Upper case

A S D F G H J K L Y

DataInputStream

The DataInputStream is used in the context of DataOutput-
Stream and can be used to read primitives.

Following is the constructor to create an InputStream:

```
InputStream in = DataInputStream(InputStream in);
```

Once you have *DataInputStream* object in hand, then there
is a list of helper methods, which can be used to read the
stream or to do other operations on the stream.

Sr. No.	Methods with Description
1	**public final int read(byte[] r, int off, int len)throws IOException** Reads up to len bytes of data from the input stream into an array of bytes. Returns the total number of bytes read into the buffer otherwise -1 if it is end of file.
2	**Public final int read(byte [] b)throws IOException** Reads some bytes from the inputstream an stores in to the byte array. Returns the total number of bytes read into the buffer otherwise -1 if it is end of file.
3	**(a) public final Boolean readBooolean()throws IOException** **(b) public final byte readByte()throws IOException** **(c) public final short readShort()throws IOException** **(d) public final Int readInt()throws IOException** These methods will read the bytes from the contained InputStream. Returns the next two bytes of the InputStream as the specific primitive type.
4	**public String readLine() throws IOException** Reads the next line of text from the input stream. It reads successive bytes, converting each byte separately into a character, until it encounters a line terminator or end of file; the characters read are then returned as a String.

Example

Following is an example to demonstrate DataInputStream and DataOutputStream. This example reads 5 lines given in a file test.txt and converts those lines into capital letters and finally copies them into another file test1.txt.

```java
import java.io.*;
public class DataInput_Stream{
public static void main(String args[])throws
IOException{
//writing string to a file encoded as modified
UTF-8
DataOutputStream dataOut = new
DataOutputStream(new
```

```
FileOutputStream("E:\\file.txt"));
dataOut.writeUTF("hello");
//Reading data from the same file
DataInputStream dataIn = new DataInputStream(new
FileInputStream("E:\\file.txt"));
while(dataIn.available()>0){
String k = dataIn.readUTF(); System.out.print(k+"
");
}
}
}
```

Following is the sample run of the above program:

hello

FileOutputStream

FileOutputStream is used to create a file and write data into it. The stream would create a file, if it doesn't already exist, before opening it for output.

Here are two constructors which can be used to create a FileOutputStream object. Following constructor takes a file name as a string to create an input stream object to write the file:

```
OutputStream f = new
FileOutputStream("C:/java/hello")
```

Following constructor takes a file object to create an output stream object to write the file. First, we create a file object using File() method as follows:

```
File f = new File("C:/java/hello"); OutputStream
f = new FileOutputStream(f);
```

Once you have *OutputStream* object in hand, then there is a list of helper methods, which can be used to write to stream or to do other operations on the stream.

Sr. No.	Methods with Description
1	**public void close() throws IOException{}** This method closes the file output stream. Releases any system resources associated with the file. Throws an IOException.
2	**protected void finalize()throws IOException {}** This method cleans up the connection to the file. Ensures that the close method of this file output stream is called when there are no more references to this stream. Throws an IOException.
3	**public void write(int w)throws IOException{}** This method writes the specified byte to the output stream.
4	**public void write(byte[] w)** Writes w.length bytes from the mentioned byte array to the OutputStream.

There are other important output streams available, for more detail you can refer to the following:

- ByteArrayOutputStream
- DataOutputStream

ByteArrayOutputStream

The ByteArrayOutputStream class stream creates a buffer in memory and all the data sent to the stream is stored in the buffer. Following is the list of the constructors to be provided by ByteArrayOutputStream class.

Sr. No.	Constructors and Description
1	**ByteArrayOutputStream()** This constructor creates a ByteArrayOutputStream having buffer of 32 byte
2	**ByteArrayOutputStream(int a)** This constructor creates a ByteArrayOutputStream having buffer of the given size

Once you have *ByteArrayOutputStream* object in hand, then there is a list of helper methods which can be used to write the stream or to do other operations on the stream.

Methods with Description

- **public void reset()** This method resets the number of valid bytes of the byte array output stream to zero, so all the accumulated output in the stream will be discarded.
- **public byte[] toByteArray()** This method creates a newly allocated Byte array. Its size would be the current size of the output stream and the contents of the buffer will be copied into it. Returns the current contents of the outputstream as a byte array.
- **public String toString()** Converts the buffer content into a string. Translation will be done according to the default character encoding. Returns the String

translated from the buffer's content.

- **public void write(int w)** Writes the specified array to the output stream.
- **public void write(byte []b, int of, int len)** Writes len number of bytes starting from offset off to the stream.
- **public void writeTo(OutputStream outSt)** Writes the entire content of this Stream to the specified stream argument.

Example

Following is an example to demonstrate ByteArrayOutputS tream and ByteArrayInputStream.

```
import java.io.*;
public class ByteStreamTest {
public static void main(String args[])throws
IOException { ByteArrayOutputStream bOutput =
newByteArrayOutputStream(12);
while( bOutput.size()!= 10 ) {
// Gets the inputs from the user
bOutput.write(System.in.read());
}
byte b [] = bOutput.toByteArray();
System.out.println("Print the content"); for(int
x= 0 ; x < b.length; x++) {
//printing the characters
System.out.print((char)b[x] + "   ");
}
System.out.println("   ");
int c;
ByteArrayInputStream bInput = new
ByteArrayInputStream(b);
System.out.println("Converting characters to
```

```
Upper case " ); for(int y = 0 ; y < 1; y++ ) {
while(( c= bInput.read())!= -1) {
System.out.println(Character.toUpperCase((char)c));
}
bInput.reset();
}
}
}
```

Here is the sample run of the above program:

asdfghjkly

Print the content

a s d f g h j k l y

Converting characters to Upper case

A S D F G H J K L Y

DataOutputStream

The DataOutputStream stream lets you write the primitives to an output source. Following is the constructor to create a DataOutputStream.

```
DataOutputStream out =
DataOutputStream(OutputStreamout);
```

Once you have *DataOutputStream* object in hand, then there is a list of helper methods, which can be used to write the stream or to do other operations on the stream.

Sr. No.	Methods with Description
1	**public final void write(byte[] w, int off, int len)throws IOException** Writes len bytes from the specified byte array starting at point off, to the underlying stream.
2	**Public final int write(byte [] b)throws IOException** Writes the current number of bytes written to this data output stream. Returns the total number of bytes written into the buffer.
3	**(a) public final void writeBooolean()throws IOException,** **(b) public final void writeByte()throws IOException,** **(c) public final void writeShort()throws IOException** **(d) public final void writeInt()throws IOException** These methods will write the specific primitive type data into the output stream as bytes.
4	**Public void flush()throws IOException** Flushes the data output stream.
5	**public final void writeBytes(String s) throws IOException** Writes out the string to the underlying output stream as a sequence of bytes. Each character in the string is written out, in sequence, by discarding its high eight bits.

Example

Following is an example to demonstrate DataInputStream and DataOutputStream. This example reads 5 lines given in a file test.txt and converts those lines into capital letters and finally copies them into another file test1.txt.

```java
import java.io.*;
public class DataInput_Stream{
public static void main(String args[])throws
IOException{
```

```
//writing string to a file encoded as modified
UTF-8
DataOutputStream dataOut = new
DataOutputStream(new
FileOutputStream("E:\\file.txt"));
dataOut.writeUTF("hello");
//Reading data from the same file
DataInputStream dataIn = new DataInputStream(new
FileInputStream("E:\\file.txt"));
while(dataIn.available()>0){
String k = dataIn.readUTF(); System.out.print(k+"
");
}
}
}
```

Here is the sample run of the above program:

THIS IS TEST 1,

   THIS IS TEST 2,

   THIS IS TEST3,

   THIS IS TEST 4,

   THIS IS TEST 5,

Example

Following is the example to demonstrate InputStream and OutputStream:

```
import java.io.*;
public class fileStreamTest{
```

```
public static void main(String args[]){
try{
byte bWrite [] = {11,21,3,40,5};
OutputStream os = new
FileOutputStream("test.txt");
for(int x=0; x < bWrite.length ; x++){
os.write( bWrite[x] ); // writes the bytes
}
os.close();
InputStream is = new FileInputStream("test.txt");
int size = is.available();
for(int i=0; i< size; i++){
System.out.print((char)is.read() + "   ");
}
is.close();
}catch(IOException e){
System.out.print("Exception");
}
}
}
```

The above code would create file test.txtand would write given numbers in binary format. Same would be the output on the stdout screen.

File Navigation and I/O

There are several other classes that we would be going through to get to know the basics of File Navigation and I/O.

- File Class
- FileReader Class
- FileWriter Class

File Class

Java File class represents the files and directory path names in an abstract manner. This class is used for creation of files and directories, file searching, file deletion, etc.

The File object represents the actual file/directory on the disk. Following is the list of constructors to create a File object.

Sr. No.	Methods with Description
1	**File(File parent, String child)** This constructor creates a new File instance from a parent abstract pathname and a child pathname string.
2	**File(String pathname)** This constructor creates a new File instance by converting the given pathname string into an abstract pathname.
3	**File(String parent, String child)** This constructor creates a new File instance from a parent pathname string and a child pathname string.
4	**File(URI uri)** This constructor creates a new File instance by converting the given file: URI into an abstract pathname.

Once you have *File* object in hand, then there is a list of helper methods which can be used to manipulate the files.

Methods with Description

- **public String getName()** Returns the name of the file or directory denoted by this abstract pathname.
- **public String getParent()** Returns the pathname string of this abstract pathname's parent, or null if this pathname does not name a parent directory.
- **public File getParentFile()** Returns the abstract pathname of this abstract pathname's parent, or null if this pathname does not name a parent directory.
- **public String getPath()** Converts this abstract pathname into a pathname string.
- **public boolean isAbsolute()** Tests whether this abstract pathname is absolute. Returns true if this abstract pathname is absolute, false otherwise.
- **public String getAbsolutePath()** Returns the absolute pathname string of this abstract pathname.
- **public boolean canRead()** Tests whether the application can read the file denoted by this abstract pathname. Returns true if and only if the file specified by this abstract pathname exists and can be read by the application; false otherwise.
- **public boolean canWrite()** Tests whether the application can modify to the file denoted by this abstract pathname. Returns true if and only if the file system actually contains a file denoted by this abstract pathname and the application is allowed to write to the file; false otherwise.
- **public boolean exists()** Tests whether the file or directory denoted by this abstract pathname exists. Returns true if and only if the file or directory denoted by this

abstract pathname exists; false otherwise.

- **public boolean isDirectory()** Tests whether the file denoted by this abstract pathname is a directory. Returns true if and only if the file denoted by this abstract pathname exists and is a directory; false otherwise.
- **public boolean isFile()** Tests whether the file denoted by this abstract pathname is a normal file. A file is normal if it is not a directory and, in addition, satisfies other system- dependent criteria. Any non-directory file created by a Java application is guaranteed to be a normal file. Returns true if and only if the file denoted by this abstract pathname exists and is a normal file; false otherwise.
- **public long lastModified()** Returns the time that the file denoted by this abstract pathname was last modified. Returns a long value representing the time the file was last modified, measured in milliseconds since the epoch (00:00:00 GMT,January 1, 1970), or 0L if the file does not exist or if an I/O error occurs.
- **public long length()** Returns the length of the file denoted by this abstract pathname. The return value is unspecified if this pathname denotes a directory.
- **public boolean createNewFile() throws IOException** Atomically creates a new, empty file named by this abstract pathname if and only if a file with this name does not yet exist. Returns true if the named file does not exist and was successfully created; false if the named file already exists.
- **public boolean delete()** Deletes the file or directory denoted by this abstract pathname. If this pathname denotes a directory, then the directory must be empty

in order to be deleted. Returns true if and only if the file or directory is successfully deleted; false otherwise.

- **public void deleteOnExit()** Requests that the file or directory denoted by this abstract pathname be deleted when the virtual machine terminates.
- **public String[] list()** Returns an array of strings naming the files and directories in the directory denoted by this abstract pathname.
- **public String[] list(FilenameFilter filter)** Returns an array of strings naming the files and directories in the directory denoted by this abstract pathname that satisfy the specified filter.
- **public File[] listFiles()** Returns an array of abstract pathnames denoting the files in the directory denoted by this abstract pathname.
- **public File[] listFiles(FileFilter filter)** Returns an array of abstract pathnames denoting the files and directories in the directory denoted by this abstract pathname that satisfy the specified filter.
- **public boolean mkdir()** Creates the directory named by this abstract pathname. Returns true if and only if the directory was created; false otherwise.
- **public boolean mkdirs()** Creates the directory named by this abstract pathname, including any necessary but nonexistent parent directories. Returns true if and only if the directory was created, along with all necessary parent directories; false otherwise.
- **public boolean renameTo(File dest)** Renames the file denoted by this abstractpathname. Returns true if and only if the renaming succeeded; false otherwise.
- **public boolean setLastModified(long time)** Sets the

last-modified time of the file or directory named by this abstract pathname. Returns true if and only if the operation succeeded; false otherwise.

- **public boolean setReadOnly()** Marks the file or directory named by this abstractpathname so that only read operations are allowed. Returns true if and only if the operation succeeded; false otherwise.
- **public static File createTempFile(String prefix, String suffix, File directory) throws IOException** Creates a new empty file in the specified directory, using the given prefix and suffix strings to generate its name. Returns an abstract pathname denoting a newly-created empty file.
- **public static File createTempFile(String prefix, String suffix) throws IOException** Creates anempty file in the default temporary-file directory, using the given prefix and suffix to generate its name. Invoking this method is equivalent toinvoking createTempFile(prefix, suffix, null). Returns abstractpathname denoting a newly-created empty file.
- **public int compareTo(File pathname)** Compares two abstract pathnames lexicographically. Returns zero if the argument is equal to this abstract pathname, a value less than zero if this abstract pathname is lexicographically less than the argument, or a value greater than zero if this abstract pathname is lexicographically greater than the argument.
- **public int compareTo(Object o)** Compares this abstract pathname to another object. Returns zero if the argument is equal to this abstract pathname, a value less than zero if this abstract pathname is lexicographically

less than the argument, or a value greater than zero if this abstract pathname is lexicographically greater than the argument.

- **public boolean equals(Object obj)** Tests this abstract pathname for equality with the given object.Returns true if and only if the argument is not null and is an abstract pathname that denotes the same file or directory as this abstract pathname.
- **public String toString()** Returns the pathname string of this abstract pathname. This is just the string returned by the getPath() method.

Example

Following is an example to demonstrate File object:

```java
import java.io.File;
public class FileDemo {
public static void main(String[] args) {
File f = null;
String[] strs = {"test1.txt", "test2.txt"};
try{
// for each string in string array for(String
s:strs )
{
// create new file f=new File(s);
// true if the file is executable boolean bool =
f.canExecute();
// find the absolute path
String a = f.getAbsolutePath();
// prints absolutepath
System.out.print(a);
// prints
```

```
System.out.println(" is executable: "+ bool);
}
}catch(Exception e){
// if any I/O error occurs e.printStackTrace();
}
}
}
```

Consider there is an executable file test1.txt and another file test2.txt is non executable in the current directory. Let us compile and run the above program, this will produce the following result:

test1.txt is executable: true test2.txt is executable: false

FileReader Class

This class inherits from the InputStreamReader class. FileReader is used for reading streams of characters.

This class has several constructors to create required objects. Following is the list of constructors provided by the FileReader class.

Sr. No.	Constructors and Description
1	**FileReader(File file)** This constructor creates a new FileReader, given the File to read from.
2	**FileReader(FileDescriptor fd)** This constructor creates a new FileReader, given the FileDescriptor to read from.
3	**FileReader(String fileName)** This constructor creates a new FileReader, given the name of the file to read from.

Once you have FileReader object in hand then there is a list of helper methods which can be used to manipulate the files.

Sr. No.	Methods with Description
1	**public int read() throws IOException** Reads a single character. Returns an int, which represents the character read.
2	**public int read(char [] c, int offset, int len)** Reads characters into an array. Returns the number of characters read.

Example

Following is an example to demonstrate class:

```java
import java.io.*;
public class FileRead{
public static void main(String args[])throws
IOException{ File file = new File("Hello1.txt");
// creates the file file.createNewFile();
// creates a FileWriter Object
```

```
FileWriter writer = new FileWriter(file);
// Writes the content to the file
writer.write("This\n is\n an\n example\n");
writer.flush();
writer.close();
//Creates a FileReader Object FileReader fr = new
FileReader(file); char [] a = new char[50];
fr.read(a); // reads the content to the array
for(char c : a)
System.out.print(c); //prints the characters one
by one fr.close();
}
}
```

This will produce the following result:

This is an example

FileWriter Class

This class inherits from the OutputStreamWriter class. The class is used for writing streams of characters.

This class has several constructors to create required objects. Following is a list.

Sr. No.	Constructors and Description
1	**FileWriter(File file)** This constructor creates a FileWriter object given a File object.
2	**FileWriter(File file, boolean append)** This constructor creates a FileWriter object given a File object with a boolean indicating whether or not to append the data written.
3	**FileWriter(FileDescriptor fd)** This constructor creates a FileWriter object associated with the given file descriptor.
4	**FileWriter(String fileName)** This constructor creates a FileWriter object, given a file name.
5	**FileWriter(String fileName, boolean append)** This constructor creates a FileWriter object given a file name with a boolean indicating whether or not to append the data written.

Once you have *FileWriter* object in hand, then there is a list of helper methods, which can be used to manipulate the files.

Sr. No.	Methods with Description
1	**public void write(int c) throws IOException** Writes a single character.
2	**public void write(char [] c, int offset, int len)** Writes a portion of an array of characters starting from offset and with a length of len.
3	**public void write(String s, int offset, int len)** Write a portion of a String starting from offset and with a length of len.

Example

Following is an example to demonstrate class:

```java
import java.io.*;
public class FileRead{
public static void main(String args[])throws
IOException{ File file = new File("Hello1.txt");
// creates the file file.createNewFile();
// creates a FileWriter Object
FileWriter writer = new FileWriter(file);
// Writes the content to the file
writer.write("This\n is\n an\n example\n");
writer.flush();
writer.close();
//Creates a FileReader Object FileReader fr = new
FileReader(file); char [] a = new char[50];
fr.read(a); // reads the content to the array
for(char c : a)
System.out.print(c); //prints the characters one
by one
fr.close();
}
}
```

This will produce the following result:

This is an example

Directories in Java

A directory is a File which can contain a list of other files and directories.You use **File** object to create directories, to list down files available in a directory. For complete detail, check a list of all the methods which you can call on File object and what are related to directories.

Creating Directories

There are two useful **File** utility methods, which can be used to create directories:

- The **mkdir( )** method creates a directory, returning true on success and false on failure. Failure indicates that the path specified in the File object already exists, or that the directory cannot be created because the entire path does not exist yet.
- The **mkdirs()** method creates both a directory and all the parents of the directory. Following example creates "/tmp/user/java/bin" directory:

```java
import java.io.File;
public class CreateDir {
public static void main(String args[]) { String
dirname = "/tmp/user/java/bin"; File d =
newFile(dirname);
// Create directory now.
d.mkdirs();
}
}
```

Compile and execute the above code to create "/tmp/user/-java/bin".

Note: Java automatically takes care of path separators on UNIX and Windows as per conventions. If you use a forward slash (/) on a Windows version of Java, the path will still resolve correctly.

Listing Directories

You can use **list( )** method provided by **File** object to list down all the files and directories available in a directory as follows:

```java
import java.io.File;
public class ReadDir {
public static void main(String[] args) {
File file = null; String[] paths; try{
// create new file object
file = newFile("/tmp");
// array of files and directory paths =
file.list();
// for each name in the path array for(String
path:paths)
{
// prints filenameand directory name
System.out.println(path);
}
}catch(Exception e){
// if any error occurs e.printStackTrace();
}
}
}
```

This will produce the following result based on the directories and files available in your **/tmp** directory:

test1.txt

test2.txt

ReadDir.java

ReadDir.class

Exceptions

An exception (or exceptional event) is a problem that arises during the execution of a program. When an **Exception** occurs the normal flow of the program is disrupted and the program/Application terminates abnormally, which is not recommended, therefore, these exceptions are to be handled.

An exception can occur for many different reasons. Following are some scenarios where an exception occurs.

- A user has entered an invalid data.
- A file that needs to be opened cannot be found.
- A network connection has been lost in the middle of communications or the JVM has run out of memory.

Some of these exceptions are caused by user error, others by programmer error, and others by physical resources that have failed in some manner.

Based on these, we have three categories of Exceptions. You need to understand them to know how exception handling works in Java.

- **Checked exceptions:** A checked exception is an exception that occurs at the compile time, these are also called as compile time exceptions. These exceptions cannot simply be ignored at the time of compilation, the programmer should take care of (handle) these exceptions.

For example, if you use **FileReader** class in your program to read data from a file, if the file specified in its constructor doesn't exist, then a *FileNotFoundException* occurs, and the compiler prompts the programmer to handle the exception.

```
import java.io.File;
import java.io.FileReader;
public class FilenotFound_Demo {
public static void main(String args[]){ File
file=new File("E://file.txt");
FileReader fr = new FileReader(file);
}
}
```

If you try to compile the above program, you will get the following exceptions.

```
C:\>javac FilenotFound_Demo.java
FilenotFound_Demo.java:8: error: unreported
```

```
exception FileNotFoundException; must be caught
or declared to be thrown
FileReader fr = new FileReader(file);
                ^
1 error
```

Note: Since the methods **read()** and **close()** of FileReader class throws IOException, you can observe that the compiler notifies to handle IOException, along with FileNotFoundEx ception.

- **Unchecked exceptions:** An unchecked exception is an exception that occurs at the time of execution. These are also called as **Runtime Exceptions**. These include programming bugs, such as logic errors or improper use of an API. Runtime exceptions are ignored at the time of compilation.

For example, if you have declared an array of size 5 in your program, and trying to call the 6th element of the array then an *ArrayIndexOutOfBoundsExceptionexception* occurs.

```
public class Unchecked_Demo {
public static void main(String args[]){
int num[]={1,2,3,4}; System.out.println(num[5]);
}
}
```

If you compile and execute the above program, you will get the following exception.

```
Exception in thread
"main"java.lang.ArrayIndexOutOfBoundsException: 5
at
Exceptions.Unchecked_Demo.main(Unchecked_Demo.java:8)
```

- **Errors:** These are not exceptions at all, but problems that arise beyond the control of the user or the programmer. Errors are typically ignored in your code because you can rarely do anything about an error. For example, if a stack overflow occurs, an error will arise. They are also ignored at the time of compilation.

Exception Hierarchy

All exception classes are subtypes of the java.lang.Exception class. The exception class is a subclass of the Throwable class. Other than the exception class there is another subclass called Error which is derived from the Throwable class.

Errors are abnormal conditions that happen in case of severe failures, these are not handled by the Java programs. Errors are generated to indicate errors generated by the runtime environment. Example: JVM is out of memory. Normally, programs cannot recover from errors.

The Exception class has two main subclasses: IOException

class and RuntimeException Class.

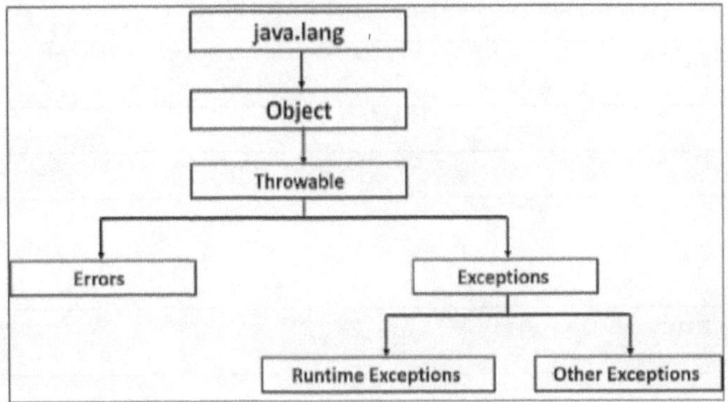

Following is a list of most common checked and unchecked Java's Built-in Exceptions.

Built-in Exceptions

Java defines several exception classes inside the standard package **java.lang**. The most general of these exceptions are subclasses of the standard type RuntimeException. Since java.lang is implicitly imported into all Java programs, most exceptions derived from RuntimeException are automatically available.

Java defines several other types of exceptions that relate to its various class libraries. Following is the list of Java Unchecked RuntimeException.

Exception	Description
ArithmeticException	Arithmetic error, such as divide-by-zero.
ArrayIndexOutOfBoundsException	Array index is out-of-bounds.
ArrayStoreException	Assignment to an array element of an incompatible type.
ClassCastException	Invalid cast.
IllegalArgumentException	Illegal argument used to invoke a method.

IllegalMonitorStateException	Illegal monitor operation, such as waiting on an unlocked thread.
IllegalStateException	Environment or application is in incorrect state.
IllegalThreadStateException	Requested operation not compatible with the current thread state.
IndexOutOfBoundsException	Some type of index is out-of-bounds.
NegativeArraySizeException	Array created with a negative size.
NullPointerException	Invalid use of a null reference.
NumberFormatException	Invalid conversion of a string to a numeric format.
SecurityException	Attempt to violate security.
StringIndexOutOfBounds	Attempt to index outside the bounds of a string.
UnsupportedOperationException	An unsupported operation was encountered.

Following is the list of Java Checked Exceptions Defined in java.lang.

Exception	Description
ClassNotFoundException	Class not found.
CloneNotSupportedException	Attempt to clone an object that does not implement the Cloneable interface.
IllegalAccessException	Access to a class is denied.
InstantiationException	Attempt to create an object of an abstract class or interface.
InterruptedException	One thread has been interrupted by another thread.
NoSuchFieldException	A requested field does not exist.
NoSuchMethodException	A requested method does not exist.

Exceptions Methods

Following is the list of important methods available in the Throwable class.

Sr. No.	Methods with Description
1	**public String getMessage()** Returns a detailed message about the exception that has occurred. This message is initialized in the Throwable constructor.
2	**public Throwable getCause()** Returns the cause of the exception as represented by a Throwable object.
3	**public String toString()** Returns the name of the class concatenated with the result of getMessage().
4	**public void printStackTrace()** Prints the result of toString() along with the stack trace to System.err, the error output stream.
5	**public StackTraceElement [] getStackTrace()** Returns an array containing each element on the stack trace. The element at index 0 represents the top of the call stack, and the last element in the array represents the method at the bottom of the call stack.
6	**public Throwable fillInStackTrace()** Fills the stack trace of this Throwable object with the current stack trace, adding to any previous information in the stack trace.

Catching Exceptions

A method catches an exception using a combination of the **try** and **catch** keywords. A try/catch block is placed around the code that might generate an exception. Code within a try/catch block is referred to as protected code, and the syntax for using try/catch looks like the following:

```
try
{
//Protected code
}catch(ExceptionName e1)
```

```
{
//Catch block
}
```

The code which is prone to exceptions is placed in the try block. When an exception occurs, that exception occurred is handled by catchblock associated with it. Every try block should be immediately followed either by a catch block or finally block.

A catch statement involves declaring the type of exception you are trying to catch. If an exception occurs in protected code, the catch block (or blocks) that follows the try is checked. If the type of exception that occurred is listed in a catch block, the exception is passed to the catch block much as an argument is passed into a method parameter.

Example

The following is an array declared with 2 elements. Then the code tries to access the 3rd element of the array which throws an exception.

```
// File Name : ExcepTest.java import java.io.*;
public class ExcepTest{
public static void main(String args[]){
try{
int a[] = new int[2];
System.out.println("Access element three :" +
a[3]);
```

```
}catch(ArrayIndexOutOfBoundsException e){
System.out.println("Exception thrown :" + e);
}
System.out.println("Out of the block");
}
}
```

This will produce the following result:

```
Exception thrown :java.lang.ArrayIndexOutOfBoundsException: 3
   Out of the block
```

Multiple Catch Blocks

A try block can be followed by multiple catch blocks. The syntax for multiple catch blocks looks like the following:

```
try
{
//Protected code
}catch(ExceptionType1 e1)
{
//Catch block
}catch(ExceptionType2 e2)
{
//Catch block
}catch(ExceptionType3 e3)
{
//Catch block
}
```

The previous statements demonstrate three catch blocks,

but you can have any number of them after a single try. If an exception occurs in the protected code, the exception is thrown to the first catch block in the list. If the data type of the exception thrown matches ExceptionType1, it gets caught there. If not, the exception passes down to the second catch statement. This continues until the exception either is caught or falls through all catches, in which case the current method stops execution and the exception is thrown down to the previous method on the call stack.

Example

Here is code segment showing how to use multiple try/catch statements.

```
try
{
file = new FileInputStream(fileName);
x = (byte) file.read();
}catch(IOException i)
{
i.printStackTrace();
return -1;
}catch(FileNotFoundException f) //Not valid!
{
f.printStackTrace();
return -1;
}
```

Catching Multiple Type of Exceptions

Since Java 7, you can handle more than one exception using a single catch block, this feature simplifies the code. Here is how you would do it:

```
catch (IOException|FileNotFoundException ex) {
logger.log(ex);
throw ex;
```

The Throws/Throw Keywords

If a method does not handle a checked exception, the method must declare it using the **throws** keyword. The throws keyword appears at the end of a method's signature.

You can throw an exception, either a newly instantiated one or an exception that you just caught, by using the **throw** keyword.

Try to understand the difference between throws and throw keywords, *throws* is used to postpone the handling of a checked exception and *throw* is used to invoke an exception explicitly.

The following method declares that it throws a RemoteException:

```
import java.io.*;
public class className
{
public void deposit(doubleamount) throws
RemoteException
```

```
{
// Method implementation throw new
RemoteException();
}
//Remainder of class definition
}
```

A method can declare that it throws more than one exception, in which case the exceptions are declared in a list separated by commas. For example, the following method declares that it throws a RemoteException and an InsufficientFundsException:

```
import java.io.*;
public class className
{
public void withdraw(double amount) throws
RemoteException, InsufficientFundsException
{
// Method implementation
}
//Remainder of class definition
}
```

The Finally Block

The finally block follows a try block or a catch block. A finally block of code always executes, irrespective of occurrence of an Exception.

Using a finally block allows you to run any cleanup-type statements that you want to execute, no matter what happens in the protected code.

A finally block appears at the end of the catch blocks and has the following syntax:

```
try
{
//Protected code
}catch(ExceptionType1 e1)
{
//Catch block
}catch(ExceptionType2 e2)
{
//Catch block
}catch(ExceptionType3 e3)
{
//Catch block
}finally
{
//The finally block always executes.
}
```

Example

```
public class ExcepTest{
public static void main(String args[]){
int a[] = new int[2];
try{
System.out.println("Access element three :" +
a[3]);
}catch(ArrayIndexOutOfBoundsException e){
System.out.println("Exception thrown :" + e);
}
finally{
a[0] = 6;
System.out.println("First element value: "
+a[0]); System.out.println("The finally statement
is executed");
```

```
    }
  }
}
```

This will produce the following result:

```
Exception thrown :java.lang.ArrayIndexOutOfBoundsException: 3
    First element value: 6
    The finally statement is executed
```

Note the following:

- A catch clause cannot exist without a try statement.
- It is not compulsory to have finally clauses whenever a try/catch block is present.
- The try block cannot be present without either catch clause or finally clause.
- Any code cannot be present in between the try, catch, finally blocks.

The try-with-resources

Generally, when we use any resources like streams, connections, etc. we have to close them explicitly using finally block. In the following program, we are reading data from a file using **FileReader** and we are closing it using finally block.

```java
import java.io.File;
import java.io.FileReader;
import java.io.IOException;
public class ReadData_Demo {
public static void main(String args[]){
FileReader fr=null;
try{
File file=new File("file.txt");
fr = new FileReader(file); char [] a = new
char[50];
fr.read(a); // reads the content to the array
for(char c : a)
System.out.print(c); //prints the characters one
by one
}catch(IOException e){
e.printStackTrace();
}
finally{
try{
fr.close();
}catch(IOException ex){
ex.printStackTrace();
}
}
}
}
```

try-with-resources, also referred as **automatic resource management**, is a new exception handling mechanism that was introduced in Java 7, which automatically closes the resources used within the try catch block.

To use this statement, you simply need to declare the required resources within the parenthesis, and the created resource will be closed automatically at the end of the block.

Following is the syntax of try-with-resources statement.

```
try(FileReader fr=new FileReader("file path"))
{
//use the resource
}catch(){
//body of catch
}
}
```

Following is the program that reads the data in a file using try-with-resources statement.

```
import java.io.FileReader;
import java.io.IOException;
public class Try_withDemo {
public static void main(String args[]){
try(FileReader fr=new FileReader("E://file.txt")){
char [] a =new char[50];
fr.read(a); // reads the contentto the array
for(char c : a)
System.out.print(c); //prints the characters one
by one
}catch(IOException e){
e.printStackTrace();
}
}
}
```

Following points are to be kept in mind while working with try-with-resources statement.

- To use a class with try-with-resources statement it should implement **AutoCloseable** interface and the

close() method of it gets invoked automatically at runtime.

- You can declare more than one class in try-with-resources statement.
- While you declare multiple classes in the try block of try-with-resources statement these classes are closed in reverse order.
- Except the deceleration of resources within the parenthesis everything is the same as normal try/catch block of a try block.
- The resource declared in try gets instantiated just before the start of the try-block.
- The resource declared at the try block is implicitly declared as final.

User-defined Exceptions

You can create your own exceptions in Java. Keep the following points in mind when writing your own exception classes:

- All exceptions must be a child of Throwable.
- If you want to write a checked exception that is automatically enforced by the Handle or Declare Rule, you need to extend the Exception class.
- If you want to write a runtime exception, you need to extend the RuntimeException class.

We can define our own Exception class as below:

```
class MyException extends Exception{}
```

You just need to extend the predefined **Exception** class to create your own Exception. These are considered to be checked exceptions. The following **InsufficientFundsE xception** class is a user-defined exception that extends the Exception class, making it a checked exception. An exception class is like any other class, containing useful fields and methods.

Example

```java
// File Name InsufficientFundsException.java
importjava.io.*;
public class InsufficientFundsException extends
Exception
{
private double amount;
public InsufficientFundsException(double amount)
{
this.amount = amount;
}
public double getAmount()
{
return amount;
}
}
```

To demonstrate using our user-defined exception, the following CheckingAccount class contains a withdraw() method that throws an InsufficientFundsException.

```java
// File Name CheckingAccount.java importjava.io.*;
public class CheckingAccount
{
private double balance;
private int number;
public CheckingAccount(int number)
{
this.number = number;
}
public void deposit(doubleamount)
{
balance += amount;
}
public void withdraw(double amount) throws
InsufficientFundsException
{
if(amount <= balance)
{
balance -= amount;
}
else
{
double needs = amount - balance;
throw new InsufficientFundsException(needs);
}
}
public double getBalance()
{
return balance;
}
public int getNumber()
{
return number;
}
}
```

The following BankDemo program demonstrates invoking

the deposit() and withdraw() methods of CheckingAccount.

```java
// File Name BankDemo.java public class BankDemo
{
public static void main(String [] args)
{
CheckingAccount c = new CheckingAccount(101);
System.out.println("Depositing $500...");
c.deposit(500.00);
try
{
System.out.println("\nWithdrawing $100...");
c.withdraw(100.00);
System.out.println("\nWithdrawing $600...");
c.withdraw(600.00);
}catch(InsufficientFundsException e)
{
System.out.println("Sorry, but you are short $" +
e.getAmount());
e.printStackTrace();
}
}
}
```

Compile all the above three files and run BankDemo. This will produce the following result:

Depositing $500...

Withdrawing $100... Withdrawing $600...

Sorry, but you are short $200.0

InsufficientFundsException

at CheckingAccount.withdraw(CheckingAccount.java:25)

at BankDemo.main(BankDemo.java:13)

Common Exceptions

In Java, it is possible to define two categories of Exceptions and Errors.

- **JVM Exceptions:** These are exceptions/errors that are exclusively or logically thrown by the JVM. Examples: NullPointerException, ArrayIndexOutOfBoundsException, ClassCastException.
- **Programmatic Exceptions:** These exceptions are thrown explicitly by the application or the API programmers. Examples: IllegalArgumentException, IllegalStateException.

Inner Classes

In this chapter, we will discuss inner classes of Java.

Nested Classes

In Java, just like methods, variables of a class too can have another class as its member. Writing a class within another is allowed in Java. The class written within is called the **nested class**, and the class that holds the inner class is called the **outerclass**.

Syntax

Following is the syntax to write a nested class. Here, the class **Outer_Demo** is the outer class and the class **Inner_Demo** is the nested class.

```
class Outer_Demo{
class Nested_Demo{
}
}
```

Nested classes are divided into two types:

- **Non-static nested classes:** These are the non-static members of a class.
- **Static nested classes:** These are the static members of a class.

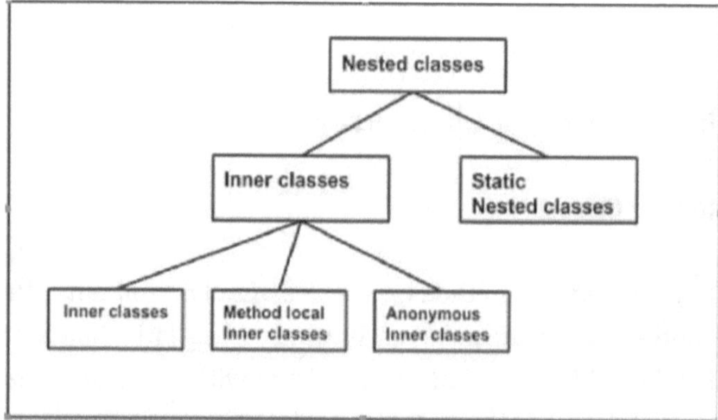

Inner Classes (Non-static Nested Classes)

Inner classes are a security mechanism in Java. We know a class cannot be associated with the access modifier **private**, but if we have the class as a member of other class, then the inner class can be made private. And this is also used to access the private members of a class.

Inner classes are of three types depending on how and where you define them. They are:

- Inner Class
- Method-local Inner Class

- Anonymous Inner Class

Inner Class

Creating an inner class is quite simple. You just need to write a class within a class. Unlike a class, an inner class can be private and once you declare an inner class private, it cannot be accessed from an object outside the class.

Following is the program to create an inner class and access it. In the given example, we make the inner class private and access the class through a method.

```
class Outer_Demo{
int num;
//inner class
private class Inner_Demo{
public void print(){
System.out.println("This is an inner class");
}
}
//Accessing he inner class from the method within
voiddisplay_Inner(){
Inner_Demo inner = newInner_Demo();
inner.print();
}
}
public class My_class{
public static void main(String args[]){
//Instantiating the outer class
Outer_Demo outer = newOuter_Demo();
//Accessing the display_Inner() method.
outer.display_Inner();
```

```
    }
  }
```

Here you can observe that **Outer_Demo** is the outer class, **Inner_Demo** is the inner class, **display_Inner()** is the method inside which we are instantiating the inner class, and this method is invoked from the **main** method.

If you compile and execute the above program, you will get the following result.

This is an inner class.

Accessing the Private Members

As mentioned earlier, inner classes are also used to access the private members of a class. Suppose, a class is having private members to access them. Write an inner class in it, return the private members from a method within the inner class, say, **getValue()**, and finally from another class (from which you want to access the private members) call the getValue() method of the inner class.

To instantiate the inner class, initially you have to instantiate the outer class. Thereafter, using the object of the outer class, following is the way in which you can instantiate the inner class.

```
Outer_Demo outer=new Outer_Demo();
Outer_Demo.Inner_Demo inner=outer.new
Inner_Demo();
```

The following program shows how to access the private members of a class using inner class.

```
class Outer_Demo {
//private variable of the outer class private int
num= 175;
//inner class
public class Inner_Demo{
public int getNum(){
System.out.println("This is the getnum method of
the inner class");
return num;
}
}
}
public class My_class2{
public static void main(String args[]){
//Instantiating the outer class
Outer_Demo outer=new Outer_Demo();
//Instantiating the inner class
Outer_Demo.Inner_Demo inner=outer.new
Inner_Demo(); System.out.println(inner.getNum());
}
}
```

If you compile and execute the above program, you will get the following result.

The value of num in the class Test is: 175

Method-local Inner Class

In Java, we can write a class within a method and this will be a local type. Like local variables, the scope of the inner class is restricted within the method.

A method-local inner class can be instantiated only within the method where the inner class is defined. The following program shows how to use a method-local inner class.

```java
public class Outerclass{
//instance method of the outer class void
my_Method(){
int num = 23;
//method-local inner class class MethodInner_Demo{
public void print(){
System.out.println("This is method inner class
"+num);
}
}//end of inner class
//Accessing the inner class
MethodInner_Demo inner = new MethodInner_Demo();
inner.print();
}
public static void main(String args[]){
Outerclass outer = newOuterclass();
outer.my_Method();
}
}
```

If you compile and execute the above program, you will get the following result.

This is method inner class 23

Anonymous Inner Class

An inner class declared without a class name is known as an **anonymous inner class**. In case of anonymous inner classes, we declare and instantiate them at the same time. Generally, they are used whenever you need to override the method of a class or an interface. The syntax of an anonymous inner class is as follows:

```
AnonymousInner an_inner = new AnonymousInner(){
public void my_method(){
........
........
}
};
```

The following program shows how to override the method of a class using anonymous inner class.

```
abstract class AnonymousInner{
public abstract void mymethod();
}
public class Outer_class {
public static void main(String args[]){
AnonymousInner inner = new AnonymousInner(){
public void mymethod(){
System.out.println("This is an example of
anonymous inner class");
}
};
inner.mymethod();
}
}
```

If you compile and execute the above program, you will get the following result.

This is an example of anonymous inner class

In the same way, you can override the methods of the concrete class as well as the interface using an anonymous inner class.

Anonymous Inner Class as Argument

Generally, if a method accepts an object of an interface, an abstract class, or a concrete class, then we can implement the interface, extend the abstract class, and pass the object to the method. If it is a class, then we can directly pass it to the method.

But in all the three cases, you can pass an anonymous inner class to the method. Here is the syntax of passing an anonymous inner class as a method argument:

```
obj.my_Method(new My_Class(){
public void Do(){
 . . . . .

 . . . . .

}
});
```

The following program shows how to pass an anonymous inner class as a method argument.

```java
//interface interface Message{
String greet();
}
public class My_class {
//method which accepts the object of interface
Message public void displayMessage(Message m){
System.out.println(m.greet() +", This is an
example of anonymous inner calss as an argument");
}
public static void main(String args[]){
//Instantiating the class
My_class obj = new My_class();
//Passing an anonymous inner class as an argument
obj.displayMessage(new Message(){
public String greet(){
return "Hello";
}
});
}
}
```

If you compile and execute the above program, it gives you the following result.

Hello This is an example of anonymous inner class as an argument

Static Nested Class

A static inner class is a nested class which is a static member of the outer class. It can be accessed without instantiating the outer class, using other static members. Just like static members, a static nested class does not have access to the instance variables and methods of the outer class. The syntax of static nested class is as follows:

```
class MyOuter {
static class Nested_Demo{
}
}
```

Instantiating a static nested class is a bit different from instantiating an inner class. The following program shows how to use a static nested class.

```
public class Outer{
static class Nested_Demo{
public void my_method(){
System.out.println("This is my nested class");
}
}
public static void main(String args[]){
Outer.Nested_Demo nested = new
Outer.Nested_Demo();
nested.my_method();
}
}
```

If you compile and execute the above program, you will get the following result.

This is my nested class

II

Java Object Oriented

Inheritance

Inheritance can be defined as the process where one class acquires the properties (methods and fields) of another. With the use of inheritance the information is made manageable in a hierarchical order.

The class which inherits the properties of other is known as subclass (derived class, child class) and the class whose properties are inherited is known as superclass (base class, parent class).

extends Keyword

extends is the keyword used to inherit the properties of a class. Following is the syntax of extends keyword.

```
class Super{
   .....
   .....
}
class Sub extends Super{
   .....
   .....
```

```
}
```

Sample Code

Following is an example demonstrating Java inheritance. In this example, you can observe two classes namely Calculation and My_Calculation.

Using extends keyword, the My_Calculation inherits the methods addition() and Subtraction() of Calculation class.

Copy and paste the following program in a file with name My_Calculation.java

```java
class Calculation{
int z;
public void addition(int x, int y){
z = x+y;
System.out.println("The sum of the given
numbers:"+z);
}
public void Substraction(int x,int y){
z = x-y;
System.out.println("The difference between the
given numbers:"+z);
}
}
public class My_Calculation extends Calculation{
public void multiplication(int x, int y){
z = x*y;
System.out.println("The product of the given
numbers:"+z);
}
public static void main(String args[]){
```

```
int a = 20, b = 10;
My_Calculation demo = new My_Calculation();
demo.addition(a, b);
demo.Substraction(a, b);
demo.multiplication(a, b);
}
}
```

Compile and execute the above code as shown below.

```
javac My_Calculation.java java My_Calculation
```

After executing the program, it will produce the following result.

The sum of the given numbers:30

The difference between the given numbers:10

The product of the given numbers:200

In the given program, when an object to **My_Calculation** class is created, a copy of the contents of the superclass is made within it. That is why, using the object of the subclass you can access the members of a superclass.

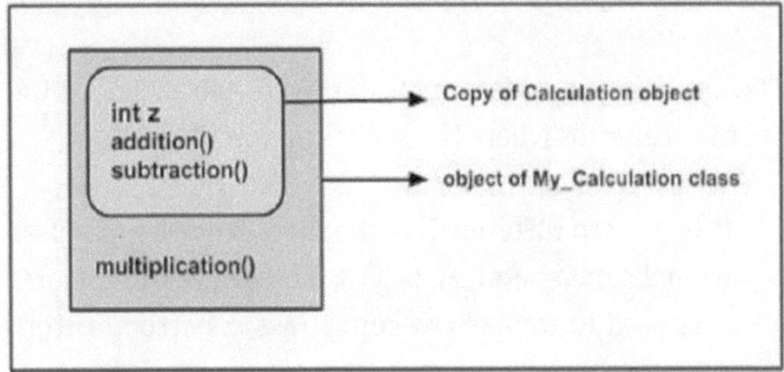

The Superclass reference variable can hold the subclass object, but using that variable you can access only the members of the superclass, so to access the members of both classes it is recommended to always create reference variable to the subclass.

If you consider the above program, you can instantiate the class as given below. But using the superclass reference variable (**cal** in this case) you cannot call the method **multiplication()**, which belongs to the subclass My_Calculation.

```
Calculation cal = new My_Calculation();
demo.addition(a, b);
demo.Subtraction(a, b);
```

Note – A subclass inherits all the members (fields, methods, and nested classes) from its superclass. Constructors are not members, so they are not inherited by subclasses, but the constructor of the superclass can be invoked from the subclass.

The super keyword

The **super** keyword is similar to **this** keyword. Following are the scenarios where the super keyword is used.

- It is used to **differentiate the members** of superclass from the members of subclass, if they have same names.
- It is used to **invoke the superclass** constructor from subclass.

Differentiating the Members

If a class is inheriting the properties of another class. And if the members of the superclass have the names same as the sub class, to differentiate these variables we use super keyword as shown below.

```
super.variable super.method();
```

Sample Code

This chapter provides you a program that demonstrates the usage of the **super** keyword.

In the given program, you have two classes namely *Sub_class* and *Super_class*, both have a method named display() with different implementations, and a variable named num with different values. We are invoking display() method of both classes and printing the value of the variable num of both classes. Here you can observe that we have used super keyword to differentiate the members of superclass from subclass.

Copy and paste the program in a file with name Sub_class.java.

```java
class Super_class{
int num = 20;
//display method of superclass public void
display(){
System.out.println("This is the display method of
superclass");
}
}
public class Sub_class extends Super_class {
int num = 10;
//display method of sub class public void
display(){
System.out.println("This is the display method of
subclass");
}
public void my_method(){
//Instantiating subclass
Sub_class sub = new Sub_class();
//Invoking the display()method of sub class
sub.display();
//Invoking the display()method of superclass
super.display();
//printing the value of variable num of subclass
System.out.println("value of the variable named
num in sub class:"+ sub.num);
//printing the value of variable num of superclass
System.out.println("value of the variable named
num in super class:"+
super.num);
}
public static void main(String args[]){ Sub_class
```

```
obj = new Sub_class();
obj.my_method();
}
}
```

Compile and execute the above code using the following syntax.

```
javac Super_Demo javaSuper
```

On executing the program, you will get the following result -

This is the display method of subclass

This is the display method of superclass

value of the variable named num in sub class:10 valueof the variable named num in sup

Invoking Superclass Constructor

If a class is inheriting the properties of another class, the subclass automatically acquires the default constructor of the superclass. But if you want to call a parameterized constructor of the superclass, you need to use the super keyword as shown below.

```
super(values);
```

Sample Code

The program given in this chapter demonstrates how to use

the super keyword to invoke the parametrized constructor of the superclass. This program contains a superclass and a subclass, where the superclass contains a parameterized constructor which accepts a string value, and we used the super keyword to invoke the parameterized constructor of the superclass.

Copy and paste the following program in a file with the name Subclass.java

```
class Superclass{
int age;
Superclass(int age){
this.age = age;
}
public void getAge(){
System.out.println("The value of the variable
named age in super class is: " +age);
}
}
public class Subclass extends Superclass {
Subclass(int age){
super(age);
}
public static void main(String argd[]){ Subclass
s = new Subclass(24);
s.getAge();
}
}
```

Compile and execute the above code using the following syntax.

```
javac Subclass java Subclass
```

On executing the program, you will get the following result
–

The value of the variable named age in super class is: 24

IS-ARelationship

IS-A is a way of saying: This object is a type of that object. Let us see how the **extends** keyword is used to achieve inheritance.

```
public class Animal{
}
public class Mammal extends Animal{
}
public class Reptile extends Animal{
}
public class Dog extends Mammal{
}
```

Now, based on the above example, in Object-Oriented terms, the following are true –

- Animal is the superclass of Mammal class.
- Animal is the superclass of Reptile class.
- Mammal and Reptile are subclasses of Animal class.
- Dog is the subclass of both Mammal and Animal classes.

Now, if we consider the IS-A relationship, we can say –

- Mammal IS-A Animal

- Reptile IS-A Animal
- Dog IS-A Mammal
- Hence: Dog IS-A Animal as well

With the use of the extends keyword, the subclasses will be able to inherit all the properties of the superclass except for the private properties of the superclass.

We can assure that Mammal is actually an Animal with the use of the instance operator.

Example

```
class Animal{
}
class Mammal extends Animal{
}
class Reptile extends Animal{
}
public class Dog extends Mammal{
public static void main(String args[]){ Animal a
= new Animal();
Mammal m = new Mammal(); Dog d = new Dog();
System.out.println(m instanceof Animal);
System.out.println(d instanceof Mammal);
System.out.println(d instanceof Animal);
}
}
```

This will produce the following result –

true true true

Since we have a good understanding of the **extends** keyword, let us look into how the **implements** keyword is used to get the IS-A relationship.

Generally, the **implements** keyword is used with classes to inherit the properties of an interface. Interfaces can never be extended by a class.

Example

```
public interface Animal {
}
public class Mammal implements Animal{
}
public class Dog extends Mammal{
}
```

The instanceof Keyword

Let us use the **instanceof** operator to check determine whether Mammal is actually an Animal, and dog is actually an Animal.

```
interface Animal{}
class Mammal implements Animal{}
public class Dog extends Mammal{
public static void main(String args[]){
Mammal m = new Mammal(); Dog d = new Dog();
System.out.println(m instanceof Animal);
System.out.println(d instanceof Mammal);
System.out.println(d instanceof Animal);
}
}
```

This will produce the following result:

```
true true

   true
```

HAS-Arelationship

These relationships are mainly based on the usage. This determines whether a certain class **HAS-A** certain thing. This relationship helps to reduce duplication of code as well as bugs.

Lets look into an example –

```java
public class Vehicle{}
public class Speed{}
public class Van extends Vehicle{
private Speed sp;
}
```

This shows that class Van HAS-A Speed. By having a separate class for Speed, we do not have to put the entire code that belongs to speed inside the Van class, which makes it possible to reuse the Speed class in multiple applications.

In Object-Oriented feature, the users do not need to bother about which object is doing the real work. To achieve this, the Van class hides the implementation details from the users of the Van class. So, basically what happens is the users would ask the Van class to do a certain action and the Van class will either do the work by itself or ask another class to perform the action.

Types of Inheritance

There are various types of inheritance as demonstrated below.

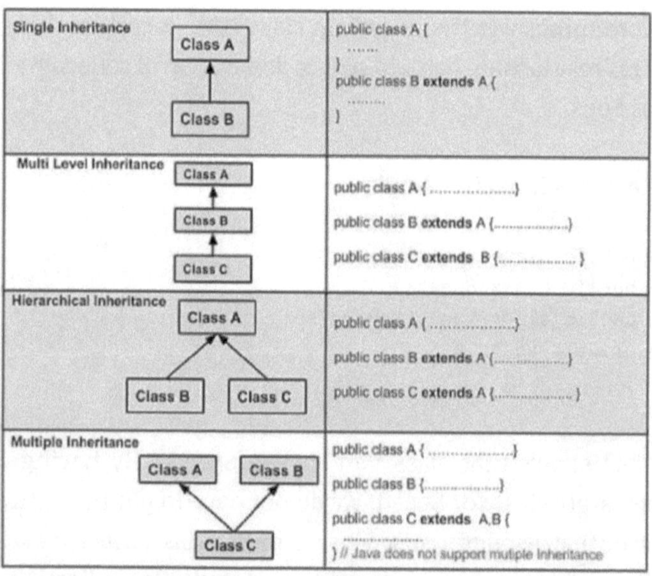

A very important fact to remember is that Java does not support multiple inheritance. This means that a class cannot extend more than one class. Therefore following is illegal –

```
public class extends Animal, Mammal{}
```

However, a class can implement one or more interfaces, which ha helped Java get rid of the impossibility of multiple inheritance.

Overriding

In the previous chapter, we talked about superclasses and subclasses. If a class inherits a method from its superclass, then there is a chance to override the method provided that it is not marked final.

The benefit of overriding is: ability to define a behavior that's specific to the subclass type, which means a subclass can implement a parent class method based on its requirement.

In object-oriented terms, overriding means to override the functionality of an existing method.

Example

Let us look at an example.

```
class Animal{
public void move(){
System.out.println("Animals can move");
}
}
```

```
class Dog extends Animal{
public void move(){
System.out.println("Dogs can walk and run");
}
}
public class TestDog{
public static void main(String args[]){
Animal a = new Animal(); // Animal reference and
object
Animal b = new Dog(); // Animal reference but Dog
object
a.move();// runs the method in Animal class
b.move();//Runs the method in Dog class
}
}
```

This will produce the following result:

Animals can move

Dogs can walk and run

In the above example, you can see that even though **b** is a type of Animal it runs the move method in the Dog class. The reason for this is: In compile time, the check is made on the reference type. However, in the runtime, JVM figures out the object type and would run the method that belongs to that particular object.

Therefore, in the above example, the program will compile properly since Animal class has the method move. Then, at the runtime, it runs the method specific for that object.

Consider the following example:

```java
class Animal{
public void move(){
System.out.println("Animals can move");
}
}
class Dog extends Animal{
public void move(){
System.out.println("Dogs can walk and run");
}
public void bark(){ System.out.println("Dogs can
bark");
}
}
public class TestDog{
public static void main(String args[]){
Animal a = new Animal(); // Animal reference and
object
Animal b = new Dog(); // Animal reference but Dog
object
a.move();// runs the method in Animal class
b.move();//Runs the method in Dog class
b.bark();
}
}
```

This will produce the following result:

TestDog.java:30: cannot find symbol

symbol : method bark()

location: class Animal

b.bark();

^

This program will throw a compile time error since b's reference type Animal doesn't have a method by the name of bark.

Rules for Method Overriding

- The argument list should be exactly the same as that of the overridden method.
- The return type should be the same or a subtype of the return type declared in the original overridden method in the superclass.
- The access level cannot be more restrictive than the overridden method's access level. For example: If the superclass method is declared public then the overriding method in the sub lass cannot be either private or protected.
- Instance methods can be overridden only if they are inherited by the subclass.
- A method declared final cannot be overridden.
- A method declared static cannot be overridden but can be re-declared.
- If a method cannot be inherited, then it cannot be overridden.
- A subclass within the same package as the instance's superclass can override any superclass method that is not declared private or final.
- A subclass in a different package can only override the non-final methods declared public or protected.
- An overriding method can throw any uncheck exceptions, regardless of whether the overridden method throws exceptions or not. However, the overriding

method should not throw checked exceptions that are new or broader than the ones declared by the overridden method. The overriding method can throw narrower or fewer exceptions than the overridden method.
- Constructors cannot be overridden.

Using the super Keyword

When invoking a superclass version of an overridden method the **super** keyword is used.

```
class Animal{
public void move(){
System.out.println("Animals can move");
}
}
class Dog extends Animal{
public void move(){
super.move(); // invokesthe super class method
System.out.println("Dogs can walk and run");
}
}
public class TestDog{
public static void main(String args[]){
Animal b = new Dog(); // Animal reference but Dog
object b.move(); //Runs the method in Dog class
}
}
```

This will produce the following result:

Animals can move

Dogs can walk and run

Polymorphism

Polymorphism is the ability of an object to take on many forms. The most common use of polymorphism in OOP occurs when a parent class reference is used to refer to a child class object.

Any Java object that can pass more than one IS-A test is considered to be polymorphic. In Java, all Java objects are polymorphic since any object will pass the IS-A test for their own type and for the class Object.

It is important to know that the only possible way to access an object is through a reference variable. A reference variable can be of only one type. Once declared, the type of a reference variable cannot be changed.

The reference variable can be reassigned to other objects provided that it is not declared final. The type of the reference variable would determine the methods that it can invoke on the object.

A reference variable can refer to any object of its declared type or any subtype of its declared type. A reference variable can be declared as a class or interface type.

Example

Let us look at an example.

```
public interface Vegetarian{}
public class Animal{}
public class Deer extends Animal implements
Vegetarian{}
```

Now, the Deer class is considered to be polymorphic since this has multiple inheritance. Following are true for the above examples:

- A Deer IS-A Animal
- A Deer IS-A Vegetarian
- A Deer IS-A Deer
- A Deer IS-A Object

When we apply the reference variable facts to a Deer object reference, the following declarations are legal:

```
Deer d = new Deer();
Animal a = d;
Vegetarian v = d;
Object o = d;
```

All the reference variables d, a, v, o refer to the same Deer object in the heap.

Virtual Methods

In this chapter, I will show you how the behavior of over-ridden methods in Java allows you to take advantage of polymorphism when designing your classes.

We already have discussed method overriding, where a child class can override a method in its parent. An overridden method is essentially hidden in the parent class, and is not invoked unless the child class uses the super keyword within the overriding method.

```java
/* File name : Employee.java */
public class Employee
{
private String name; private String address;
private int number;
public Employee(String name, String address, int
number)
{
System.out.println("Constructing an Employee");
this.name = name; this.address = address;
this.number = number;
}
public void mailCheck()
{
System.out.println("Mailing a check to "+
this.name
+ " " + this.address);
}
public String toString()
{
return name + " " + address + " " + number;
}
public String getName()
{
return name;
```

```
}
public String getAddress()
{
return address;
}
public void setAddress(String newAddress)
{
address = newAddress;
}
public int getNumber()
{
return number;
}
}
}
```

Now suppose we extend Employee class as follows:

```
/* File name : Salary.java */
public class Salary extends Employee
{
private double salary; //Annual salary
public Salary(String name, String address, int
number, double salary)
{
super(name, address, number);
setSalary(salary);
}
public void mailCheck()
{
System.out.println("Within mailCheck of Salary
class "); System.out.println("Mailing check to "
+ getName()
+ " with salary " + salary);
}
public double getSalary()
{
```

```
return salary;
}
public void setSalary(double newSalary)
{
if(newSalary >= 0.0)
{
salary = newSalary;
}
}
public double computePay()
{
System.out.println("Computing salary pay for " +
getName());
return salary/52;
}
}
```

Now, you study the following program carefully and try to
determine its output:

```
/* File name : VirtualDemo.java */
public class VirtualDemo
{
public static void main(String [] args)
{
Salary s = new Salary("Mohd Mohtashim", "Ambehta,
UP",3, 3600.00); Employee e = new Salary("John
Adams", "Boston, MA", 2, 2400.00);
System.out.println("Call mailCheck using Salary
reference --"); s.mailCheck();
System.out.println("\n Call mailCheck using
Employee reference--");
e.mailCheck();
}
}
```

This will produce the following result:

Constructing an Employee
    Constructing an Employee
    Call mailCheck using Salary reference —
    WithinmailCheck of Salary class
    ailing check to Mohd Mohtashim with salary 3600.0

 Call mailCheck using Employeereference—
    Within mailCheck of Salary class
    ailing check to John Adams with salary 2400.0

Here, we instantiate two Salary objects. One using a Salary reference **s**, and the other using an Employee reference **e**.

While invoking *s.mailCheck()*, the compiler sees mailCheck() in the Salary class at compile time, and the JVM invokes mailCheck() in the Salary class at run time. Invoking mailCheck() on **e** is quite different because **e** is an Employee reference. When the compiler sees *e.mailCheck()*, the compiler sees the mailCheck() method in the Employee class.

Here, at compile time, the compiler used mailCheck() in Employee to validate this statement. At run time, however, the JVM invokes mailCheck() in the Salary class.

This behavior is referred to as virtual method invocation, and the methods are referred to as virtual methods. All methods in Java behave inthis manner, whereby an over-ridden method is invoked at run time, no matter what data type the reference is that was used in the source code at compile time.

Abstraction

As per dictionary, **abstraction** is the quality of dealing with ideas rather than events. For example, when you consider the case of e-mail, complex details such as what happens as soon as you send an e-mail, the protocol your e-mail server uses are hidden from the user. Therefore, to send an e-mail you just need to type the content, mention the address of the receiver, and click send.

Likewise in Object-oriented programming, abstraction is a process of hiding the implementation details from the user, only the functionality will be provided to the user. In other words, the user will have the information on what the object does instead of how it does it.

In Java, abstraction is achieved using Abstract classes and interfaces.

Abstract Class

A class which contains the **abstract** keyword in its declaration is known as abstract class.

- Abstract classes may or may not contain *abstract methods*, i.e., methods without body (public void get();)
- But, if a class has at least one abstract method, then the class **must** be declared abstract.
- If a class is declared abstract, it cannot be instantiated.
- To use an abstract class, you have to inherit it from another class, provide implementations to the abstract methods in it.
- If you inherit an abstract class, you have to provide implementations to all the abstract methods in it.

Example

This chapter provides you an example of the abstract class. To create an abstract class, just use the **abstract** keyword before the class keyword, in the class declaration.

```
/* File name : Employee.java */
public abstract class Employee
{
private String name; private String address;
private int number;
public Employee(String name, String address, int
number)
{
System.out.println("Constructing an Employee");
this.name = name; this.address = address;
this.number = number;
}
public double computePay()
{
System.out.println("Inside Employee computePay");
return 0.0;
```

```java
}
public void mailCheck()
{
System.out.println("Mailing a check to "+
this.name
+ " " + this.address);
}
public String toString()
{
return name + " " + address + " " + number;
}
public String getName()
{
return name;
}
public String getAddress()
{
return address;
}
public void setAddress(String newAddress)
{
address = newAddress;
}
public int getNumber()
{
return number;
}
}
```

You can observe that except abstract methods the Employee class is same as normal class in Java. The class is now abstract, but it still has three fields, seven methods, and one constructor.

Now you can try to instantiate the Employee class in the

following way:

```java
/* File name : AbstractDemo.java */
public class AbstractDemo
{
public static void main(String [] args)
{
/* Following is not allowed and would raise error
*/ Employee e = new Employee("George W.",
"Houston, TX", 43);
System.out.println("\n Call mailCheck using
Employee reference--");
e.mailCheck();
}
}
```

When you compile the above class, it gives you the following error:

Employee.java:46: Employee is abstract; cannot be instantiated

　　Employee e = new Employee("George W.", "Houston, TX", 43);

　　^

　1 error

Inheriting the Abstract Class

We can inherit the properties of Employee class just like concrete class in the following way:

```java
/* File name : Salary.java */
public class Salary extends Employee
{
private double salary; //Annual salary
```

```java
public Salary(String name, String address, int
number, double salary)
{
super(name, address, number);
setSalary(salary);
}
public void mailCheck()
{
System.out.println("Within mailCheck of Salary
class "); System.out.println("Mailing check to "
+ getName()
+ " with salary " + salary);
}
public double getSalary()
{
return salary;
}
public void setSalary(double newSalary)
{
if(newSalary >= 0.0)
{
salary = newSalary;
}
}
public double computePay()
{
System.out.println("Computing salary pay for " +
getName());
return salary/52;
}
}
```

Here, you cannot instantiate the Employee class, but you can instantiate the Salary Class, and using this instance you can access all the three fields and seven methods of Employee class as shown below.

```java
/* File name : AbstractDemo.java */
public class AbstractDemo
{
public static void main(String [] args)
{
Salary s = new Salary("Mohd Mohtashim", "Ambehta,
UP",3, 3600.00); Employee e = new Salary("John
Adams", "Boston, MA", 2, 2400.00);
System.out.println("Call mailCheck using Salary
reference --");
s.mailCheck();
System.out.println("\n Call mailCheck using
Employee reference--");
e.mailCheck();
}
}
```

This produces the following result:

Constructing an Employee

   Constructing an Employee

Call mailCheck using Salary reference —

   WithinmailCheck of Salary class

   ailing check to Mohd Mohtashim with salary 3600.0

Call mailCheck using Employeereference—

   Within mailCheck of Salary class

   ailing check to John Adams with salary 2400.

Abstract Methods

If you want a class to contain a particular method but

you want the actual implementation of that method to be determined by child classes, you can declare the method in the parent class as an abstract.

- **abstract** keyword is used to declare the method as abstract.
- You have to place the **abstract** keyword before the method name in the method declaration.
- An abstract method contains a method signature, but no method body.
- Instead of curly braces, an abstract method will have a semi colon (;) at the end.

Following is an example of the abstract method.

```java
public abstract class Employee
{
private String name; private String address;
private int number;
public abstract double computePay();
//Remainder of class definition
}
```

Declaring a method as abstract has two consequences:

- The class containing it must be declared as abstract.
- Any class inheriting the current class must either override the abstract method or declare itself as abstract.

Note: Eventually, a descendant class has to implement the abstract method; otherwise, you would have a hierarchy of abstract classes that cannot be instantiated.

Suppose Salary class inherits the Employee class, then it should implement the **computePay()** method as shown below:

```
/* File name : Salary.java */
public class Salary extends Employee
{
private double salary; // Annual salary
public double computePay()
{
System.out.println("Computing salary pay for " +
getName());
return salary/52;
}
//Remainder of class definition
}
```

Encapsulation

Encapsulation is one of the four fundamental OOP concepts. The other three are inheritance, polymorphism, and abstraction.

Encapsulation in Java is a mechanism of wrapping the data (variables) and code acting on the data (methods) together as a single unit. In encapsulation, the variables of a class will be hidden from other classes, and can be accessed only through the methods of their current class. Therefore, it is also known as **data hiding**.

To achieve encapsulation in Java:

- Declare the variables of a class as private.
- Provide public setter and getter methods to modify and view the variables values.

Example

Following is an example that demonstrates how to achieve Encapsulation in Java:

```java
/* File name : EncapTest.java */
public class EncapTest{
private String name; private String idNum;
private int age;
public int getAge(){
return age;
}
public String getName(){
return name;
}
public String getIdNum(){
return idNum;
}
public void setAge( int newAge){
age = newAge;
}
public void setName(StringnewName){
name = newName;
}
public void setIdNum( String newId){
idNum = newId;
}
}
```

The public setXXX() and getXXX() methods are the access points of the instance variables of the EncapTest class. Normally, these methods are referred as getters and setters. Therefore, any class that wants to access the variables should access them through these getters and setters.

The variables of the EncapTest class can be accessed using the following program:

```
/* File name : RunEncap.java */
public class RunEncap{
public static void main(String args[]){ EncapTest
encap = newEncapTest(); encap.setName("James");
encap.setAge(20); encap.setIdNum("12343ms");
System.out.print("Name : " + encap.getName() +
"Age : "+
encap.getAge());
}
}
```

This will produce the following result:

Name : James Age : 20

Benefits of Encapsulation

- The fields of a class can be made read-only or write-only.
- A class can have total control over what is stored in its fields.
- The users of a class do not know how the class stores its data. A class can change the data type of a field and users of the class do not need to change any of their code.

Interfaces

An interface is a reference type in Java. It is similar to class. It is a collection of abstract methods. A class implements an interface, thereby inheriting the abstract methods of the interface.

Along with abstract methods, an interface may also contain constants, default methods, static methods, and nested types. Method bodies exist only for default methods and static methods.

Writing an interface is similar to writing a class. But a class describes the attributes and behaviors of an object. And an interface contains behaviors that a class implements.

Unless the class that implements the interface is abstract, all the methods of the interface need to be defined in the class.

An interface is similar to a class in the following ways:

- An interface can contain any number of methods.
- An interface is written in a file with a **.java** extension,

with the name of the interface matching the name of the file.

- The byte code of an interface appears in a **.class** file.
- Interfaces appear in packages, and their corresponding bytecode file must be in a directory structure that matches the package name.

However, an interface is different from a class in several ways, including:

- You cannot instantiate an interface.
- An interface does not contain any constructors.
- All of the methods in an interface are abstract.
- An interface cannot contain instance fields. The only fields that can appear in an interface must be declared both static and final.
- An interface is not extended by a class; it is implemented by a class.
- An interface can extend multiple interfaces.

Declaring Interfaces

The **interface** keyword is used to declare an interface. Here is a simple example to declare an interface.

Example

Following is an example of an interface:

```
/* File name : NameOfInterface.java */
import java.lang.*;
//Any number of import statements
public interface NameOfInterface
{
//Any number of final, static fields
//Any number of abstract method declarations\
}
```

Interfaces have the following properties:

- An interface is implicitly abstract. You do not need to use the **abstract** keyword while declaring an interface.
- Each method in an interface is also implicitly abstract, so the abstract keyword is not needed.
- Methods in an interface are implicitly public.

Example

```
/* File name : Animal.java */
interface Animal {
public void eat();
public void travel();
}
```

Implementing Interfaces

When a class implements an interface, you can think of the class as signing a contract, agreeing to perform the specific behaviors of the interface. If a class does not perform all the behaviors of the interface, the class must declare itself as abstract.

A class uses the **implements** keyword to implement an interface. The implements keyword appears in the class declaration following the extends portion of the declaration.

```
/* File name : MammalInt.java */
public class MammalInt implements Animal{
public void eat(){ System.out.println("Mammal
eats");
}
public void travel(){ System.out.println("Mammal
travels");
}
public int noOfLegs(){
return 0;
}
public static void main(String args[]){ MammalInt
m = new MammalInt(); m.eat();
m.travel();
}
}
```

This will produce the following result:

Mammal eats

Mammal travels

When overriding methods defined in interfaces, there are several rules to be followed:

- Checked exceptions should not be declared on imple-mentation methods other than the ones declared by the interface method or subclasses of those declared by the interface method.

- The signature of the interface method and the same return type or subtype should be maintained when overriding the methods.
- An implementation class itself can be abstract and if so, interface methods need not be implemented.

When implementation interfaces, there are several rules:

- A class can implement more than one interface at a time.
- A class can extend only one class, but implement many interfaces.
- An interface can extend another interface, in a similar way as a class can extend another class.

Extending Interfaces

An interface can extend another interface in the same way that a class can extend another class. The **extends** keyword is used to extend an interface, and the child interface inherits the methods of the parent interface.

The following Sports interface is extended by Hockey and Football interfaces.

```java
//Filename: Sports.java public interface Sports
{
public void setHomeTeam(String name);
public void setVisitingTeam(String name);
}
//Filename: Football.java
public interface Football extends Sports
```

```java
{
public void homeTeamScored(int points); public
void visitingTeamScored(int points); public void
endOfQuarter(int quarter);
}
//Filename: Hockey.java
public interface Hockey extends Sports
{
public void homeGoalScored(); public
void visitingGoalScored(); public
void endOfPeriod(int period); public
void overtimePeriod(int ot);
}
```

The Hockey interface has four methods, but it inherits two from Sports; thus, a class that implements Hockey needs to implement all six methods. Similarly, a class that implements Football needs to define the three methods from Football and the two methods from Sports.

Extending Multiple Interfaces

A Java class can only extend one parent class. Multiple inheritance is not allowed. Interfaces are not classes, however, and an interface can extend more than one parent interface.

The extends keyword is used once, and the parent interfaces are declared in a comma- separated list.

For example, if the Hockey interface extended both Sports and Event, it would be declared as:

public interface Hockey extends Sports, Event

Tagging Interfaces

The most common use of extending interfaces occurs when the parent interface does not contain any methods. For example, the MouseListener interface in the java.awt.event package extended java.util.EventListener, which is defined as:

```
package java.util;
public interface EventListener
{}
```

An interface with no methods in it is referred to as a **tagging** interface. There are two basic design purposes of tagging interfaces:

Creates a common parent: As with the EventListener interface, which is extended by dozens of other interfaces in the Java API, you can use a tagging interface to create a common parent among a group of interfaces. For example, when an interface extends EventListener, the JVM knows that this particular interface is going to be used in an event delegation scenario.

Adds a data type to a class: This situation is where the term, tagging comes from. A class that implements a tagging interface does not need to define any methods (since the interface does not have any), but the class becomes an interface type through polymorphism.

Packages

Packages are used in Java in order to prevent naming conflicts, to control access, to make searching/locating and usage of classes, interfaces, enumerations and annotations easier, etc.

A **Package** can be defined as a grouping of related types (classes, interfaces, enumerations and annotations) providing access protection and namespace management.

Some of the existing packages in Java are:

- **java.lang** - bundles the fundamental classes
- **java.io** - classes for input, output functions are bundled in this package

Programmers can define their own packages to bundle group of classes/interfaces, etc. It is a good practice to group related classes implemented by you so that a programmer can easily determine that the classes, interfaces, enumerations, and annotations are related.

Since the package creates a new namespace there won't be

any name conflicts with names in other packages. Using packages, it is easier to provide access control and it is also easier to locate the related classes.

Creating a Package

While creating a package, you should choose a name for the package and include a **package** statement along with that name at the top of every source file that contains the classes, interfaces, enumerations, and annotation types that you want to include in the package.

The package statement should be the first line in the source file. There can be only one package statement in each source file, and it applies to all types in the file.

If a package statement is not used then the class, interfaces, enumerations, and annotation types will be placed in the current default package.

To compile the Java programs with package statements, you have to use -d option as shown below.

```
javac -d Destination_folder file_name.java
```

Then a folder with the given package name is created in the specified destination, and the compiled class files will be placed in that folder.

Example

Let us look at an example that creates a package called **animals**. It is a good practice to use names of packages with lower case letters to avoid any conflicts with the names of classes and interfaces.

Following package example contains interface named *animals*:

```
/* File name : Animal.java */
package animals;
interface Animal {
public void eat();
public void travel();
}
```

Now, let us implement the above interface in the same package *animals*:

```
package animals;
/* File name : MammalInt.java */
public class MammalInt implements Animal{
public void eat(){ System.out.println("Mammal
eats");
}
public void travel(){ System.out.println("Mammal
travels");
}
public int noOfLegs(){
return 0;
}
public static void main(String args[]){ MammalInt
m = new MammalInt(); m.eat();
m.travel();
}
```

```
}
```

Now compile the java files as shown below:

```
$ javac -d . Animal.java
$ javac -d . MammalInt.java
```

Now a package/folder with the name **animals** will be created in the current directory and these class files will be placed in it as shown below.

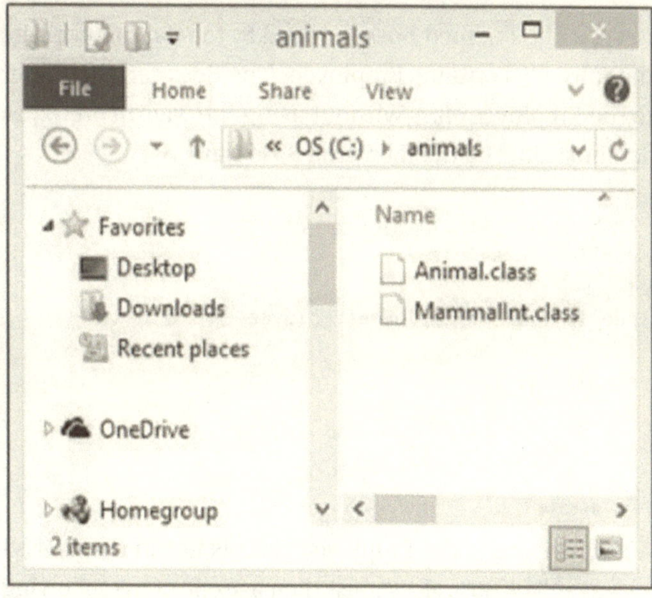

You can execute the class file within the package and get the result as shown below.

```
$ java animals.MammalInt
   ammal eats
   ammal travels
```

The import Keyword

If a class wants to use another class in the same package, the package name need not be used. Classes in the same package find each other without any special syntax.

Example

Here, a class named Boss is added to the payroll package that already contains Employee. The Boss can then refer to the Employee class without using the payroll prefix, as demonstrated by the following Boss class.

```
package payroll;
public class Boss
{
public void payEmployee(Employee e)
{
e.mailCheck();
}
}
```

What happens if the Employee class is not in the payroll package? The Boss class must then use one of the following techniques for referring to a class in a different package.

- The fully qualified name of the class can be used. For example:

payroll.Employee

- The package can be imported using the import keyword and the wild card (*). For example:

import payroll.*;

- The class itself can be imported using the import key-word. For example:

import payroll.Employee;

Note: A class file can contain any number of import statements. The import statements must appear after the package statement and before the class declaration.

The Directory Structure of Packages

Two major results occur when a class is placed in a package:

- The name of the package becomes a part of the name of the class, as we just discussed in the previous chapter.
- The name of the package must match the directory structure where the corresponding bytecode resides.

Here is simple way of managing your files in Java:

Put the source code for a class, interface, enumeration, or

annotation type in a text file whose name is the simple name of the type and whose extension is **.java**.For example:

```
// File Name :  Car.java
package vehicle;
public class Car {
// Class implementation.
}
```

Now, put the source file in a directory whose name reflects the name of the package to which the class belongs:

```
....\vehicle\Car.java
```

Now, the qualified class name and path name would be as follows:

- Class name -> vehicle.Car
- Path name -> vehicle\Car.java (in windows)

In general, a company uses its reversed Internet domain name for its package names. **Example**: A company's Internet domain name is apple.com, then all its package names would start with com.apple. Each component of the package name corresponds to a subdirectory.

Example: The company had a com.apple.computers package that contained a Dell.java source file, it would be contained in a series of subdirectories like this:

```
....\com\apple\computers\Dell.java
```

At the time of compilation, the compiler creates a different output file for each class, interface and enumeration defined in it. The base name of the output file is the name of the type, and its extension is **.class**.

For example:

```
// File Name: Dell.java
package com.apple.computers;
public class Dell{
}
class Ups{
}
```

Now, compile this file as follows using -d option:

```
$javac -d . Dell.java
```

The files will be compiled as follows:

```
.\com\apple\computers\Dell.class
.\com\apple\computers\Ups.class
```

You can import all the classes or interfaces defined in \com\apple\computers\ as follows:

```
import com.apple.computers.*;
```

Like the .java source files, the compiled .class files should be in a series of directories that reflect the package name.

However, the path to the .class files does not have to be the same as the path to the .java source files. You can arrange your source and class directories separately, as:

```
<path-one>\sources\com\apple\computers\Dell.java
<path-two>\classes\com\apple\computers\Dell.class
```

By doing this, it is possible to give access to the classes directory to other programmers without revealing your sources. You also need to manage source and class files in this manner so that the compiler and the Java Virtual Machine (JVM) can find all the types your program uses.

The full path to the classes directory, <path-two>\classes, is called the class path, and is set with the CLASSPATH system variable. Both the compiler and the JVM construct the path to your .class files by adding the package name to the class path.

Say <path-two>\classes is the class path, and the package name is com.apple.computers, then the compiler and JVM will look for .class files in <path- two>\classes\com\apple\computers.

A class path may include several paths. Multiple paths should be separated by a semicolon (Windows) or colon (Unix). By default, the compiler and the JVM search the current directory and the JAR file containing the Java platform classes so that these directories are automatically in the class path.

Set CLASSPATH System Variable

To display the current CLASSPATH variable, use the following commands in Windows and UNIX (Bourne shell):

- In Windows -> C:\> set CLASSPATH
- In UNIX -> % echo $CLASSPATH

To delete the current contents of the CLASSPATH variable, use:

- In Windows -> C:\> set CLASSPATH=
- In UNIX -> % unset CLASSPATH; export CLASSPATH

To set the CLASSPATH variable:

- In Windows -> set CLASSPATH=C:\users\jack\java\classes
- In UNIX -> % CLASSPATH=/home/jack/java/classes; export CLASSPATH

III

Java Advanced

Data Structures

The data structures provided by the Java utility package are very powerful and perform a wide range of functions. These data structures consist of the following interface and classes:

- Enumeration
- BitSet
- Vector
- Stack
- Dictionary
- Hashtable
- Properties

All these classes are now legacy and Java-2 has introduced a new framework called Collections Framework, which is discussed in the next chapter.

The Enumeration

The Enumeration interface isn't itself a data structure, but it is very important within the context of other data structures. The Enumeration interface defines a means to retrieve successive elements from a data structure.

For example, Enumeration defines a method called nextElement that is used to get the next element in a data structure that contains multiple elements.

The Enumeration Interface

The Enumeration interface defines the methods by which you can enumerate (obtain one at a time) the elements in a collection of objects.

This legacy interface has been superseded by Iterator. Although not deprecated, Enumeration is considered obsolete for new code. However, it is used by several methods defined by the legacy classes such as Vector and Properties, is used by several other API classes, and is currently in widespread use in application code.

The methods declared by Enumeration are summarized in the following table:

Sr. No.	Methods with Description
1	**boolean hasMoreElements( )** When implemented, it must return true while there are still more elements to extract, and false when all the elements have been enumerated.
2	**Object nextElement( )** This returns the next object in the enumeration as a generic Object reference.

Example

Following is an example showing usage of Enumeration.

```java
import java.util.Vector;
import java.util.Enumeration;
public class EnumerationTester {
public static void main(String args[]) {
Enumeration days;
Vector dayNames = newVector();
dayNames.add("Sunday");
dayNames.add("Monday");
dayNames.add("Tuesday");
dayNames.add("Wednesday");
dayNames.add("Thursday");
dayNames.add("Friday");
dayNames.add("Saturday");
days = dayNames.elements();
while (days.hasMoreElements()){
System.out.println(days.nextElement());
}
}
}
```

This will produce the following result:

Sunday

Monday

Tuesday

Wednesday

Thursday

Friday

Saturday

The BitSet

The BitSet class implements a group of bits or flags that can be set and cleared individually. This class is very useful in cases where you need to keep up with a set of Boolean values; you just assign a bit to each value and set or clear it as appropriate.

The BitSet Class

The BitSet class creates a special type of array that holds bit values. The BitSet array can increase in size as needed. This makes it similar to a vector of bits. This is a legacy class but it has been completely re-engineered in Java 2, version 1.4.

The BitSet defines the following two constructors.

Sr. No.	Constructor and Description
1	**BitSet( )** This constructor creates a default object
2	**BitSet(int size)** This constructor allows you to specify its initial size, i.e., the number of bits that it can hold. All bits are initialized to zero

BitSet implements the Cloneable interface and defines the methods listed in the following table:

Methods with Description

- **void and(BitSet bitSet)** ANDsthe contents of the invoking BitSet object with those specified by bitSet. The result is placed into the invoking object.

- **void andNot(BitSet bitSet)** For each1 bit in bitSet,the corresponding bit in the invoking BitSet is cleared.
- **int cardinality( )** Returns the number of set bits in the invoking object.
- **void clear( )** Zeros all bits.
- **void clear(int index)** Zeros the bit specified by index.
- **void clear(int startIndex, int endIndex)** Zeros the bits from startIndex to endIndex.
- **Objectclone( )** Duplicates the invoking BitSet object.
- **boolean equals(Object bitSet)**
- Returns true if the invoking bit set is equivalent to the one passed in bitSet. Otherwise, the method returns false.
- **void flip(int index)** Reverses the bit specified by the index.
- **void flip(int startIndex, int endIndex)** Reverses the bits from startIndex to endIndex.
- **boolean get(int index)** Returns the current state of the bit at the specified index.
- **BitSet get(int startIndex, int endIndex)** Returns a Bit-Set that consists of the bits from startIndex to endIndex. The invoking object is not changed.
- **int hashCode( )** Returns the hash code for the invoking object.
- **boolean intersects(BitSet bitSet)** Returns true if at least one pair of corresponding bits within the invoking object and bitSet are 1.
- **boolean isEmpty( )** Returns true if all bits in the invoking object are zero.

- **int length()** Returns the number of bits required to hold the contents of the invoking BitSet. This value is determined by the location of the last 1 bit.
- **int nextClearBit(int startIndex)** Returns the index of the next cleared bit, (that is, the next zero bit), starting from the index specified by startIndex.
- **int nextSetBit(int startIndex)** Returns the index of the next set bit (thatis, the next 1 bit), starting from the index specified by startIndex. If no bit is set, -1 is returned.
- **void or(BitSetbitSet)** ORs the contents of the invoking BitSet object with that specified by bitSet. The result is placed into the invoking object.
- **void set(int index)** Sets the bit specified by index.
- **void set(int index,boolean v)** Sets the bit specified by index to the value passed in v. True sets the bit, false clears the bit.
- **void set(int startIndex, int endIndex)** Sets the bits from startIndex to endIndex.
- **void set(int startIndex, int endIndex, boolean v)** Sets the bits from startIndex to endIndex, to the value passed in v. true sets the bits, false clears the bits.
- **int size( )** Returns the number of bits in the invoking BitSet object.
- **String toString( )** Returns the string equivalent of the invoking BitSet object.
- **void xor(BitSet bitSet)** XORsthe contents of the invoking BitSet object with that specified by bitSet. The result is placed into the invoking object.

Example

The following program illustrates several of the methods supported by this data structure:

```java
import java.util.BitSet;
public class BitSetDemo {
public static void main(String args[]) { BitSet
bits1 = new BitSet(16);
BitSet bits2 = new BitSet(16);
// set some bits
for(int i=0; i<16; i++) {
if((i%2) == 0) bits1.set(i);
if((i%5) != 0) bits2.set(i);
}
System.out.println("Initial pattern in bits1: ");
System.out.println(bits1);
System.out.println("\nInitial pattern in bits2:
"); System.out.println(bits2);
// AND bits bits2.and(bits1);
System.out.println("\nbits2 AND bits1: ");
System.out.println(bits2);
// OR bits bits2.or(bits1);
System.out.println("\nbits2 OR bits1: ");
System.out.println(bits2);
// XOR bits bits2.xor(bits1);
System.out.println("\nbits2 XOR bits1: ");
System.out.println(bits2);
}
}
```

This will produce the following result:

Initial pattern in bits1:

{0, 2, 4, 6, 8, 10, 12, 14}

Initial pattern in bits2:

{1, 2, 3, 4, 6, 7, 8, 9, 11, 12, 13, 14}

bits2 AND bits1:

{2, 4, 6, 8, 12, 14}

bits2 OR bits1:

{0, 2, 4, 6, 8, 10, 12, 14}

bits2 XOR bits1:

{}

The Vector

The Vector class is similar to a traditional Java array, except that it can grow as necessary to accommodate new elements. Like an array, elements of a Vector object can be accessed via an index into the vector. The nice thing about using the Vector class is that you don't have to worry about setting it to a specific size upon creation; it shrinks and grows automatically when necessary.

The Vector Class

Vector implements a dynamic array. It is similar to ArrayList, but with two differences:

- Vector is synchronized.
- Vector contains many legacy methods that are not part of the collections framework.

Vector proves to be very useful if you don't know the size of the array in advance or you just need one that can change sizes over the lifetime of a program.

Following is the list of constructors provided by the vector class.

Constructor and Description

- **Vector( )**This constructor creates a default vector, which has an initial size of 10
- **Vector(int size)** This constructor accepts an argument that equals to the required size, and creates a vector whose initial capacity is specified by size
- **Vector(int size, int incr)** This constructor creates a vector whose initial capacity is specified by size and whose increment is specified by incr. The increment specifies the number of elements to allocate each time that a vector is resized upward
- **Vector(Collection c)** This constructor creates a vector that contains the elements of collection c

Apart from the methods inherited from its parent classes, Vector defines the following methods and description:

- **void add(int index, Object element)** Inserts the specified element at the specified position in this Vector.
- **boolean add(Object o)** Appends the specified element to the end of this Vector.
- **boolean addAll(Collection c)** Appends all of the elements in the specified Collection to the end of this Vector, in the order that they are returned by the specified Collection's Iterator.
- **boolean addAll(int index, Collection c)** Inserts all of the elements in in the specified Collection into this Vector at the specified position.

- **void addElement(Object obj)** Adds the specified component to the end of this vector, increasing its size by one.
- **int capacity()** Returns the current capacity of this vector.
- **void clear()** Removes all of the elements from this vector.
- **Objectclone()** Returns a clone of this vector.
- **boolean contains(Object elem)** Tests if the specified object is a component in this vector.
- **boolean containsAll(Collection c)** Returns true if this vector contains all of the elements in the specified Collection.
- **void copyInto(Object[] anArray)** Copies the components of this vector into the specified array.
- **ObjectelementAt(int index)** Returns the component at the specified index.
- **Enumeration elements()** Returns an enumeration of the components of this vector.
- **void ensureCapacity(int minCapacity)** Increases the capacity of this vector, if necessary, to ensure that it can hold at least the number of components specified by the minimum capacity argument.
- **boolean equals(Object o)** Compares the specified Object with this vector for equality.
- **ObjectfirstElement()** Returns the first component (the item at index 0) of this vector.
- **Objectget(int index)** Returns the element at the specified position in this vector.
- **int hashCode()** Returns the hash code value for this vector.

- **int indexOf(Object elem)** Searches for the first occurrence of the given argument, testing for equality using the equals method.
- **int indexOf(Object elem, int index)** Searches for the first occurrence of the given argument, beginning the search at index, and testing for equality using the equals method.
- **void insertElementAt(Object obj, int index)** Inserts the specified object as a component in this vector at the specified index.
- **boolean isEmpty()** Tests if this vector has no components.
- **ObjectlastElement()** Returns the last component of the vector.
- **int lastIndexOf(Object elem)** Returns the index of the last occurrence of the specified object in this vector.
- **int lastIndexOf(Object elem, int index)** Searches backwards for the specified object,starting from the specified index, and returns an index to it.
- **Objectremove(int index)** Removes the element at the specified position in this vector.
- **boolean remove(Object o)** Removes the first occurrence of the specified element in this vector, If the vector does not contain the element, it is unchanged.
- **boolean removeAll(Collection c)** Removes from this vector all of its elements that are contained in the specified Collection.
- **void removeAllElements()** Removes all components from this vector and sets its size to zero.
- **boolean removeElement(Objectobj)** Removes the first (lowest-indexed) occurrence of the argument from this

vector.

- **void removeElementAt(int index)** removeElementAt(int index)
- **protected void removeRange(int fromIndex, int toIndex)** Removes from this List all of the elements whose index is between fromIndex, inclusive and toIndex, exclusive.
- **boolean retainAll(Collectionc)** Retains only the elements in this vector that are contained in the specified Collection.
- **Objectset(int index, Objectelement)** Replaces the element at the specified position in this vector with the specified element.
- **void setElementAt(Object obj, int index)** Sets the component at the specified index of this vector to be the specified object.
- **void setSize(int newSize)** Sets the size of this vector.
- **int size()** Returns the number of components in this vector.
- **List subList(int fromIndex, int toIndex)** Returns a view of the portion of this List between fromIndex, inclusive, and toIndex, exclusive.
- **Object[] toArray()** Returns an array containing all of the elements in this vector in the correct order.
- **Object[] toArray(Object[] a)** Returns an array containing all of the elements in this vector in the correct order; the runtime type of the returned array is that of the specified array.
- **String toString()** Returns a string representation of this vector, containing the String representation of each element.

- **void trimToSize()** Trims the capacity of this vector to be the vector's current size.

Example

The following program illustrates several of the methods supported by this collection:

```java
import java.util.*;
public class VectorDemo {
public static void main(String args[]) {
// initial size is 3, increment is 2
Vector v = new Vector(3, 2);
System.out.println("Initial size: " + v.size());
System.out.println("Initial capacity: "+
v.capacity()); v.addElement(new Integer(1));
v.addElement(new Integer(2)); v.addElement(new
Integer(3)); v.addElement(new Integer(4));
System.out.println("Capacity after four
additions: " +
v.capacity()); v.addElement(new Double(5.45));
System.out.println("Current capacity: "+
v.capacity());
v.addElement(new Double(6.08)); v.addElement(new
Integer(7)); System.out.println("Current
capacity: " + v.capacity());
v.addElement(new Float(9.4));
v.addElement(new Integer(10));
System.out.println("Current capacity: " +
v.capacity());
v.addElement(new Integer(11)); v.addElement(new
Integer(12)); System.out.println("First element:
" +
(Integer)v.firstElement());
System.out.println("Last element: " +
(Integer)v.lastElement());
```

```java
if(v.contains(new Integer(3)))
System.out.println("Vector contains 3.");
// enumerate the elements in the vector.
Enumeration vEnum = v.elements();
System.out.println("\nElements in vector:");
while(vEnum.hasMoreElements())
System.out.print(vEnum.nextElement() + " ");
System.out.println();
}
}
```

This will produce the following result:

Initial size: 0

Initial capacity: 3

Capacity after four additions: 5

Current capacity: 5

Current capacity: 7

Current capacity: 9

First element: 1

Last element: 12

Vector contains 3.

Elements in vector:

1 2 3 4 5.45 6.08 7 9.4 10 1112

The Stack

The Stack class implements a last-in-first-out (LIFO) stack of elements.

You can think of a stack literally as a vertical stack of objects;

when you add a new element, it gets stacked on top of the others.

When you pull an element off the stack, it comes off the top. In other words, the last element you added to the stack is the first one to come back off.

The Stack Class

Stack is a subclass of Vector that implements a standard last-in, first-out stack.

Stack only defines the default constructor, which creates an empty stack. Stack includes all the methods defined by Vector, and adds several of its own.

```
Stack( )
```

Apart from the methods inherited from its parent class Vector, Stack defines the following methods:

Methods with Description

- **boolean empty()** Tests if this stack is empty. Returns true if the stack is empty, and returns false if the stack contains elements.
- **Objectpeek( )** Returns the element on the top of the stack, but does not remove it.
- **Objectpop( )** Returns the element on the top of the stack, removing it in the process.

- **Objectpush(Object element)** Pushes the element onto the stack. Element is also returned.
- **int search(Object element)** Searches for element in the stack. If found, its offset from the top of the stack is returned. Otherwise, .1 is returned.

Example

The following program illustrates several of the methods supported by this collection:

```java
import java.util.*;
public class StackDemo {
static void showpush(Stack st, int a) {
st.push(new Integer(a));
System.out.println("push(" + a + ")");
System.out.println("stack: " + st);
}
static void showpop(Stack st) {
System.out.print("pop-> "); Integer a = (Integer)
st.pop(); System.out.println(a);
System.out.println("stack: " + st);
}
public static void main(String args[]) { Stack st
= new Stack(); System.out.println("stack: "+ st);
showpush(st, 42);
showpush(st, 66); showpush(st, 99); showpop(st);
showpop(st); showpop(st);
try {
showpop(st);
} catch (EmptyStackException e) {
System.out.println("empty stack");
}
}
}
```

This will produce the following result:

```
stack: [ ]
    push(42) stack: [42] push(66)
    stack: [42, 66]
    push(99)
    stack: [42, 66, 99]
    pop -> 99
    stack: [42, 66]
    pop -> 66 stack: [42] pop-> 42 stack: [ ]
    pop -> empty stack
```

The Dictionary

The Dictionary class is an abstract class that defines a data structure for mapping keys to values.

This is useful in cases where you want to be able to access data via a particular key rather than an integer index.

Since the Dictionary class is abstract, it provides only the framework for a key-mapped data structure rather than a specific implementation.

The Dictionary Class

Dictionary is an abstract class that represents a key/value storage repository and operates much like Map.

Given a key and value, you can store the value in a Dictionary object. Once the value is stored, you can retrieve it by using its key. Thus, like a map, a dictionary can be thought of as a list of key/value pairs.

The abstract methods defined by Dictionary are listed below:

Methods with Description

- **Enumeration elements( )** Returns an enumeration of the values contained in the dictionary.
- **Objectget(Object key)** Returns the object that contains the value associated with the key. If the key is not in the dictionary, a null object is returned.
- **boolean isEmpty( )** Returns true if the dictionary is empty, and returns false if it contains at least one key.
- **Enumeration keys( )** Returns an enumeration of the keys contained in the dictionary.
- **Object put(Object key, Objectvalue)** Inserts a key and its value into the dictionary. Returns null if the key is not already in the dictionary; returns the previous value associated with the key if the key is already in the dictionary.
- **Object remove(Object key)** Removes the key and its value. Returns the value associated with the key. If the key is not in the dictionary, a null is returned.
- **int size( )** Returns the number of entries in the dictionary.

The Dictionary class is obsolete. You should implement the Map interface to obtain key/value storage functionality.

The Map Interface

The Map interface maps unique keys to values. A key is an object that you use to retrieve a value at a later date.

- Given a key and a value, you can store the value in a Map object. After the value is stored, you can retrieve it by using its key.
- Several methods throw a NoSuchElementException when no items exist in the invoking map.
- A ClassCastException is thrown when an object is incompatible with the elements in a map.
- A NullPointerException is thrown if an attempt is made to use a null object and null is not allowed in the map.
- An UnsupportedOperationException is thrown when an attempt is made to change an unmodifiable map.

Methods with Description

- **void clear( )** Removes all key/value pairs from the invoking map.
- **boolean containsKey(Objectk)** Returns true if the invoking map contains **k** as a key. Otherwise, returns false.
- **boolean containsValue(Object v)** Returns true if the map contains **v** as a value. Otherwise, returns false.
- **Set entrySet( )** Returns a Set that contains the entries in the map. The set contains objects of type Map.Entry. This method provides a set-view of the invoking map.
- **boolean equals(Object obj)** Returns true if obj is a Map and contains the same entries. Otherwise, returns false.

- **Objectget(Object k)** Returns the value associated with the key **k**.
- **int hashCode( )** Returns the hash code for the invoking map.
- **boolean isEmpty( )** Returns true if the invoking map is empty. Otherwise, returns false.
- **Set keySet( )** Returns a Set that contains the keys in the invoking map. This method provides a set-view of the keys in the invoking map.
- **Object put(Object k, Objectv)** Puts an entry in the invoking map, overwriting any previous value associated with the key. The key and value are k and v, respectively. Returns null if the key did not already exist. Otherwise, the previous value linked to the key is returned.
- **void putAll(Map m)** Puts all the entries from **m** into this map.
- **Objectremove(Object k)** Removes the entry whose key equals **k**.
- **int size( )** Returns the number of key/value pairs in the map.
- **Collection values( )** Returns a collection containing the values in the map. This method provides a collection-view of the values in the map.

Example

Map has its implementation in various classes like HashMap. Following is an example to explain map functionality:

```java
import java.util.*;
public class CollectionsDemo {
public static void main(String[] args) { Map m1 =
newHashMap();
m1.put("Zara", "8");
m1.put("Mahnaz", "31"); m1.put("Ayan","12");
m1.put("Daisy", "14"); System.out.println();
System.out.println(" Map Elements");
System.out.print("\t"+ m1);
}
}
```

This will produce the following result:

ap Elements

   {Mahnaz=31, Ayan=12, Daisy=14, Zara=8}

The Hashtable

The Hashtable class provides a means of organizing data based on some user-defined key structure.

For example, in an address list hash table you could store and sort data based on a key such as ZIP code rather than on a person's name.

The specific meaning of keys with regard to hash tables is totally dependent on the usage of the hash table and the data it contains.

The Hashtable Class

Hashtable was part of the original java.util and is a concrete implementation of a Dictionary.

However, Java 2 re-engineered Hashtable so that it also implements the Map interface. Thus, Hashtable is now integrated into the collections framework. It is similar to HashMap, but is synchronized.

Like HashMap, Hashtable stores key/value pairs in a hash table. When using a Hashtable, you specify an object that is used as a key, and the value that you want linked to that key. The key is then hashed, and the resulting hash code is used as the index at which the value is stored within the table.

Following is the list of constructors provided by the HashTable class.

Constructor and Description

- **Hashtable( )** This is the default constructor of the hash table it instantiates the Hashtable class.
- **Hashtable(int size)** This constructor accepts an integer parameter and creates a hash table that has an initial size specified by integer value size.
- **Hashtable(int size, float fillRatio)** This creates a hash table that has an initial size specified by size and a fill ratio specified by fillRatio. This ratio must be between 0.0 and 1.0, and it determines how full the hash table can be before it is resized upward.
- **Hashtable(Map<? extends K, ? extends V> t)** This constructs a Hashtable with the given mappings.

Apart from the methods defined by Map interface, Hashtable defines the following methods:

Methods with Description

- **void clear( )** Resets and empties the hash table.
- **Objectclone( )** Returns a duplicate of the invoking object.
- **boolean contains(Object value)** Returns true if some value equal to the value exists within the hash table. Returns false if the value isn't found.
- **boolean containsKey(Objectkey)** Returns true if some key equal to the key exists within the hash table. Returns false if the key isn't found.
- **boolean containsValue(Object value)** Returns true if some value equal to the value exists within the hash table. Returns false if the value isn't found.
- **Enumeration elements( )** Returns an enumeration of the values contained in the hash table.
- **Objectget(Object key)** Returns the object that contains the value associated with the key. If the key is not in the hash table, a null object is returned.
- **boolean isEmpty( )** Returns true if the hash table is empty; returns false if it contains at least one key.
- **Enumeration keys( )** Returns an enumeration of the keys contained in the hash table.
- **Object put(Object key, Objectvalue)** Inserts a key and a value into the hash table. Returns null if the key isn't already in the hash table; returns the previous value associated with the key if the key is already in the hash table.

- **void rehash( )** Increases the size of the hash table and rehashes all of its keys.
- **Objectremove(Object key)** Removes the key and its value. Returns the value associated with the key. If the key is not in the hash table, a null object is returned.
- **int size( )** Returns the number of entries in the hash table.
- **String toString( )** Returns the string equivalent of a hash table.

Example

The following program illustrates several of the methods supported by this data structure:

```java
import java.util.*;
public class HashTableDemo {
public static void main(String args[]) {
// Create a hash map
Hashtable balance = new Hashtable(); Enumeration
names;
String str;
double bal;
balance.put("Zara", new Double(3434.34));
balance.put("Mahnaz",new Double(123.22));
balance.put("Ayan", new Double(1378.00));
balance.put("Daisy", new Double(99.22));
balance.put("Qadir", new Double(-19.08));
// Show all balances in hash table. names =
balance.keys(); while(names.hasMoreElements()) {
str = (String) names.nextElement();
System.out.println(str + ": " +
balance.get(str));
} System.out.println();
```

```
// Deposit 1,000 into Zara's account
bal =
((Double)balance.get("Zara")).doubleValue();
balance.put("Zara", new Double(bal+1000));
System.out.println("Zara's new balance: " +
balance.get("Zara"));
    }
}
```

This will produce the following result:

```
Qadir: -19.08
  Zara: 3434.34 ahnaz: 123.22
  Daisy: 99.22
  Ayan: 1378.0
  Zara's new balance: 4434.34
```

The Properties

Properties is a subclass of Hashtable. It is used to maintain lists of values in which the key is a String and the value is also a String.

The Properties class is used by many other Java classes. For example, it is the type of object returned by System.getProperties( ) when obtaining environmental values.

The Properties Class

Properties is a subclass of Hashtable. It is used to maintain lists of values in which the key is a String and the value is also a String.

The Properties class is used by many other Java classes. For example, it is the type of object returned by System.getProperties( ) when obtaining environmental values.

Properties define the following instance variable. This variable holds a default property list associated with a Properties object. Properties defaults;

Following is the list of constructors provided by the properties class.

Constructors and Description

- **Properties( )** This constructor creates a Properties object that has no default values.
- **Properties(Properties propDefault)** Creates an object that uses propDefault for its default values. In both cases, the property list is empty.

Apart from the methods defined by Hashtable, Properties define the following methods:

Methods with Description

- **String getProperty(String key)** Returns the value associated with the key. A null object is returned if the key is neither in the list nor in the default property list.
- **String getProperty(String key, String defaultProperty)** Returns the value associated with the key; defaultProp-

erty is returned if the key is neither in the list nor in the default property list.

- **void list(PrintStream streamOut)** Sends the property list to the output stream linked to streamOut.
- **void list(PrintWriter streamOut)** Sends the property list to the output stream linked to streamOut.
- **void load(InputStream streamIn) throws IOException** Inputs a property list from the input stream linked to streamIn.
- **Enumeration propertyNames( )** Returns an enumeration of the keys. This includes those keys found in the default property list,too.
- **ObjectsetProperty(String key, String value)** Associates value with the key. Returns the previous value associated with the key, or returns null if no such association exists.
- **void store(OutputStream streamOut, String description)** After writing the string specified by description, the property list is written to the outputstream linked to streamOut.

Example

The following program illustrates several of the methods supported by this data structure:

```
import java.util.*;
public class PropDemo {
public static void main(String args[]) {
Properties capitals = new Properties(); Set
states;
```

```
String str;
capitals.put("Illinois", "Springfield");
capitals.put("Missouri", "Jefferson City");
capitals.put("Washington", "Olympia");
capitals.put("California", "Sacramento");
capitals.put("Indiana","Indianapolis");
// Show all states and capitals in hashtable.
states = capitals.keySet(); // get set-view of
keys Iterator itr = states.iterator();
while(itr.hasNext()) {
str = (String) itr.next();
System.out.println("The capital of " +
str + "is " + capitals.getProperty(str) + ".");
} System.out.println();
// look for state not in list -- specify default
str = capitals.getProperty("Florida",
"NotFound"); System.out.println("Thecapital of
Florida is "
+ str + ".");
}
}
```

This will produce the following result:

The capital of Missouri is Jefferson City.

The capital of Illinois is Springfield.

The capital of Indiana is Indianapolis.

The capital of California is Sacramento.

The capital of Washington is Olympia.

The capital of Florida is Not Found.

Collections Framework

Prior to Java 2, Java provided ad hoc classes such as **Dictionary, Vector, Stack**, and **Properties** to store and manipulate groups of objects. Although these classes were quite useful, they lacked a central, unifying theme. Thus, the way that you used Vector was different from the way that you used Properties.

The collections framework was designed to meet several goals, such as:

- The framework had to be high-performance. The implementations for the fundamental collections (dynamic arrays, linked lists, trees, and hashtables) were to be highly efficient.
- The framework had to allow different types of collections to work in a similar manner and with a high degree of interoperability.
- The framework had to extend and/or adapt a collection easily.

Towards this end, the entire collections framework is designed around a set of standard interfaces. Several standard implementations such as **LinkedList, HashSet,** and **TreeSet**, of these interfaces are provided that you may use as-is and you may also implement your own collection, if you choose.

A collections framework is a unified architecture for representing and manipulating collections. All collections frameworks contain the following:

- **Interfaces:** These are abstract data types that represent collections. Interfaces allow collections to be manipulated independently of the details of their representation. In object-oriented languages, interfaces generally form a hierarchy.
- **Implementations, i.e., Classes:** These are the concrete implementations of the collection interfaces. In essence, they are reusable data structures.
- **Algorithms:** These are the methods that perform useful computations, such as searching and sorting, on objects that implement collection interfaces. The algorithms are said to be polymorphic: that is, the same method can be used on many different implementations of the appropriate collection interface.

In addition to collections, the framework defines several map interfaces and classes. Maps store key/value pairs. Although maps are not *collections* in the proper use of the term, but they are fully integrated with collections.

The Collection Interfaces

The collections framework defines several interfaces. This

chapter provides an overview of each interface:

Interfaces with Description

- **The Collection Interface** This enables you to work with groups of objects;it is at the top of the collections hierarchy.
- **The List Interface** This extends **Collection** and an instance of List stores an ordered collection of elements.
- **The Set** This extends Collection to handle sets, which must contain unique elements
- **The SortedSet** This extends Set to handle sorted sets.
- **The Map** This maps unique keys to values.
- **The Map.Entry** This describes an element (a key/value pair) in a map. This is an inner class of Map.
- **The SortedMap** This extends Map so that the keys are maintained in an ascending order.
- **The Enumeration** This is legacy interface defines the methods by which you can enumerate (obtain one at a time) the elements in a collection of objects. This legacy interface has been superseded by Iterator.

The Collection Interface

The Collection interface is the foundation upon which the collections framework is built. It declares the core methods that all collections will have. These methods are summarized in the following table.

Because all collections implement Collection, familiarity with its methods is necessary for a clear understanding

of the framework. Several of these methods can throw an
UnsupportedOperationException.

Methods with Description

- **boolean add(Object obj)** Adds obj to the invoking collection. Returns true if obj was added to the collection. Returns false if obj is already a member of the collection, or if the collection does not allow duplicates.
- **boolean addAll(Collection c)** Adds all the elements of **c** to the invoking collection. Returns true if the operation succeeds (i.e., the elements were added). Otherwise, returns false.
- **void clear( )** Removes all elements from the invoking collection.
- **boolean contains(Object obj)** Returns true if obj is an element of the invoking collection. Otherwise, returns false.
- **boolean containsAll(Collection c)** Returns true if the invoking collection contains all elements of **c**. Otherwise, returns false.
- **boolean equals(Object obj)** Returns true if the invoking collection and obj are equal. Otherwise, returns false.
- **int hashCode( )** Returns the hash code for the invoking collection.
- **boolean isEmpty( )** Returns true if the invoking collection is empty. Otherwise, returns false.
- **Iterator iterator( )** Returns an iterator for the invoking collection.
- **boolean remove(Object obj)** Removes one instance of obj from the invoking collection. Returns true if the

element was removed. Otherwise, returns false.

- **boolean removeAll(Collection c)** Removes all elements of **c** from the invoking collection. Returns true if the collection changed (i.e., elements were removed). Otherwise, returns false.
- **boolean retainAll(Collection c)** Removes all elements from the invoking collection except those in **c**.Returns true if the collection changed (i.e., elements were removed). Otherwise, returns false.
- **int size( )** Returns the number of elements held in the invoking collection.
- **Object[ ] toArray( )** Returns an array that contains all the elements stored in the invoking collection. The array elements are copies of the collection elements.
- **Object[] toArray(Object array[ ])** Returns an array containing only those collection elements whose type matches that of array.

Example

Following is an example to explain few methods from various class implementations of the above collection methods:

```
import java.util.*;
public class CollectionsDemo {
public static void main(String[] args) {
//ArrayList
List a1 = new ArrayList(); a1.add("Zara");
a1.add("Mahnaz"); a1.add("Ayan");
System.out.println(" ArrayList Elements");
System.out.print("\t" + a1);
//LinkedList
```

```java
List l1 = new LinkedList(); l1.add("Zara");
l1.add("Mahnaz"); l1.add("Ayan");
System.out.println();
System.out.println(" LinkedList Elements");
System.out.print("\t" + l1);
//HashSet
Set s1 = newHashSet(); s1.add("Zara");
s1.add("Mahnaz"); s1.add("Ayan");
System.out.println();
System.out.println(" Set Elements");
System.out.print("\t" + s1);
//HashMap
Map m1 = newHashMap(); m1.put("Zara","8");
m1.put("Mahnaz", "31"); m1.put("Ayan", "12");
m1.put("Daisy", "14");
System.out.println();
System.out.println(" Map Elements");
System.out.print("\t" + m1);
}
}
```

This will produce the following result:

ArrayList Elements

[Zara, Mahnaz, Ayan] LinkedList Elements

[Zara, Mahnaz, Ayan]

Set Elements

[Zara, Mahnaz, Ayan] Map Elements

{Mahnaz=31, Ayan=12, Daisy=14, Zara=8}

The List Interface

The List interface extends **Collection** and declares the behavior of a collection that stores a sequence of elements.

- Elements can be inserted or accessed by their position in the list, using a zero- based index.
- A list may contain duplicate elements.
- In addition to the methods defined by **Collection**, List defines some of its own, which are summarized in the following table.
- Several of the list methods will throw an UnsupportedO perationException if the collection cannot be modified, and a ClassCastException is generated when one object is incompatible with another.

Methods with Description

- **void add(int index, Object obj)** Inserts obj into the invoking list at the index passed in the index. Any preexisting elements at or beyond the point of insertion are shifted up. Thus, no elements are overwritten.
- **boolean addAll(int index, Collection c)** Inserts all elements of **c** into the invoking list at the index passed in the index. Any preexisting elements at or beyond the point of insertion are shifted up. Thus, no elements are overwritten. Returns true if the invoking list changes and returns false otherwise.
- **Object get(int index)** Returns the object stored at the specified index within the invoking collection.
- **int indexOf(Objectobj)** Returns the index of the first instance of obj in the invoking list. If obj is not an element of the list, .1 is returned.

- **int lastIndexOf(Object obj)** Returns the index of the last instance of obj in the invoking list. If obj is not an element of the list, .1 is returned.
- **ListIterator listIterator( )** Returns an iterator to the start of the invoking list.
- **ListIterator listIterator(int index)** Returns an iterator to the invoking list that begins at the specified index.
- **Object remove(int index)** Removes the element at position index from the invoking list and returns the deleted element. The resulting list is compacted. That is, the indexes of subsequent elements are decremented by one.
- **Object set(int index, Objectobj)** Assigns obj to the location specified by index within the invoking list.
- **List subList(int start, int end)** Returns a list that includes elements from start to end.1 in the invoking list. Elements in the returned list are also referenced by the invoking object.

Example

The above interface has been implemented in various classes like ArrayList or LinkedList, etc. Following is the example to explain few methods from various class implementation of the above collection methods:

```java
import java.util.*;
public class CollectionsDemo {
public static void main(String[] args) { List a1
= new ArrayList(); a1.add("Zara");
a1.add("Mahnaz");
```

```java
a1.add("Ayan");
System.out.println(" ArrayList Elements");
System.out.print("\t" + a1);
List l1 = new LinkedList(); l1.add("Zara");
l1.add("Mahnaz"); l1.add("Ayan");
System.out.println();
System.out.println(" LinkedList Elements");
System.out.print("\t" + l1);
}
}
```

This will produce the following result:

ArrayList Elements

   [Zara, Mahnaz, Ayan] LinkedList Elements

   [Zara, Mahnaz, Ayan]

The Set Interface

A Set is a Collection that cannot contain duplicate elements. It models the mathematical set abstraction.

The Set interface contains only methods inherited from Collection and adds the restriction that duplicate elements are prohibited.

Set also adds a stronger contract on the behavior of the equals and hashCode operations, allowing Set instances to be compared meaningfully even if their implementation types differ.

The methods declared by Set are summarized in the following table:

Methods with Description

- **add( )** Adds an object to the collection.
- **clear( )** Removes all objects from the collection.
- **contains( )** Returns true if a specified object is an element within the collection.
- **isEmpty( )** Returns true if the collection has no elements.
- **iterator( )** Returns an Iterator object for the collection, which may be used to retrieve an object.
- **remove( )** Removes a specified object from the collection.
- **size( )** Returns the number of elements in the collection.

Example

Set has its implementation in various classes like HashSet, TreeSet, LinkedHashSet. Following is an example to explain Set functionality:

```java
import java.util.*;
public class SetDemo {
public static void main(String args[]) { int
count[] = {34, 22,10,60,30,22}; Set<Integer> set
= newHashSet<Integer>(); try{
for(int i = 0; i<5; i++){
set.add(count[i]);
} System.out.println(set);
TreeSet sortedSet = new TreeSet<Integer>(set);
```

```
System.out.println("The sorted list is:");
System.out.println(sortedSet);
System.out.println("The First element of the set
is: "+ (Integer)sortedSet.first());
System.out.println("The last element of the set
is: "+
(Integer)sortedSet.last());
}
catch(Exception e){}
}
}
```

This will produce the following result:

[amrood]$ java SetDemo [34,30, 60, 10, 22]

   The sorted list is: [10,22, 30, 34, 60]

   The First element of the set is: 10

   The last element of the set is: 60

The SortedSet Interface

The SortedSet interface extends Set and declares the behavior of a set sorted in an ascending order. In addition to those methods defined by Set, the SortedSet interface declares the methods summarized in the following table:

Several methods throw a NoSuchElementException when no items are contained in the invoking set. A ClassCastException is thrown when an object is incompatible with the elements in a set.

A NullPointerException is thrown if an attempt is made to

use a null object and null is not allowed in the set.

Methods with Description

- **Comparator comparator()** Returns the invoking sorted set's comparator. If the natural ordering is used for this set, null is returned.
- **Object first( )** Returns the first element in the invoking sorted set.
- **SortedSet headSet(Object end)** Returns a SortedSet containing those elements less than end that are contained in the invoking sorted set. Elements in the returned sorted set are also referenced by the invoking sorted set.
- **Object last()** Returns the last element in the invoking sorted set.
- **SortedSet subSet(Object start, Object end)** Returns a SortedSet that includes those elements between start and end.1. Elements in the returned collection are also referenced by the invoking object.
- **SortedSet tailSet(Object start)** Returns a SortedSet that contains those elements greater than or equal to start that are contained in the sorted set. Elements in the returned set are also referenced by the invoking object.

Example

SortedSet have its implementation in various classes like TreeSet. Following is an example of a TreeSet class:

```java
import java.util.*;
public class SortedSetTest {
public static void main(String[] args) {
// Create the sorted set
SortedSet set = new TreeSet();
// Add elements to the set set.add("b");
set.add("c");
set.add("a");
// Iterating over the elements in the set
Iterator it = set.iterator();
while (it.hasNext()) {
// Get element
Object element = it.next();
System.out.println(element.toString());
}
}
}
```

This will produce the following result:

a b c

The Map Interface

The Map interface maps unique keys to values. A key is an object that you use to retrieve a value at a later date.

- Given a key and a value, you can store the value in a Map object. After the value is stored, you can retrieve it by using its key.
- Several methods throw a NoSuchElementException when no items exist in the invoking map.

- A ClassCastException is thrown when an object is incompatible with the elements in a map.
- A NullPointerException is thrown if an attempt is made to use a null object and null is not allowed in the map.
- An UnsupportedOperationException is thrown when an attempt is made to change an unmodifiable map.

Methods with Description

- **void clear( )** Removes all key/value pairs from the invoking map.
- **boolean containsKey(Objectk)** Returns true if the invoking map contains **k** as a key. Otherwise, returns false.
- **boolean containsValue(Object v)** Returns true if the map contains **v** as a value. Otherwise, returns false.
- **Set entrySet( )** Returns a Set that contains the entries in the map. The set contains objects of type Map.Entry. This method provides a set-view of the invoking map.
- **boolean equals(Object obj)** Returns true if obj is a Map and contains the same entries. Otherwise, returns false.
- **Object get(Object k)** Returns the value associated with the key **k**.
- **int hashCode( )** Returns the hash code for the invoking map.
- **boolean isEmpty( )** Returns true if the invoking map is empty. Otherwise, returns false.
- **Set keySet( )** Returns a Set that contains the keys in the invoking map. This method provides a set-view of the keys in the invoking map.
- **Object put(Object k, Object v)** Puts an entry in the in-

voking map, overwriting any previous value associated with the key. The key and value are **k** and **v**, respectively. Returns null if the key did not already exist. Otherwise, the previous value linked to the key is returned.

- **void putAll(Map m)** Puts all the entries from m into this map.
- **Objectremove(Object k)** Removes the entry whose key equals **k**.
- **int size( )** Returns the number of key/value pairs in the map.
- **Collection values( )** Returns a collection containing the values in the map. This method provides a collection-view of the values in the map.

Example

Map has its implementation in various classes like HashMap. Following is an example to explain map functionality:

```java
import java.util.*;
public class CollectionsDemo {
public static void main(String[] args) { Map m1 =
new HashMap();
m1.put("Zara", "8"); m1.put("Mahnaz", "31");
m1.put("Ayan","12");
m1.put("Daisy", "14");
System.out.println();
System.out.println("Map Elements");
System.out.print("\t" + m1);
}
}
```

This will produce the following result:

ap Elements

{Mahnaz=31, Ayan=12, Daisy=14, Zara=8}

The Map.Entry Interface

The Map.Entry interface enables you to work with a map entry.

The **entrySet( )** method declared by the Map interface returns a Set containing the map entries. Each of these set elements is a Map.Entry object.

Following table summarizes the methods declared by this interface:

Methods with Description

- **boolean equals(Object obj)** Returns true if obj is a Map.Entry whose key and value are equal to that of the invoking object.
- **Object getKey( )** Returns the key for this map entry.
- **ObjectgetValue( )** Returns the value for this map entry.
- **int hashCode( )** Returns the hash code for this map entry.
- **Object setValue(Object v)** Sets the value for this map entry to **v**.A ClassCastException is thrown if **v** is not the correct type for the map. A NullPointerException is thrown if **v** is null and the map does not permit null keys. An UnsupportedOperationException is thrown if

the map cannot be changed.

Example

Following is an example showing how **Map.Entry** can be used:

```java
import java.util.*;
public class HashMapDemo {
public static void main(String args[]) {
// Create a hash map
HashMap hm = new HashMap();
// Put elements to the map hm.put("Zara",new
Double(3434.34)); hm.put("Mahnaz", new
Double(123.22)); hm.put("Ayan", new
Double(1378.00)); hm.put("Daisy", new
Double(99.22)); hm.put("Qadir", new
Double(-19.08));
// Get a set of the entries
Set set = hm.entrySet();
// Get an iterator
Iterator i = set.iterator();
// Display elements while(i.hasNext()) {
Map.Entry me = (Map.Entry)i.next();
System.out.print(me.getKey() + ": ");
System.out.println(me.getValue());}
System.out.println();
// Deposit 1000 into Zara's account
double balance =
((Double)hm.get("Zara")).doubleValue();
hm.put("Zara", new Double(balance + 1000));
System.out.println("Zara's new balance: "+
hm.get("Zara"));
}
}
```

This will produce the following result:

```
Daisy 99.22
Qadir: -19.08
Zara: 3434.34
Ayan: 1378.0 ahnaz: 123.22
Zara's new balance: 4434.34
```

The SortedMap Interface

The SortedMap interface extends Map. It ensures that the entries are maintained in an ascending key order.

Several methods throw a NoSuchElementException when no items are in the invoking map. A ClassCastException is thrown when an object is incompatible with the elements in a map. A NullPointerException is thrown if an attempt is made to use a null object when null is not allowed in the map.

The methods declared by SortedMap are summarized in the following table:

Methods with Description

- **Comparator comparator()** Returns the invoking sorted map's comparator. If the natural ordering is used for the invoking map, null is returned.
- **ObjectfirstKey( )** Returns the first key in the invoking map.
- **SortedMap headMap(Object end)** Returns a sorted map for those map entries with keys that are less than end.

- **ObjectlastKey( )** Returns the last key in the invoking map.
- **SortedMap subMap(Object start, Object end)** Returns a map containing those entries with keys that are greater than or equal to start and less than end.
- **SortedMap tailMap(Object start)** Returns a map containing those entries with keys that are greater than or equal to start.

Example

SortedMap has its implementation in various classes like TreeMap. Following is the example to explain SortedMap functionlaity:

```java
import java.util.*;
public class TreeMapDemo {
public static void main(String args[]) {
// Create a hash map
TreeMap tm = new TreeMap();
// Put elements to the map tm.put("Zara",new
Double(3434.34)); tm.put("Mahnaz", new
Double(123.22)); tm.put("Ayan", new
Double(1378.00)); tm.put("Daisy", new
Double(99.22)); tm.put("Qadir", new
Double(-19.08));
// Get a set of the entries
Set set = tm.entrySet();
// Get an iterator
Iterator i = set.iterator();
// Display elements while(i.hasNext()) {
Map.Entry me = (Map.Entry)i.next();
System.out.print(me.getKey() + ": ");
System.out.println(me.getValue());
```

```
} System.out.println();
// Deposit 1000 into Zara's account
double balance =
((Double)tm.get("Zara")).doubleValue();
tm.put("Zara", new Double(balance + 1000));
System.out.println("Zara's new balance: " +
tm.get("Zara"));
}
}
```

This will produce the following result:

Ayan: 1378.0

Daisy 99.22 ahnaz: 123.22

Qadir: -19.08

Zara: 3434.34

Zara.s current balance: 4434.34

The Enumeration Interface

The Enumeration interface defines the methods by which you can enumerate (obtain one at a time) the elements in a collection of objects.

This legacy interface has been superseded by Iterator. Although not deprecated, Enumeration is considered obsolete for new code. However, it is used by several methods defined by the legacy classes such as Vector and Properties, is used by several other API classes, and is currently in widespread use in application code.

The methods declared by Enumeration are summarized in

the following table:

Methods with Description

- **boolean hasMoreElements( )** When implemented, it must return true while there are still more elements to extract, and false when all the elements have been enumerated.
- **ObjectnextElement( )** This returns the next object in the enumeration as a generic Object reference.

Example

Following is an example showing usage of Enumeration.

```java
import java.util.Vector;
import java.util.Enumeration;
public class EnumerationTester{
public static void main(String args[]) {
Enumeration days;
Vector dayNames = newVector();
dayNames.add("Sunday");
dayNames.add("Monday");
dayNames.add("Tuesday");
dayNames.add("Wednesday");
dayNames.add("Thursday");
dayNames.add("Friday");
dayNames.add("Saturday");
days = dayNames.elements();
while (days.hasMoreElements()){
System.out.println(days.nextElement());
}
}
}
```

This will produce the following result:

Sunday

Monday

Tuesday

Wednesday

Thursday

Friday

Saturday

The Collection Classes

Java provides a set of standard collection classes that implement Collection interfaces. Some of the classes provide full implementations that can be used as-is and others are abstract class, providing skeletal implementations that are used as starting points for creating concrete collections.

The standard collection classes are summarized in the following table:

Classes with Description

- **AbstractCollection** Implements most of the Collection interface.
- **AbstractList** Extends AbstractCollection and implements most of the List interface.
- **AbstractSequentialList** Extends AbstractList for use by a collection that uses sequential rather than random access of its elements.
- **LinkedList** Implements a linked list by extending AbstractSequentialList.

- **ArrayList** Implements a dynamic array by extending AbstractList.
- **AbstractSet** Extends AbstractCollection and implements most of the Set interface.
- **HashSet** Extends AbstractSet for use with a hash table.
- **LinkedHashSet** Extends HashSet to allow insertion-order iterations.
- **TreeSet** Implements a set stored in a tree.Extends AbstractSet.
- **AbstractMap** Implements most of the Map interface.
- **HashMap** Extends AbstractMap to use a hash table.
- **TreeMap** Extends AbstractMap to use a tree.
- **WeakHashMap** Extends AbstractMap to use a hash table with weak keys.
- **LinkedHashMap** Extends HashMap to allow insertion-order iterations.
- **IdentityHashMap** Extends AbstractMap and uses reference equality when comparing documents.

The *AbstractCollection, AbstractSet, AbstractList, AbstractSeq uentialList* and *AbstractMap* classes provide skeletal implementations of the core collection interfaces, to minimize the effort required to implement them.

The LinkedList Class

The LinkedList classextends AbstractSequentialList and implements the List interface. It provides a linked-list data structure.

Following are the constructors supported by the LinkedList

class.

Constructors and Description

- **LinkedList( )** This constructor builds an empty linked list.
- **LnkedList(Collection c)** This constructor builds a linked list that is initialized with the elements of the collection **c**.

Apart from the methods inherited from its parent classes, LinkedList defines the following methods:

Methods with Description

- **void add(int index, Object element)** Inserts the specified elementat the specified position index in this list. Throws IndexOutOfBoundsException if the specified index is out of range (index < 0|| index > size()).
- **boolean add(Object o)** Appends the specified element to the end of this list.
- **boolean addAll(Collection c)** Appends all of the elements in the specified collection to the end of this list, in the order that they are returned by the specified collection's iterator. Throws NullPointerException if the specified collection is null.
- **boolean addAll(int index, Collection c)** Inserts all of the elements inthe specified collection into this list, starting at the specified position. Throws NullPointerException if the specified collection is null.
- **void addFirst(Object o)** Inserts the given element at the

beginning of this list.

- **void addLast(Object o)** Appends the given element to the end of this list.
- **void clear()** Removes all of the elements from this list.
- **Objectclone()** Returns a shallow copy of this LinkedList.
- **boolean contains(Object o)** Returns true if this list contains the specified element. More formally, returns true if and only if this list contains at least one element **e** such that (o==null? e==null : o.equals(e)).
- **Objectget(int index)** Returns the element at the specified position in this list. Throws IndexOutOfBoundsExc eption if the specified index is out of range (index <0|| index >= size()).
- **Object getFirst()** Returns the first element in this list. Throws NoSuchElementException if this list is empty.
- **Object getLast()** Returns the last element in this list. Throws NoSuchElementException if this list is empty.
- **int indexOf(Objecto)** Returns the index in this list of the first occurrence of the specified element, or -1 if the list does not contain this element.
- **int lastIndexOf(Object o)** Returns the index in this list of the last occurrence of the specified element, or -1 if the list does not contain this element.
- **ListIterator listIterator(int index)** Returns a list-iterator of the elements in this list (in proper sequence), starting at the specified position in the list. Throws IndexOutOfBoundsException if the specified index is out of range (index < 0 ||index >= size()).
- **Object remove(int index)** Removes the element at the specified position in this list. Throws NoSuchElementE xception if this list is empty.

- **boolean remove(Object o)** Removes the first occurrence of the specified element in this list. Throws NoSuchElementException if this list is empty. Throws IndexOutOfBoundsException if the specified index is out of range (index < 0|| index >=size()).
- **Object removeFirst()** Removes and returns the first element from this list. Throws NoSuchElementExce ption if this list is empty.
- **Object removeLast()** Removes and returns the last element from this list. Throws NoSuchElementExce ption if this list is empty.
- **Object set(int index,Object element)** Replaces the element at the specified position in this list with the specified element. Throws IndexOutOfBoundsExcep tion if the specified index is out of range (index < 0 || index >= size()).
- **int size()** Returns the number of elements in this list.
- **Object[] toArray()** Returns an array containing all of the elements in this list in the correct order. Throws NullPointerException if the specified array is null.
- **Object[] toArray(Object[]a)** Returns an array containing all of the elements in this list in the correct order; the runtime type of the returned array is that of the specified array.

Example

The following program illustrates several of the methods supported by LinkedList:

```
import java.util.*;
public class LinkedListDemo {
public static void main(String args[]) {
// create a linked list
LinkedList ll = new LinkedList();
// add elements to the linked list ll.add("F");
ll.add("B");
ll.add("D"); ll.add("E"); ll.add("C");
ll.addLast("Z"); ll.addFirst("A"); ll.add(1,
"A2");
System.out.println("Original contents of ll: " +
ll);
// remove elements from the linked list
ll.remove("F");
ll.remove(2);
System.out.println("Contents of ll after
deletion: "
+ ll);
// remove first and last elements
ll.removeFirst();
ll.removeLast();
System.out.println("ll after deleting first and
last: "
+ ll);
// get and set a value
Object val = ll.get(2);
ll.set(2, (String) val + "Changed");
System.out.println("ll after change: " + ll);
}
}
```

This will produce the following result:

Original contents of ll: [A, A2, F, B, D, E, C, Z]

Contents of ll

after deletion: [A, A2, D, E, C, Z] ll

after deleting first and last: [A2, D, E, C]ll

after change: [A2, D, E Changed, C]

The ArrayList Class

The ArrayList class extends AbstractList and implements the List interface. ArrayList supports dynamic arrays that can grow as needed.

Standard Java arrays are of a fixed length. After arrays are created, they cannot grow or shrink, which means that you must know in advance how many elements an array will hold.

Array lists are created with an initial size. When this size is exceeded, the collection is automatically enlarged. When objects are removed, the array may be shrunk.

Following is the list of the constructors provided by the ArrayList class.

Constructors and Description

- **ArrayList( )** This constructor builds an empty array list.
- **ArrayList(Collection c)** This constructor builds an array list that is initialized with the elements of the collection c.
- **ArrayList(int capacity)** This constructor builds an array list that has the specified initial capacity. The capacity is the size of the underlying array that is used to store the elements. The capacity grows automatically as

elements are added to an array list.

Apart from the methods inherited from its parent classes, ArrayList defines the following methods:

Methods with Description

- **void add(int index, Objectelement)** Inserts the specified element at the specified position index in this list. Throws IndexOutOfBoundsException if the specified index is out of range (index < 0 || index > size()).
- **boolean add(Object o)** Appends the specified element to the end of this list.
- **boolean addAll(Collection c)** Appends all of the elements in the specified collection to the end of this list, in the order that they are returned by the specified collection's iterator. Throws NullPointerException, if the specified collection is null.
- **boolean addAll(int index, Collection c)** Inserts all of the elements in the specified collection into this list, starting at the specified position. Throws NullPointerException if the specified collection is null.
- **void clear()** Removes all of the elements from this list.
- **Objectclone()** Returns a shallow copy of this ArrayList.
- **boolean contains(Object o)** Returns true if this list contains the specified element. More formally, returns true if and only if this list contains at least one element e such that (o==null ? e==null : o.equals(e)).
- **void ensureCapacity(int minCapacity)** Increases the capacity of this ArrayList instance, if necessary, to ensure that it can hold at least the number of elements

specified by the minimum capacity argument.

- **Object get(int index)** Returns the element at the specified position in this list. Throws IndexOutOfBoundsException if the specified index is out of range (index<0 || index >=size()).
- **int indexOf(Objecto)** Returns the index in this list of the first occurrence of the specified element, or -1 if the List does not contain this element.
- **int lastIndexOf(Object o)** Returns the index in this list of the last occurrence of the specified element, or -1 if the list does not contain this element.
- **Object remove(int index)** Removes the element at the specified position in this list. Throws IndexOutOfBou ndsException if the index is out of range (index < 0 || index>= size()).
- **protected void removeRange(int fromIndex, int toIndex)** Removes from this List all of the elements whose index is between from Index, inclusive and to Index, exclusive.
- **Object set(int index,Object element)** Replaces the element at the specified position in this list with the specified element. Throws IndexOutOfBoundsException if the specified index is out of range (index < 0 || index >= size()).
- **int size()** Returns the number of elements in this list.
- **Object[] toArray()** Returns an array containing all of the elements in this list in the correct order. Throws NullPointerException if the specified array is null.
- **Object[] toArray(Object[]a)** Returns an array containing all of the elements in this list in the correct order; the runtime type of the returned array is that of the

specified array.

- **void trimToSize()** Trims the capacity of this ArrayList instance to be the list's current size.

Example

The following program illustrates several of the methods supported by ArrayList:

```java
import java.util.*;
public class ArrayListDemo {
public static void main(String args[]) {
// create an array list ArrayList al = new
ArrayList(); System.out.println("Initial size of
al: " + al.size());
// add elements to the array list al.add("C");
al.add("A"); al.add("E"); al.add("B");
al.add("D"); al.add("F"); al.add(1, "A2");
System.out.println("Size of al after additions: "
+ al.size());
// display the array list
System.out.println("Contents of al: " + al);
// Remove elements from the array list
al.remove("F");
al.remove(2);
System.out.println("Size of al after deletions: "
+ al.size()); System.out.println("Contents of al:
" + al);
}
}
```

This will produce the following result:

Initial size of al: 0

Size of al after additions: 7

Contents of al: [C, A2, A, E, B, D, F]

Size of al after deletions: 5

Contents of al: [C, A2, E, B, D]

The HashSet Class

HashSet extends AbstractSet and implements the Set interface. It creates a collection that uses a hash table for storage.

A hash table stores information by using a mechanism called **hashing**. In hashing, the informational content of a key is used to determine a unique value, called its hash code.

The hash code is then used as the index at which the data associated with the key is stored. The transformation of the key into its hash code is performed automatically.

Following is the list of constructors provided by theHashSet class.

Constructors and Description

- **HashSet( )** This constructor constructs a default HashSet.
- **HashSet(Collection c)** This constructor initializes the hash set by using the elements of the collection **c**.
- **HashSet(int capacity)** This constructor initializes the capacity of the hash set to the given integer value capacity. The capacity grows automatically as elements

are added to the HashSet.

- **HashSet(int capacity, float fillRatio)** This constructor initializes both the capacity and the fill ratio (also called load capacity) of the hash set from its arguments. Here the fill ratio must be between 0.0 and 1.0, and it determines how full the hash set can be before it is resized upward. Specifically, when the number of elements is greater than the capacity of the hash set multiplied by its fill ratio, the hash set is expanded.

Apart from the methods inherited from its parent classes, HashSet defines following methods:

Methods with Description

- **boolean add(Object o)** Adds the specified element to this set if it is not already present.
- **void clear()** Removes all of the elements from this set.
- **Object clone()** Returns a shallow copy of this HashSet instance: the elements themselves are not cloned.
- **boolean contains(Object o)** Returns true if this set contains the specified element.
- **boolean isEmpty()** Returns true if this set contains no elements.
- **Iterator iterator()** Returns an iterator over the elements in this set.
- **boolean remove(Object o)** Removes the specified element from this set if it is present.
- **int size()** Returns the number of elements in this set (its cardinality).

Example

The following program illustrates several of the methods supported by HashSet:

```java
import java.util.*;
public class HashSetDemo {
public static void main(String args[]) {
// create a hash set
HashSet hs = new HashSet();
// add elements to the hash set hs.add("B");
hs.add("A"); hs.add("D"); hs.add("E");
hs.add("C"); hs.add("F");
System.out.println(hs);
}
}
```

This will produce the following result:

[A, B, C,D, E, F]

The LinkedHashSet Class

This class extends HashSet, but adds no members of its own.

LinkedHashSet maintains a linked list of the entries in the set, in the order in which they were inserted. This allows insertion-order iteration over the set.

That is, when cycling through a LinkedHashSet using an iterator, the elements will be returned in the order in which they were inserted.

The hash code is then used as the index at which the data associated with the key is stored. The transformation of the key into its hash code is performed automatically.

Following is the list of constructors supported by the LinkedHashSet.

Constructors and Description

- **HashSet( )** This constructor constructs a default HashSet.
- **HashSet(Collection c)** This constructor initializes the hash set by using the elements of the collection **c**.
- **LinkedHashSet(int capacity)** This constructor initializes the capacity of the linkedhashset to the given integer value capacity. The capacity grows automatically as elements are added to the HashSet.
- **LinkedHashSet(int capacity, float fillRatio)** This constructor initializes both the capacity and the fill ratio (also called load capacity) of the hash set from its arguments.

Example

The following program illustrates several of the methods supported by LinkedHashSet:

```
import java.util.*;
public class HashSetDemo {
public static void main(String args[]) {
// create a hash set
```

```
LinkedHashSet hs = new LinkedHashSet();
// add elements to the hash set hs.add("B");
hs.add("A"); hs.add("D"); hs.add("E");
hs.add("C"); hs.add("F"); System.out.println(hs);
}
}
```

This will produce the following result:

[B, A, D, E, C

The TreeSet Class

TreeSet provides an implementation of the Set interface that uses a tree for storage. Objects are stored in a sorted and ascending order.

Access and retrieval times are quite fast, which makes TreeSet an excellent choice when storing large amounts of sorted information that must be found quickly.

Following is the list of the constructors supported by the TreeSet class.

Constructors with Description

- **TreeSet( )** This constructor constructs an empty tree set that will be sorted in an ascending order according to the natural order of its elements.
- **TreeSet(Collection c)** This constructor builds a tree set

that contains the elements of the collection **c**.

- **TreeSet(Comparator comp)** This constructor constructs an empty tree set that will be sorted according to the given comparator.
- **TreeSet(SortedSet ss)**
- This constructor builds a TreeSet that contains the elements of the given SortedSet.

Apart from the methods inherited from its parent classes, TreeSet defines the following methods:

Methods with Description

- **void add(Objecto)** Adds the specified element to this set if it is not already present.
- **boolean addAll(Collection c)** Adds all of the elements in the specified collection to this set.
- **void clear()** Removes all of the elements from this set.
- **Objectclone()** Returns a shallow copy of this TreeSet instance.
- **Comparator comparator()** Returns the comparator used to order this sorted set, or null if this tree set uses its elements natural ordering.
- **boolean contains(Object o)** Returns true if this set contains the specified element.
- **Object first()** Returns the first (lowest) element currently in this sorted set.
- **SortedSet headSet(Object toElement)** Returns a view of the portion of this set whose elements are strictly less than to Element.
- **boolean isEmpty()** Returns true if this set contains no

elements.

- **Iterator iterator()** Returns an iterator over the elements in this set.
- **Objectlast()** Returns the last (highest)element currently in this sorted set.
- **boolean remove(Object o)** Removes the specified element from this set if it is present.
- **int size()** Returns the number of elements in this set (its cardinality).
- **SortedSet subSet(Object fromElement, Object toElement)** Returns a view of the portion of this set whose elements range from fromElement, inclusive, to toElement, exclusive.
- **SortedSet tailSet(Object fromElement)** Returns a view of the portion of this set whose elements are greater than or equal to fromElement.

Example

The following program illustrates several of the methods supported by this collection:

```
import java.util.*;
public class TreeSetDemo {
public static void main(String args[]) {
// Create a tree set
TreeSet ts = new TreeSet();
// Add elements to the tree set ts.add("C");
ts.add("A"); ts.add("B"); ts.add("E");
ts.add("F"); ts.add("D");
System.out.println(ts);
}
```

```
}
```

This will produce the following result:

[A, B, C, D, E, F]

The HashMap Class

The HashMap class uses a hashtable to implement the Map interface. This allows the execution time of basic operations, such as get( ) and put( ), to remain constant even for large sets.

Following is the list of constructors supported by the HashMap class.

Constructors and Description

- **HashMap( )** This constructor constructs a default HashMap.
- **HashMap(Map m)** This constructor initializes the hash map by using the elements of the given Map object **m**.
- **HashMap(int capacity)**This constructor initializes the capacity of the hash map to the given integer value, capacity.
- **HashMap(int capacity, float fillRatio)** This constructor initializes both the capacity and fill ratio of the hash map by using its arguments.

Apart from the methods inherited from its parent classes,

HashMap defines the following methods:

Methods with Description

- **void clear()** Removes all mappings from this map.
- **Object clone()** Returns a shallow copy of this HashMap instance: the keys and values themselves are not cloned.
- **boolean containsKey(Objectkey)** Returns true if this map contains a mapping for the specified key.
- **boolean containsValue(Object value)** Returns true if this map maps one or more keys to the specified value.
- **Set entrySet()** Returns a collection view of the mappings contained in this map.
- **Object get(Object key)** Returns the value to which the specified key is mapped in this identity hash map, or null if the map contains no mapping for this key.
- **boolean isEmpty()** Returns true if this map contains no key-value mappings.
- **Set keySet()** Returns a set view of the keys contained in this map.
- **Objectput(Object key, Object value)** Associates the specified value with the specified key in this map.
- **putAll(Map m)** Copies all of the mappings from the specified map to this map. These mappings will replace any mappings that this map had for any of the keys currently in the specified map.
- **Objectremove(Object key)** Removes the mapping for this key from this map if present.
- **int size()** Returns the number of key-value mappings in this map.
- **Collection values()** Returns a collection view of the

values contained in this map.

Example

The following program illustrates several of the methods supported by this collection:

```java
import java.util.*;
public class HashMapDemo {
public static void main(String args[]) {
// Create a hash map
HashMap hm = new HashMap();
// Put elements to the map hm.put("Zara",new
Double(3434.34));
hm.put("Mahnaz", new Double(123.22));
hm.put("Ayan", new Double(1378.00));
hm.put("Daisy", new Double(99.22));
hm.put("Qadir", new Double(-19.08));
// Get a set of the entries
Set set = hm.entrySet();
// Get an iterator
Iterator i = set.iterator();
// Display elements while(i.hasNext()) {
Map.Entry me = (Map.Entry)i.next();
System.out.print(me.getKey() + ": ");
System.out.println(me.getValue());
} System.out.println();
// Deposit 1000 into Zara's account
double balance =
((Double)hm.get("Zara")).doubleValue();
hm.put("Zara", new Double(balance + 1000));
System.out.println("Zara's new balance: "+
hm.get("Zara"));
}
}
```

This will produce the following result:

Zara: 3434.34 ahnaz: 123.22

    Daisy: 99.22

    Ayan: 1378.0

    Qadir: -19.08

    Zara's new balance: 4434.34

The TreeMap Class

The TreeMap class implements the Map interface by using a tree. A TreeMap provides an efficient means of storing key/value pairs in sorted order, and allows rapid retrieval.

You should note that, unlike a hash map, a tree map guarantees that its elements will be sorted in an ascending key order.

Following is the list of the constructors supported by the TreeMap class.

Constructors and Description

- **TreeMap( )** This constructor constructs an empty tree map that will be sorted using the natural order of its keys.
- **TreeMap(Comparatorcomp)** This constructor constructs an empty tree-based map that will be sorted using the Comparator comp.
- **TreeMap(Map m)** This constructor initializes a tree map with the entries from **m**,which will be sorted using

the natural order of the keys.

- **TreeMap(SortedMap sm)** This constructor initializes a tree map with the entries from the SortedMap **sm**, which will be sorted in the same order as **sm**.

Apart from the methods inherited from its parent classes, TreeMap defines the following methods:

Methods with Description

- **void clear()** Removes all mappings from this TreeMap.
- **Object clone()** Returns a shallow copy of this TreeMap instance.
- **Comparator comparator()** Returns the comparator used to order this map, or null if this map uses its keys' natural order.
- **boolean containsKey(Objectkey)** Returns true if this map contains a mapping for the specified key.
- **boolean containsValue(Object value)** Returns true if this map maps one or more keys to the specified value.
- **Set entrySet()** Returns a set view of the mappings contained in this map.
- **Object firstKey()** Returns the first (lowest) key currently in this sorted map.
- **Object get(Object key)** Returns the value to which this map maps the specified key.
- **SortedMap headMap(Object toKey)** Returns a view of the portion of this map whose keys are strictly less than toKey.
- **Set keySet()** Returns a Set view of the keys contained in this map.

- **Object lastKey()** Returns the last (highest)key currently in this sorted map.
- **Objectput(Object key, Object value)**
- Associates the specified value with the specified key in this map.
- **void putAll(Map map)** Copies all of the mappings from the specified map to this map.
- **Objectremove(Object key)** Removes the mapping for this key from this TreeMap if present.
- **int size()** Returns the number of key-value mappings in this map.
- **SortedMap subMap(Object fromKey, ObjecttoKey)** Returns a view of the portion of this map whose keys range from fromKey, inclusive, to toKey, exclusive.
- **SortedMap tailMap(Object fromKey)** Returns a view of the portion of this map whose keys are greater than or equal to fromKey.
- **Collection values()** Returns a collection view of the values contained in this map.

Example

The following program illustrates several of the methods supported by this collection:

```java
import java.util.*;
public class TreeMapDemo {
public static void main(String args[]) {
// Create a hash map
TreeMap tm = new TreeMap();
// Put elements to the map tm.put("Zara",new
```

```
Double(3434.34)); tm.put("Mahnaz", new
Double(123.22)); tm.put("Ayan", new
Double(1378.00)); tm.put("Daisy", new
Double(99.22)); tm.put("Qadir", new
Double(-19.08));
// Get a set of the entries
Set set = tm.entrySet();
// Get an iterator
Iterator i = set.iterator();
// Display elements
while(i.hasNext()) {
Map.Entry me = (Map.Entry)i.next();
System.out.print(me.getKey() + ": ");
System.out.println(me.getValue());
} System.out.println();
// Deposit 1000 into Zara's account
double balance =
((Double)tm.get("Zara")).doubleValue();
tm.put("Zara", new Double(balance + 1000));
System.out.println("Zara's new balance: "+
tm.get("Zara"));
}
}
```

This will produce the following result:

Ayan: 1378.0

Daisy 99.22 ahnaz: 123.22

Qadir: -19.08

Zara: 3434.34

Zara's current balance: 4434.34

The WeakHashMapClass

WeakHashMap is an implementation of the Map interface that stores only weak references to its keys. Storing only weak references allows a key-value pair to be garbage-collected when its key is no longer referenced outside of the WeakHashMap.

This class provides the easiest way to harness the power of weak references. It is useful for implementing "registry-like" data structures, where the utility of an entry vanishes when its key is no longer reachable by any thread.

The WeakHashMap functions identically to the HashMap with one very important exception: if the Java memory manager no longer has a strong reference to the object specified as a key, then the entry in the map will be removed.

Weak Reference: If the only references to an object are weak references, the garbage collector can reclaim the object's memory at any time.it doesn't have to wait until the system runs out of memory. Usually, it will be freed the next time the garbage collector runs.

Following is the list of constructors supported by the WeakHashMap class.

Constructors and Description

- **WeakHashMap()** This constructor constructs a new, empty WeakHashMap with the default initial capacity (16) and the default load factor (0.75).
- **WeakHashMap(int initialCapacity)** This constructor

constructs a new, empty WeakHashMap with the given initial capacity and the default load factor, which is 0.75.

- **WeakHashMap(int initialCapacity, float loadFactor)** This constructor constructs a new, empty WeakHashMap with the given initial capacity and the given load factor.
- **WeakHashMap(Map t)** This constructor constructs a new WeakHashMap with the same mappings as the specified Map.

Apart from the methods inherited from its parent classes, TreeMap defines the following methods:

Methods with Description

- **void clear()** Removes all mappings from this map.
- **boolean containsKey(Objectkey)** Returns true if this map contains a mapping for the specified key.
- **boolean containsValue(Object value)** Returns true if this map maps one or more keys to the specified value.
- **Set entrySet()**Returns a collection view of the mappings contained in this map.
- **Object get(Object key)** Returns the value to which the specified key is mapped in this weak hash map, or null if the map contains no mapping for this key.
- **boolean isEmpty()** Returns true if this map contains no key-value mappings.
- **Set keySet()** Returns a set view of the keys contained in this map.
- **Objectput(Object key, Object value)** Associates the specified value with the specified key in this map.

- **void putAll(Map m)** Copies all of the mappings from the specified map to this map. These mappings will replace any mappings that this map had for any of the keys currently in the specified map.
- **Objectremove(Object key)** Removes the mapping for this key from this map if present.
- **int size()** Returns the number of key-value mappings in this map.
- **Collection values()** Returns a collection view of the values contained in this map.

Example

The following program illustrates several of the methods supported by this collection:

```java
import java.util.*;
public class WeakHashMap_Demo {
private static Map map;
public static void main (String args[]) {
map = new WeakHashMap();
map.put(new String("Maine"), "Augusta"); Runnable
runner = new Runnable() {
public void run() {
while (map.containsKey("Maine")) {
try { Thread.sleep(500);
} catch (InterruptedException ignored) {
}
System.out.println("Thread waiting"); System.gc();
}
}
};
Thread t = new Thread(runner);
```

```
t.start();
System.out.println("Main waiting");
try {
t.join();
} catch (InterruptedException ignored) {
}
}
}
```

This will produce the following result:

```
ain waiting
Thread waiting
```

If you do not include the call to System.gc(), the system may never run the garbage collector as not much memory is used by the program. For a more active program, the call would be unnecessary.

The LinkedHashMapClass

This class extends HashMap and maintains a linked list of the entries in the map, in the order in which they were inserted. This allows insertion-order iteration over the map. That is,when iterating a LinkedHashMap, the elements will be returned in the order in which they were inserted.

You can also create a LinkedHashMap that returns its elements in the order in which they were last accessed.

Following is the list of constructors supported by the LinkedHashMap class.

Constructors and Description

- **LinkedHashMap( )** This constructor constructs a default LinkedHashMap.
- **LinkedHashMap(Map m)** This constructor initializes the LinkedHashMap with the elements from the given Map class **m**.
- **LinkedHashMap(int capacity)** This constructor initializes a LinkedHashMap with the given capacity.
- **LinkedHashMap(int capacity, float fillRatio)** This constructor initializes both the capacity and the fill ratio. The meaning of capacity and fill ratio are the same as for HashMap.
- **LinkedHashMap(int capacity, float fillRatio, boolean Order)** This constructor allows you to specify whether the elements will be stored in the linked list by insertion order, or by order of last access. If Order is true, then access order is used. If Order is false, then insertion order is used.

Apart from the methods inherited from its parent classes, LinkedHashMap defines the following methods:

Methods with Description

- **void clear( )** Removes all mappings from this map.
- **boolean containsKey(Objectkey)** Returns true if this map maps one or more keys to the specified value.
- **Object get(Object key)** Returns the value to which this map maps the specified key.
- **protected boolean removeEldestEntry(Map.Entry el-**

dest) Returns true if this map should remove its eldest entry.

Example

The following program illustrates several of the methods supported by this collection:

```java
import java.util.*;
public class LinkedHashMapDemo{
public static void main(String args[]) {
// Create a hash map
LinkedHashMap lhm = new LinkedHashMap();
// Put elements to the map lhm.put("Zara", new
Double(3434.34));
lhm.put("Mahnaz", new Double(123.22));
lhm.put("Ayan", new Double(1378.00));
lhm.put("Daisy", new Double(99.22));
lhm.put("Qadir", new Double(-19.08));
// Get a set of the entries
Set set = lhm.entrySet();
// Get an iterator
Iterator i = set.iterator();
// Display elements while(i.hasNext()) {
Map.Entry me = (Map.Entry)i.next();
System.out.print(me.getKey() + ": ");
System.out.println(me.getValue());
} System.out.println();
// Deposit 1000 into Zara's account
double balance =
((Double)lhm.get("Zara")).doubleValue();
lhm.put("Zara", new Double(balance + 1000));
System.out.println("Zara's new balance: " +
lhm.get("Zara"));
}
}
```

This will produce the following result:

```
Zara: 3434.34 ahnaz: 123.22

Ayan: 1378.0

Daisy: 99.22

Qadir: -19.08

Zara's new balance: 4434.34
```

The IdentityHashMap Class

This class implements AbstractMap. It is similar to HashMap except that it uses reference equality when comparing the elements.

This class is not a general-purpose Map implementation. While this class implements the Map interface, it intentionally violates Map's general contract, which mandates the use of the equals method when comparing objects.

This class is designed for use only in rare cases wherein reference-equality semantics are required. This class provides constant-time performance for the basic operations (get and put), assuming the system identity hash function (System.identityHashCode(Object)) disperses elements properly among the buckets.

This class has one tuning parameter (which affects performance but not semantics): expected maximum size. This parameter is the maximum number of key-value mappings that the map is expected to hold.

Following is the list of the constructors supported by the

IdentityHashMap.

Constructors and Description

- **IdentityHashMap()** This constructor constructs a new, empty identity hash map with a default expected maximum size (21).
- **IdentityHashMap(int expectedMaxSize)** This constructor constructs a new, empty IdentityHashMap with the specified expected maximum size.
- **IdentityHashMap(Map m)** This constructor constructs a new identity hash map containing the keys-value mappings in the specified map.

Apart from the methods inherited from its parent classes, IdentityHashMap defines the following methods:

Methods with Description

- **void clear()** Removes all mappings from this map.
- **Objectclone()** Returns a shallow copy of this identity hash map: the keys and values themselves are not cloned.
- **boolean containsKey(Objectkey)** Tests whether the specified object reference is a key in this identity hash map.
- **boolean containsValue(Object value)** Tests whether the specified object reference is a value in this identity hash map.
- **Set entrySet()** Returns a set view of the mappings contained in this map.

- **boolean equals(Object o)** Compares the specified object with this map for equality.
- **Objectget(Object key)** Returns the value to which the specified key is mapped in this identity hash map, or null if the map contains no mapping for this key.
- **int hashCode()** Returns the hash code value for this map.
- **boolean isEmpty()** Returns true if this identity hash map contains no key-value mappings.
- **Set keySet()** Returns an identity-based set view of the keys contained in this map.
- **Object put(Object key, Object value)** Associates the specified value with the specified key in this identity hash map.
- **void putAll(Map t)** Copies all of the mappings from the specified map to this map. These mappings will replace any mappings that this map had for any of the keys currently in the specified map.
- **Object remove(Object key)** Removes the mapping for this key from this map if present.
- **int size()** Returns the number of key value mappings in this identity hash map.
- **Collection values()** Returns a collection view of the values contained in this map.

Example

The following program illustrates several of the methods supported by this collection:

```java
import java.util.*;
public class IdentityHashMapDemo {
public static void main(String args[]) {
// Create a hash map
IdentityHashMap ihm = new IdentityHashMap();
// Put elements to the map ihm.put("Zara", new
Double(3434.34)); ihm.put("Mahnaz", new
Double(123.22)); ihm.put("Ayan", new
Double(1378.00)); ihm.put("Daisy", new
Double(99.22)); ihm.put("Qadir", new
Double(-19.08));
// Get a set of the entries
Set set = ihm.entrySet();
// Get an iterator
Iterator i = set.iterator();
// Display elements while(i.hasNext()) {
Map.Entry me = (Map.Entry)i.next();
System.out.print(me.getKey() + ": ");
System.out.println(me.getValue());
} System.out.println();
// Deposit 1000 into Zara's account
double balance =
((Double)ihm.get("Zara")).doubleValue();
ihm.put("Zara", new Double(balance + 1000));
System.out.println("Zara's new balance: " +
ihm.get("Zara"));
}
}
```

This will produce the following result:

Ayan: 1378.0

Zara: 3434.34

Qadir: -19.08 ahnaz: 123.22

Daisy: 99.22

Zara's new balance: 4434.34

The following legacy classes defined by java.util have been discussed in the previous chapter:

Classes with Description

- **Vector** This implements a dynamic array. It is similar to ArrayList, but with some differences.
- **Stack** Stack is a subclass of Vector that implements a standard last-in, first-out stack.
- **Dictionary** Dictionary is an abstract class that represents a key/value storage repository and operates much like Map.
- **Hashtable** Hashtable was part of the original java.util and is a concrete implementation of a Dictionary.
- **Properties** Properties is a subclass of Hashtable. It is used to maintain lists of values in which the key is a String and the value is also a String.
- **BitSet** A BitSet class creates a special type of array that holds bit values. This array can increase in size as needed.

The Vector Class

Vector implements a dynamic array. It is similar to ArrayList, but with two differences:

- Vector is synchronized.
- Vector contains many legacy methods that are not part of the collections framework.

Vector proves to be very useful if you don't know the size of the array in advance or you just need one that can change sizes over the lifetime of a program.

Following is the list of constructors provided by the vector class.

Constructor and Description

- **Vector( )** This constructor creates a default vector, which has an initial size of 10.
- **Vector(int size)** This constructor accepts an argument that equals the required size, and creates a vector whose initial capacity is specified by size.
- **Vector(int size, int incr)** This constructor creates a vector whose initial capacity is specified by size and whose increment is specified by incr. The increment specifies the number of elements to allocate each time that a vector is resized upward.
- **Vector(Collection c)** Creates a vector that contains the elements of collection **c**.

Apart from the methods inherited from its parent classes, Vector defines the following methods:

Methods with Description

- **void add(int index, Object element)** Inserts the specified element at the specified position in this Vector.
- **boolean add(Object o)** Appends the specified element to the end of this Vector.
- **boolean addAll(Collection c)** Appends all of the ele-

ments in the specified Collection to the end of this Vector, in the order that they are returned by the specified Collection's Iterator.

- **boolean addAll(int index, Collection c** Inserts all of the elements in the specified Collection into this Vector at the specified position.
- **void addElement(Object obj)** Adds the specified component to the end of this vector, increasing its size by one.
- **int capacity()** Returns the current capacity of this vector.
- **void clear()** Removes all of the elements from this Vector.
- **Object clone()** Returns a clone of this vector.
- **boolean contains(Object elem)** Tests if the specified object is a component in this vector.
- **boolean containsAll(Collection c)** Returns true if this Vector contains all of the elements in the specified Collection.
- **void copyInto(Object[] anArray)** Copies the components of this vector into the specified array.
- **ObjectelementAt(int index)** Returns the component at the specified index.
- **Enumeration elements()** Returns an enumeration of the components of this vector.
- **void ensureCapacity(int minCapacity)** Increases the capacity of this vector, if necessary, to ensure that it can hold at least the number of components specified by the minimum capacity argument.
- **boolean equals(Object o)** Compares the specified Object with this Vector for equality.

- **Object firstElement()** Returns the first component (the item at index 0) of this vector.
- **Object get(int index)** Returns the element at the specified position in this Vector.
- **int hashCode()** Returns the hash code value for this Vector.
- **int indexOf(Objectelem)** Searches for the first occurrence of the given argument, testing for equality using the equals method.
- **int indexOf(Objectelem, int index)** Searches for the first occurrence of the given argument, beginning the search at index, and testing for equality using the equals method.
- **void insertElementAt(Object obj, int index)** Inserts the specified object as a component in this vector at the specified index.
- **boolean isEmpty()** Tests if this vector has no components.
- **Object lastElement()** Returns the last component of the vector.
- **int lastIndexOf(Object elem)** Returns the index of the last occurrence of the specified object in this vector.
- **int lastIndexOf(Object elem, int index)** Searches backwards for the specified object, starting from the specified index, and returns an index to it.
- **Object remove(int index)** Removes the element at the specified position in this Vector.
- **boolean remove(Object o)** Removes the first occurrence of the specified element in this Vector does not contain the element, it is unchanged.
- **boolean removeAll(Collection c)** Removes from this

Vector all of its elements that are contained in the specified Collection.

- **void removeAllElements()** Removes all components from this vector and sets its size to zero.
- **boolean removeElement(Objectobj)** Removes the first (lowest-indexed) occurrence of the argument from this vector.
- **void removeElementAt(int index)** removeElementAt(int index)
- **protected void removeRange(int fromIndex, int toIndex)** Removes from this List all of the elements whose index is between fromIndex, inclusive and toIndex, exclusive.
- **boolean retainAll(Collectionc)** Retains only the elements in this Vector that are contained in the specified Collection.
- **Object set(int index, Objectelement)** Replaces the element at the specified position in this Vector with the specified element.
- **void setElementAt(Object obj, int index)** Sets the component at the specified index of this vector to be the specified object.
- **void setSize(int newSize)** Sets the size of this vector.
- **int size()** Returns the number of components in this vector.
- **List subList(int fromIndex, int toIndex)** Returns a view of the portion of this List between fromIndex, inclusive, and toIndex, exclusive.
- **Object[] toArray()** Returns an array containing all of the elements in this Vector in the correct order.
- **Object[] toArray(Object[]a)** Returns an array contain-

ing all of the elements in this Vector in the correct order; the runtime type of the returned array is that of the specified array.

- **String toString()** Returns a string representation of this Vector, containing the String representation of each element.

- **void trimToSize()** Trims the capacity of this vector to be the vector's current size.

Example

The following program illustrates several of the methods supported by this collection:

```java
import java.util.*;
public class VectorDemo {
public static void main(String args[]) {
// initial size is 3, increment is 2
Vector v = new Vector(3, 2);
System.out.println("Initial size: "+ v.size());
System.out.println("Initial capacity: "+
v.capacity()); v.addElement(new Integer(1));
v.addElement(new Integer(2));
v.addElement(new Integer(3));
v.addElement(new Integer(4));
System.out.println("Capacity after four
additions: " + v.capacity());
v.addElement(new Double(5.45));
System.out.println("Current capacity: "+
v.capacity()); v.addElement(new Double(6.08));
v.addElement(new Integer(7));
System.out.println("Current capacity: "+
v.capacity());
v.addElement(new Float(9.4)); v.addElement(new
```

```
Integer(10)); System.out.println("Current
capacity: " + v.capacity()); v.addElement(new
Integer(11));
v.addElement(new Integer(12));
System.out.println("First element: " +
(Integer)v.firstElement());
System.out.println("Last element: "+
(Integer)v.lastElement()); if(v.contains(new
Integer(3)))
System.out.println("Vector contains 3.");
// enumerate the elements in the vector.
Enumeration vEnum = v.elements();
System.out.println("\nElements in vector:");
while(vEnum.hasMoreElements())
System.out.print(vEnum.nextElement() + " ");
System.out.println();
}
}
```

This will produce the following result:

Initial size: 0

Initial capacity: 3

Capacity after four additions: 5

Current capacity: 5

Current capacity: 7

Current capacity: 9

First element: 1

Last element: 12

Vector contains 3.

Elements in vector:

1 2 3 4 5.45 6.08 7 9.4 10 1112

The Stack Class

Stack is a subclass of Vector that implements a standard last-in, first-out stack.

Stack only defines the default constructor, which creates an empty stack. Stack includes all the methods defined by Vector, and adds several of its own.

```
Stack( )
```

Apart from the methods inherited from its parent class Vector, Stack defines the following methods:

Methods with Description

- **boolean empty()** Tests if this stack is empty. Returns true if the stack is empty, and returns false if the stack contains elements.
- **Object peek( )** Returns the element on the top of the stack, but does not remove it.
- **Object pop( )** Returns the element on the top of the stack, removing it in the process.
- **Object push(Object element)** Pushes the element onto the stack. The element is also returned.
- **int search(Object element)** Searches for the element in the stack.If found, its offset from the top of the stack is returned. Otherwise, .1 is returned.

Example

The following program illustrates several of the methods supported by this collection:

```java
import java.util.*;
public class StackDemo {
static void showpush(Stack st, int a) {
st.push(new Integer(a));
System.out.println("push(" + a + ")");
System.out.println("stack: "+ st);
}
static void showpop(Stack st) {
System.out.print("pop-> "); Integer a = (Integer)
st.pop(); System.out.println(a);
System.out.println("stack: "+ st);
}
public static void main(String args[]) { Stack st
= new Stack(); System.out.println("stack: " +
st); showpush(st, 42);
showpush(st, 66);
showpush(st, 99); showpop(st); showpop(st);
showpop(st);
try {
showpop(st);
} catch (EmptyStackException e) {
System.out.println("empty stack");
}
}
}
```

This will produce the following result:

stack: [ ] push(42) stack: [42] push(66)

stack: [42, 66]

push(99)

stack: [42, 66, 99]

pop -> 99

stack: [42, 66]

pop -> 66 stack: [42] pop-> 42 stack: [ ]

pop -> empty stack

The Dictionary Class

Dictionary is an abstract class that represents a key/value storage repository and operates much like Map.

Given a key and value, you can store the value in a Dictionary object. Once the value is stored, you can retrieve it by using its key. Thus, like a map, a dictionary can be thought of as a list of key/value pairs.

The abstract methods defined by Dictionary are listed below:

Methods with Description

- **Enumeration elements( )** Returns an enumeration of the values contained in the dictionary.
- **Object get(Object key)** Returns the object that contains the value associated with the key. If the key is not in the dictionary, a null object is returned.
- **boolean isEmpty( )** Returns true if the dictionary is empty, and returns false if it contains at least one key.
- **Enumeration keys( )** Returns an enumeration of the keys contained in the dictionary.
- **Object put(Object key, Objectvalue)** Inserts a key and its value into the dictionary. Returns null if the key

is not already in the dictionary; returns the previous value associated with the key if the key is already in the dictionary.

- **Object remove(Object key)** Removes the key and its value. Returns the value associated with the key. If the key is not in the dictionary, a null is returned.
- **int size( )** Returns the number of entries in the dictionary.

The Dictionary class is obsolete. You should implement the Map interface to obtain key/value storage functionality.

The Map Interface

The Map interface maps unique keys to values. A key is an object that you use to retrieve a value at a later date.

- Given a key and a value, you can store the value in a Map object. After the value is stored, you can retrieve it by using its key.
- Several methods throw a NoSuchElementException when no items exist in the invoking map.
- A ClassCastException is thrown when an object is incompatible with the elements in a map.
- A NullPointerException is thrown if an attempt is made to use a null object and null is not allowed in the map.
- An UnsupportedOperationException is thrown when an attempt is made to change an unmodifiable map.

Methods with Description

- **void clear( )** Removes all key/value pairs from the invoking map.
- **boolean containsKey(Objectk)** Returns true if the invoking map contains **k** as a key. Otherwise, returns false.
- **boolean containsValue(Object v)** Returns true if the map contains **v** as a value. Otherwise, returns false.
- **Set entrySet( )** Returns a Set that contains the entries in the map. The set contains objects of type Map.Entry. This method provides a set-view of the invoking map.
- **boolean equals(Object obj)** Returns true if obj is a Map and contains the same entries. Otherwise, returns false.
- **Object get(Object k)** Returns the value associated with the key **k**.
- **int hashCode( )** Returns the hash code for the invoking map.
- **boolean isEmpty( )** Returns true if the invoking map is empty. Otherwise, returns false.
- **Set keySet( )** Returns a Set that contains the keys in the invoking map. This method provides a set-view of the keys in the invoking map.
- **Object put(Object k, Objectv)** Puts an entry in the invoking map, overwriting any previous value associated with the key. The key and value are k and v, respectively. Returns null if the key did not already exist. Otherwise, the previous value linked to the key is returned.
- **void putAll(Map m)** Puts all the entries from **m** into this map.
- **Objectremove(Object k)** Removes the entry whose key equals **k**.
- **int size( )** Returns the number of key/value pairs in the

map.
- **Collection values( )** Returns a collection containing the values in the map. This method provides a collection-view of the values in the map.

Example

Map has its implementation in various classes like HashMap. Following is the example to explain map functionality:

```
import java.util.*;
public class CollectionsDemo {
public static void main(String[] args) { Map m1 =
newHashMap();
m1.put("Zara", "8"); m1.put("Mahnaz", "31");
m1.put("Ayan","12"); m1.put("Daisy", "14");
System.out.println();
System.out.println(" Map Elements");
System.out.print("\t" + m1);
}
}
```

This will produce the following result:

ap Elements

{Mahnaz=31, Ayan=12, Daisy=14, Zara=8}

The Hashtable Class

Hashtable was part of the original java.util and is a concrete implementation of a Dictionary. However, Java 2 re-engineered Hashtable so that it also implements the Map interface. Thus, Hashtable is now integrated into the collections framework. It is similar to HashMap, but is synchronized.

Like HashMap, Hashtable stores key/value pairs in a hash table. When using a Hashtable, you specify an object that is used as a key, and the value that you want linked to that key. The key is then hashed, and the resulting hashcode is used as the index at which the value is stored within the table.

Following is the list of constructors provided by the HashTable class.

Constructor and Description

- **Hashtable( )** This is the default constructor of the hash table. It instantiates the Hashtable class.
- **Hashtable(int size)** This constructor accepts an integer parameter and creates a hash table that has an initial size specified by the integer value size.
- **Hashtable(int size, float fillRatio)** This creates a hash table that has an initial size specified by size and a fill ratio specified by fillRatio. This ratio must be between 0.0 and 1.0,and it determines how full the hash table can be before it is resized upward.
- **Hashtable(Map<? extendsK, ? extends V> t)** This constructs a Hashtable with the given mappings.

Apart from the methods defined by Map interface, Hashtable defines the following methods:

Methods with Description

- **void clear( )** Resets and empties the hash table.
- **Object clone( )** Returns a duplicate of the invoking object.
- **boolean contains(Object value)** Returns true if some value equal to the value exists within the hash table. Returns false if the value isn't found.
- **boolean containsKey(Objectkey)** Returns true if some key equal to the key exists within the hash table. Returns false if the key isn't found.
- **boolean containsValue(Object value)** Returns true if some value equal to the value exists within the hash table. Returns false if the value isn't found.
- **Enumeration elements( )** Returns an enumeration of the values contained in the hash table.
- **Objectget(Object key)** Returns the object that contains the value associated with the key. If the key is not in the hash table, a null object is returned.
- **boolean isEmpty( )** Returns true if the hash table is empty; returns false if it contains at least one key.
- **Enumeration keys( )** Returns an enumeration of the keys contained in the hash table.
- **Object put(Object key, Objectvalue)** Inserts a key and a value into the hash table. Returns null if the key isn't already in the hash table; returns the previous value associated with the key if the key is already in the hash table.
- **void rehash( )** Increases the size of the hash table and rehashes all of its keys.
- **Object remove(Object key)** Removes key and its value.

Returns the value associated with the key. If the key is not in the hash table, a null object is returned.

- **int size( )** Returns the number of entries in the hash table.
- **String toString( )** Returns the string equivalent of a hash table.

Example

The following program illustrates several of the methods supported by this data structure:

```java
import java.util.*;
public class HashTableDemo {
public static void main(String args[]) {
// Create a hash map
Hashtable balance = new Hashtable(); Enumeration
names;
String str;
double bal;
balance.put("Zara", new Double(3434.34));
balance.put("Mahnaz",new Double(123.22));
balance.put("Ayan", new Double(1378.00));
balance.put("Daisy", new Double(99.22));
balance.put("Qadir", new Double(-19.08));
// Show all balances in hash table. names =
balance.keys(); while(names.hasMoreElements()) {
str = (String) names.nextElement();
System.out.println(str + ": " + balance.get(str));
} System.out.println();
// Deposit 1,000 into Zara's account
bal =
((Double)balance.get("Zara")).doubleValue();
balance.put("Zara", new Double(bal+1000));
System.out.println("Zara's new balance: " +
```

```
balance.get("Zara"));
    }
}
```

This will produce the following result:

Qadir: -19.08

Zara: 3434.34 ahnaz: 123.22

Daisy: 99.22

Ayan: 1378.0

Zara's new balance: 4434.34

The Properties Class

Properties is a subclass of Hashtable. It is used to maintain lists of values in which the key is a String and the value is also a String.

The Properties class is used by many other Java classes. For example, it is the type of object returned by System.getProperties( ) when obtaining the environmental values.

Properties define the following instance variable. This variable holds a default property list associated with a Properties object.

Properties defaults;

Following is the list of constructors provided by the properties class.

Constructors and Description

- **Properties( )** This constructor creates a Properties object that has no default values.
- **Properties(Properties propDefault)** Creates an object that uses propDefault for its default values. In both the cases, the property list is empty.

Apart from the methods defined by Hashtable, Properties define the following methods:

Methods with Description

- **String getProperty(String key)** Returns the value associated with the key. A null object is returned if the key is neither in the list nor in the default property list.
- **String getProperty(String key, String defaultProperty)** Returns the value associated with the key. defaultProperty is returned if the key is neither in the list nor in the default property list.
- **void list(PrintStream streamOut)** Sends the property list to the output stream linked to streamOut.
- **void list(PrintWriter streamOut)** Sends the property list to the output stream linked to streamOut.
- **void load(InputStream streamIn) throws IOException** Inputs a property list from the input stream linked to streamIn.
- **Enumeration propertyNames( )** Returns an enumeration of the keys. This includes those keys found in the default property list, too.
- **Object setProperty(String key, String value)** Associates

value with the key. Returns the previous value associated with the key, or returns null if no such association exists.

- **void store(OutputStream streamOut, String description)** After writing the string specified by the description, the property list is written to the outputstream linked to streamOut.

Example

The following program illustrates several of the methods supported by this data structure:

```
import java.util.*;
public class PropDemo {
public static void main(String args[]) {
Properties capitals = new Properties();
Set states; String str;
capitals.put("Illinois","Springfield");
capitals.put("Missouri","Jefferson City");
capitals.put("Washington", "Olympia");
capitals.put("California", "Sacramento");
capitals.put("Indiana","Indianapolis");
// Show all states and capitals in hashtable.
states = capitals.keySet(); // get set-view of
keys Iterator itr = states.iterator();
while(itr.hasNext()) {
str = (String) itr.next();
System.out.println("The capital of " +
str + " is " + capitals.getProperty(str) + ".");
} System.out.println();
// look for state not in list -- specify default
str = capitals.getProperty("Florida",
"NotFound"); System.out.println("Thecapital of
```

```
Florida is "
+ str + ".");
}
}
```

This will produce the following result:

The capital of Missouri is Jefferson City.

The capital of Illinois is Springfield.

The capital of Indiana is Indianapolis.

The capital of California is Sacramento.

Thecapital of Washington is Olympia.

The capital of Florida is NotFound.

The BitSet Class

A BitSet class creates a special type of array that holds bit values. TheBitSet array can increase in size as needed. This makes it similar to a vector of bits. This is a legacy class but it has been completely re-engineered in Java 2, version 1.4.

The BitSet defines the following two constructors:

Constructor and Description

- **BitSet( )** This constructor creates a default object.
- **BitSet(int size)** This constructor allows you to specify its initial size, i.e., the number of bits that it can hold. All bits are initialized to zero.

BitSet implements the Cloneable interface and defines the methods listed in the following table:

Methods with Description

- **void and(BitSet bitSet)** ANDs the contents of the invoking BitSet object with those specified by bitSet. The result is placed into the invoking object.
- **void andNot(BitSet bitSet)** For each 1 bit in bitSet,the corresponding bit in the invoking BitSet is cleared.
- **int cardinality( )** Returns the number of set bits in the invoking object.
- **void clear( )** Zeros all bits.
- **void clear(int index)** Zeros the bit specified by the index.
- **void clear(int startIndex, int endIndex)** Zeros the bits from startIndex to endIndex.1.
- **Object clone( )** Duplicates the invoking BitSet object.
- **boolean equals(Object bitSet)** Returns true if the invoking bit set is equivalent to the one passed in bitSet. Otherwise, the method returns false.
- **void flip(int index)** Reverses the bit specified by index.
- **void flip(int startIndex, int endIndex)** Reverses the bits from startIndex to endIndex.1.
- **boolean get(int index)** Returns the current state of the bit at the specified index.
- **BitSetget(int startIndex, int endIndex)** Returns a BitSet that consists of the bits from startIndex to endIndex.1. The invoking object is not changed.
- **int hashCode( )** Returns the hash code for the invoking object.

- **boolean intersects(BitSet bitSet)** Returns true if at least one pair of corresponding bits within the invoking object and bitSet are 1.
- **boolean isEmpty( )** Returns true if all bits in the invoking object are zero.
- **int length( )** Returns the number of bits required to hold the contents of the invoking BitSet. This value is determined by the location of the last 1 bit.
- **int nextClearBit(int startIndex)** Returns the index of the next cleared bit, (that is, the next zero bit), starting from the index specified by startIndex.
- **int nextSetBit(int startIndex)** Returns the index of the next set bit (that is, the next 1 bit), starting from the index specified by startIndex. If no bit is set, .1 is returned.
- **void or(BitSetbitSet)** ORs the contents of the invoking BitSet object with that specified by bitSet. The result is placed into the invoking object.
- **void set(int index)** Sets the bit specified by the index.
- **void set(int index,boolean v)** Sets the bit specified by the index to the value passed in **v**. True sets the bit, false clears the bit.
- **void set(int startIndex, int endIndex)** Sets the bits from startIndex to endIndex.1.
- **void set(int startIndex, int endIndex, boolean v)** Sets the bits from startIndex to endIndex.1, to the value passed in v. True sets the bits, false clears the bits.
- **int size( )** Returns the number of bits in the invoking BitSet object.
- **String toString( )** Returns the string equivalent of the invoking BitSet object.

- **void xor(BitSet bitSet)** XORs the contents of the invoking BitSet object with that specified by bitSet. The result is placed into the invoking object.

Example

The following program illustrates several of the methods supported by this data structure:

```java
import java.util.BitSet;
public class BitSetDemo {
public static void main(String args[]) { BitSet
bits1 = new BitSet(16);
BitSet bits2 = new BitSet(16);
// set some bits
for(int i=0; i<16; i++) {
if((i%2) == 0) bits1.set(i);
if((i%5) != 0) bits2.set(i);
}
System.out.println("Initial pattern in bits1: ");
System.out.println(bits1);
System.out.println("\nInitial pattern in bits2:
");
System.out.println(bits2);
// AND bits bits2.and(bits1);
System.out.println("\nbits2 AND bits1: ");
System.out.println(bits2);
// OR bits bits2.or(bits1);
System.out.println("\nbits2 OR bits1: ");
System.out.println(bits2);
// XOR bits
bits2.xor(bits1);
System.out.println("\nbits2 XOR bits1: ");
System.out.println(bits2);
}
```

```
   }
```

This will produce the following result:

```
Initial pattern in bits1:
    {0, 2, 4, 6, 8, 10, 12, 14}
    Initial pattern in bits2:
    {1, 2, 3, 4, 6, 7, 8, 9, 11, 12, 13, 14}
    bits2 AND bits1:
    {2, 4, 6, 8, 12, 14}
    bits2 OR bits1:
    {0, 2, 4, 6, 8, 10, 12, 14}
    bits2 XOR bits1:
    {}
```

The Collection Algorithms

The collections framework defines several algorithms that can be applied to collections and maps. These algorithms are defined as static methods within the Collections class.

Several of the methods can throw a **ClassCastException**, which occurs when an attempt is made to compare incompatible types, or an **UnsupportedOperationException**, which occurs when an attempt is made to modify an unmodifiable collection.

Collections define three static variables: EMPTY_SET, EMPTY_LIST, and EMPTY_MAP. All are immutable.

Algorithms with Description

The Collection Algorithms

Here is a list of all the algorithm implementation.

The Collection Algorithms

The collections framework defines several algorithms that can be applied to collections and maps. These algorithms are defined as static methods within the Collections class. Several of the methods can throw a **ClassCastException**, which occurs when an attempt is made to compare incompatible types, or an **UnsupportedOperationExcepti on**, which occurs when an attempt is made to modify an unmodifiable collection.

The methods defined in collection framework's algorithm are summarized in the following table:

Methods with Description

- **static int binarySearch(List list, Object value, Comparator c)** Searches for value in the list ordered according to **c**. Returns the position of value in list, or -1 if value is not found.
- **static int binarySearch(List list, Object value)** Searches for value in the list. The list must be sorted. Returns the position of value in list, or -1 if value is not found.
- **static void copy(List list1, List list2)** Copies the elements of list2 to list1.

- **static Enumeration enumeration(Collection c)** Returns an enumeration over **c**.
- **static void fill(List list, Object obj)** Assigns obj to each element of the list.
- **static int indexOfSubList(Listlist, List subList)** Searches list for the first occurrence of subList. Returns the index of the first match, or .1 if no match is found.
- **static int lastIndexOfSubList(List list,List subList)** Searches list for the last occurrence of subList. Returns the index of the last match, or .1 if no match is found.
- **static ArrayList list(Enumeration enum)** Returns an ArrayList that contains the elements of enum.
- **static Object max(Collection c, Comparator comp)** Returns the maximum element in c as determined by comp.
- **static Object max(Collection c)** Returns the maximum element in **c** as determined by natural ordering. The collection need not be sorted.
- **static Object min(Collection c, Comparator comp)** Returns the minimum element in c as determined by comp. The collection need not be sorted.
- **static Object min(Collection c)** Returns the minimum element in c as determined by natural ordering.
- **static List nCopies(int num,Object obj)** Returns num copies of obj contained in an immutable list. num must be greater than or equal to zero.
- **static boolean replaceAll(List list,Object old, Object new)** Replaces all occurrences of old with new in the list. Returns true if at least one replacement occurred. Returns false, otherwise.
- **static void reverse(List list)** Reverses the sequence in

list.

- **static Comparator reverseOrder( )** Returns a reverse comparator
- **static void rotate(List list, int n)** Rotates list by **n** places to the right. To rotate left, use a negative value for **n**.
- **static void shuffle(List list, Random r)** Shuffles (i.e., randomizes) the elements in the list by using **r** as a source of random numbers.
- **static void shuffle(List list)** Shuffles (i.e., randomizes) the elements in list.
- **static Set singleton(Objectobj)** Returns obj as an immutable set. This is an easy way to convert a single object into a a set.
- **static List singletonList(Object obj)** Returns obj as an immutable list. This is an easy way to convert a single object into a list.
- **static Map singletonMap(Object k, Object v)** Returns the key/value pair k/v as an immutable map. This is an easy way to convert a single key/value pair into a map.
- **static void sort(List list, Comparator comp)** Sorts the elements of list as determined by comp.
- **static void sort(List list)** Sorts the elements of the list as determined by their natural ordering.
- **static void swap(List list,int idx1, int idx2)** Exchanges the elements in the list at the indices specified by idx1 and idx2.
- **static Collection synchronizedCollection(Collection c)** Returns a thread-safe collection backed by **c**.
- **static List synchronizedList(List list)** Returns a thread-safe list backed by list.
- **static Map synchronizedMap(Map m)** Returns a

thread-safe map backed by **m**.

- **static Set synchronizedSet(Set s)** Returns a thread-safe set backed by **s**.
- **static SortedMap synchronizedSortedMap(SortedMap sm)** Returns a thread-safe sorted set backed by **sm**.
- **static SortedSet synchronizedSortedSet(SortedSet ss)** Returns a thread-safe set backed by **ss**.
- **static Collection unmodifiableCollection(Collection c)** Returns an unmodifiable collection backed by **c**.
- **static List unmodifiableList(List list)** Returns an unmodifiable list backed by the list.
- **static Map unmodifiableMap(Map m)** Returns an unmodifiable map backed by **m**.
- **static Set unmodifiableSet(Set s)** Returns an unmodifiable set backed by s.
- **static SortedMap unmodifiableSortedMap(SortedMap sm)** Returns an unmodifiable sorted map backed by **sm**.
- **static SortedSet unmodifiableSortedSet(SortedSet ss)** Returns an unmodifiable sorted set backed by ss.

Example

Following is an example, which demonstrates various algorithms.

```java
import java.util.*;
public class AlgorithmsDemo {
public static void main(String args[]) {
// Create and initialize linked list LinkedList
ll = new LinkedList(); ll.add(new Integer(-8));
ll.add(new Integer(20)); ll.add(new
```

```java
Integer(-20)); ll.add(new Integer(8));
// Create a reverse order comparator
Comparator r = Collections.reverseOrder();
// Sort list by using the comparator
Collections.sort(ll, r);
// Get iterator
Iterator li = ll.iterator();
System.out.print("List sorted in reverse: ");
while(li.hasNext()){
System.out.print(li.next() + " ");
} System.out.println(); Collections.shuffle(ll);
// display randomized list li = ll.iterator();
System.out.print("List shuffled: ");
while(li.hasNext()){
System.out.print(li.next() + " ");
} System.out.println();
System.out.println("Minimum: " +
Collections.min(ll));
System.out.println("Maximum: " +
Collections.max(ll));
}
}
```

This will produce the following result:

List sorted in reverse: 20 8 -8 -20

List shuffled: 20 -20 8 -8 minimum: -20

maximum: 20

How to Use an Iterator ?

Often, you will want to cycle through the elements in a collection. For example, you might want to display each element.

The easiest way to do this is to employ an iterator, which is an object that implements either the Iterator or the ListIterator interface.

Iterator enables you to cycle through a collection, obtaining or removing elements. ListIterator extends Iterator to allow bidirectional traversal of a list and the modification of elements.

Iterator Methods with Description

- **Using Java Iterator** Here is a list of all the methods with examples provided by Iterator and ListIterator interfaces.

How to Use Iterator?

Often, you will want to cycle through the elements in a collection. For example, you might want to display each element. The easiest way to do this is to employ an iterator, which is an object that implements either the Iterator or the ListIterator interface.

Iterator enables you to cycle through a collection, obtaining or removing elements. ListIterator extends Iterator to allow bidirectional traversal of a list, and the modification of elements.

Before you can access a collection through an iterator, you must obtain one. Each of the collection classes provides an iterator( ) method that returns an iterator to the start of the collection. By using this iterator object, you can access each element in the collection, one element at a time.

In general, to use an iterator to cycle through the contents of a collection, follow these steps:

- Obtain an iterator to the start of the collection by calling the collection's iterator()method.
- Set up a loop that makes a call to hasNext( ). Have the loop iterate as long as hasNext( ) returns true.
- Within the loop, obtain each element by calling next( ).

For collections that implement List, you can also obtain an iterator by calling ListIterator.

The Methods Declared by Iterator

Methods with Description

- **boolean hasNext( )** Returns true if there are more elements. Otherwise, returns false.
- **Object next()** Returns the next element. Throws NoSuchElementException if there is not a next element.
- **void remove( )** Removes the current element. Throws IllegalStateException if an attempt is made to call remove( ) that is not preceded by a call to next( ).

The Methods Declared by ListIterator

Methods with Description

- **void add(Objectobj)** Inserts obj into the list in front of the element that will be returned by the next call tonext( ).
- **boolean hasNext( )** Returns true if there is a next element. Otherwise, returns false.
- **boolean hasPrevious( )** Returns true if there is a previous element. Otherwise, returns false.
- **Object next()** Returns the next element. A NoSuchElem entException is thrown if there is not a next element.
- **int nextIndex( )** Returns the index of the next element. If there is not a next element, returns the size of the list.
- **Object previous( )** Returns the previous element. A NoSuchElementException is thrown if there is not a previous element.
- **int previousIndex( )** Returns the index of the previous element. If there is not a previous element, returns -1.
- **void remove( )** Removes the current element from the list.An IllegalStateException is thrown if remove( ) is called before next( ) or previous( ) is invoked.
- **void set(Object obj)** Assigns obj to the current element. This is the element last returned by a call to either next( ) or previous( ).

Example

Here is an example demonstrating both Iterator and ListIterator. It uses an ArrayList object, but the general principles apply to any type of collection.

Of course, ListIterator is available only to those collections that implement the List interface.

```java
import java.util.*;
public class IteratorDemo {
public static void main(String args[]) {
// Create an array list
ArrayList al = new ArrayList();
// add elements to the array list al.add("C");
al.add("A");
al.add("E"); al.add("B"); al.add("D");
al.add("F");
// Use iterator to display contents of al
System.out.print("Original contents of al: ");
Iterator itr = al.iterator();
while(itr.hasNext()) {
Object element = itr.next();
System.out.print(element + " ");
} System.out.println();
// Modify objects being iterated ListIterator
litr = al.listIterator(); while(litr.hasNext()) {
Object element = litr.next();
litr.set(element + "+");
}
System.out.print("Modified contents of al: ");
itr = al.iterator();
while(itr.hasNext()) {
Object element = itr.next();
System.out.print(element + " ");
} System.out.println();
// Now, display the list backwards
System.out.print("Modified list backwards: ");
while(litr.hasPrevious()) {
Object element = litr.previous();
System.out.print(element + " ");
} System.out.println();
}
}
```

This will produce the following result:

Original contents of al: C A E B D F

odified contents of al: C+ A+ E+ B+ D+ F+

odified list backwards: F+ D+ B+ E+ A+ C+

How to Use a Comparator ?

Both TreeSet and TreeMap store elements in a sorted order. However, it is the comparator that defines precisely what *sorted order* means.

This interface lets us sort a given collection any number of different ways. Also this interface can be used to sort any instances of any class (even classes we cannot modify).

Iterator Methods with Description

- **Using Java Comparator** Here is a list of all the methods with examples provided by Comparator Interface.

How to Use Comparator?

Both TreeSet and TreeMap store elements in sorted order. However, it is the comparator that defines precisely what *sorted order* means.

The Comparator interface defines two methods: compare( ) and equals( ). The compare() method, shown here, compares two elements for order:

The compare Method

```
int compare(Object obj1, Object obj2)
```

obj1 and obj2 are the objects to be compared. This method returns zero if the objects are equal. It returns a positive value if obj1 is greater than obj2. Otherwise, a negative value is returned.

By overriding compare( ), you can alter the way that objects are ordered. For example, to sort in a reverse order, you can create a comparator that reverses the outcome of a comparison.

The equals Method

The equals( ) method, shown here, tests whether an object equals the invoking comparator:

```
boolean equals(Object obj)
```

obj is the object to be tested for equality. The method returns true if obj and the invoking object are both Comparator objects and use the same ordering. Otherwise, it returns false.

Overriding equals( ) is unnecessary, and most simple comparators will not do so.

Example

```java
import java.util.*;
class Dog implements Comparator<Dog>,
Comparable<Dog>{
private String name; private int age; Dog(){
}
Dog(String n, int a){
name = n;
age = a;
}
public String getDogName(){
return name;
}
public int getDogAge(){
return age;
}
// Overriding the compareTo method public int
compareTo(Dog d){
return (this.name).compareTo(d.name);
}
// Overriding the compare method to sort the age
public int compare(Dog d, Dog d1){
return d.age - d1.age;
}
}
public class Example{
public static void main(String args[]){
// Takes a list o Dog objects
List<Dog> list = new ArrayList<Dog>();
list.add(new Dog("Shaggy",3)); list.add(new
Dog("Lacy",2)); list.add(new Dog("Roger",10));
list.add(new Dog("Tommy",4)); list.add(new
Dog("Tammy",1));
Collections.sort(list);// Sorts the array list
for(Dog a: list)//printing the sorted list of
names
System.out.print(a.getDogName() + ", ");
// Sorts the array list using comparator
```

```
Collections.sort(list,new Dog());
System.out.println(" ");
for(Dog a: list)//printing the sorted list of ages
System.out.print(a.getDogName() +" : "+
a.getDogAge() + ", ");
}
}
```

This will produce the following result:

Lacy, Roger, Shaggy, Tammy, Tommy,

Tammy : 1, Lacy : 2, Shaggy : 3,Tommy : 4, Roger : 10,

Note: Sorting of the Arrays class is as the same as the Collections.

Summary

The Java collections framework gives the programmer access to prepackaged data structures as well as to algorithms for manipulating them.

A collection is an object that can hold references to other objects. The collection interfaces declare the operations that can be performed on each type of collection.

The classes and interfaces of the collections framework are in package java.util.

Generics

It would be nice if we could write a single sort method that could sort the elements in an Integer array, a String array, or an array of any type that supports ordering.

Java **Generic** methods and generic classes enable programmers to specify, with a single method declaration, a set of related methods, or with a single class declaration, a set of related types, respectively.

Generics also provide compile-time type safety that allows programmers to catch invalid types at compile time.

Using Java Generic concept, we might write a generic method for sorting an array of objects, then invoke the generic method with Integer arrays, Double arrays, String arrays and so on, to sort the array elements.

Generic Methods

You can write a single generic method declaration that can be called with arguments of different types. Based on the types of the arguments passed to the generic method, the compiler handles each method call appropriately. Following are the rules to define Generic Methods:

- All generic method declarations have a type parameter section delimited by angle brackets (< and >) that precedes the method's return type (< E > in the next example).
- Each type parameter section contains one or more type parameters separated by commas. A type parameter, also known as a type variable, is an identifier that specifies a generic type name.
- The type parameters can be used to declare the return type and act as placeholders for the types of the arguments passed to the generic method, which are known as actual type arguments.
- A generic method's body is declared like that of any other method. Note that type parameters can represent only reference types, not primitive types (like int, double and char).

Example

Following example illustrates how we can print an array of different type using a single Generic method:

```
public class GenericMethodTest
{
// generic method printArray
public static < E > void printArray( E[]
inputArray )
{
```

```
// Display array elements
for ( E element : inputArray ){
System.out.printf("%s ", element );
} System.out.println();
}
public static void main( String args[] )
{
// Create arrays of Integer, Double and Character
Integer[] intArray = { 1, 2, 3, 4, 5 }; Double[]
doubleArray = { 1.1, 2.2, 3.3, 4.4 }; Character[]
charArray = { 'H', 'E', 'L', 'L', 'O' };
System.out.println( "Array integerArray
contains:");
printArray( intArray ); // pass an Integer array
System.out.println( "\nArray doubleArray
contains:");
printArray( doubleArray ); // pass a Double array
System.out.println( "\nArray characterArray
contains:");
printArray( charArray); // pass a Characterarray
}
}
```

This will produce the following result:

```
Array integerArray contains:

1 2 3 4 5 6

Array doubleArray contains:

1.1 2.2 3.3 4.4

Array characterArray contains: H E L L O
```

Bounded Type Parameters

There may be times when you'll want to restrict the kinds of types that are allowed to be passed to a type parameter. For example, a method that operates on numbers might only want to accept instances of Number or its subclasses. This is what bounded type parameters are for.

To declare a bounded type parameter, list the type parameter's name, followed by the extends keyword, followed by its upper bound.

Example

Following example illustrates how extends is used in a general sense to mean either "extends"(as in classes) or "implements" (as in interfaces). This example is Generic method to return the largest of three Comparable objects:

```java
public class MaximumTest
{
// determines the largest of three Comparable
objects
public static <T extends Comparable<T>> T
maximum(Tx, T y, T z)
{
T max = x; // assume x is initially the largest
if ( y.compareTo( max ) > 0 ){
max = y; // y is the largest so far
}
if ( z.compareTo( max ) > 0 ){
max = z; // z is the largest now
}
return max; // returns the largest object
}
public static void main( String args[] )
{
System.out.printf( "Maxof %d, %d and %d is
```

```
%d\n\n",
3, 4, 5, maximum( 3, 4, 5 ) );
System.out.printf( "Maxmof %.1f,%.1f and %.1f is
%.1f\n\n",
6.6, 8.8, 7.7, maximum( 6.6, 8.8, 7.7 ) );
System.out.printf( "Maxof %s, %s and %s is
%s\n","pear", "apple", "orange",maximum( "pear",
"apple", "orange") );
}
}
```

This will produce the following result:

maximum of 3, 4 and 5 is 5

maximum of 6.6, 8.8 and 7.7 is 8.8

maximum of pear, apple and orange is pear

Generic Classes

A generic class declaration looks like a non-generic class declaration, except that the class name is followed by a type parameter section.

As with generic methods, the type parameter section of a generic class can have one or more type parameters separated by commas. These classes are known as parameterized classes or parameterized types because they accept one or more parameters.

Example

Following example illustrates how we can define a generic class:

```java
public class Box<T> {
private T t;
public void add(T t) {
this.t = t;
}
public T get() {
return t;
}
public static void main(String[] args) {
Box<Integer> integerBox = new Box<Integer>();
Box<String> stringBox = new Box<String>();
integerBox.add(new Integer(10));
stringBox.add(new String("Hello World"));
System.out.printf("Integer Value
:%d\n\n",integerBox.get());
System.out.printf("String Value :%s\n",
stringBox.get());
}
}
```

This will produce the following result:

```
Integer Value :10

String Value :Hello World
```

Serialization

Java provides a mechanism,called object serialization where an object can be represented as a sequence of bytes that includes the object's data as well as information about the object's type and the types of data stored in the object.

After a serialized object has been written into a file, it can be read from the file and deserialized that is, the type information and bytes that represent the object and its data can be used to recreate the object in memory.

Most impressive is that the entire process is JVM independent, meaning an object can be serialized on one platform and deserialized on an entirely different platform.

Classes **ObjectInputStream** and **ObjectOutputStream** are high-level streams that contain the methods for serializing and deserializing an object.

The ObjectOutputStream class contains many write methods for writing various data types, but one method in particular stands out:

```
public final void writeObject(Object x) throws
IOException
```

The above method serializes an Object and sends it to the output stream. Similarly, the ObjectInputStream class contains the following method for deserializing an object:

```
public final Object readObject()throws
IOException, ClassNotFoundException
```

This method retrieves the next Object out of the stream and deserializes it. The return value is Object, so you will need to cast it to its appropriate data type.

To demonstrate how serialization works in Java, I am going to use the Employee class that we discussed early on in the book. Suppose that we have the following Employee class, which implements the Serializable interface:

```
public class Employee implements
java.io.Serializable
{
public String name; publicString address; public
transient int SSN; public int number;
public void mailCheck()
{
System.out.println("Mailing a check to "+ name +
" " + address);
}
}
```

Notice that for a class to be serialized successfully, two conditions must be met:

- The class must implement the java.io.Serializable interface.
- All of the fields in the class must be serializable. If a field is not serializable, it must be marked **transient**.

If you are curious to know if a Java Standard Class is serializable or not, check the documentation for the class. The test is simple: If the class implements java.io.Serializable, then it is serializable; otherwise, it's not.

Serializing an Object

The ObjectOutputStream class is used to serialize an Object. The following SerializeDemo program instantiates an Employee object and serializes it to a file.

When the program is done executing, a file named employee.ser is created. The program does not generate any output, but study the code and try to determine what the program is doing.

Note: When serializing an object to a file, the standard convention in Java is to give the filea **.ser** extension.

```java
import java.io.*;
public class SerializeDemo
{
public static void main(String [] args)
```

```
{
Employee e = new Employee();
e.name = "Reyan Ali";
e.address = "Phokka Kuan, Ambehta Peer";
e.SSN = 11122333;
e.number = 101;
try
{
FileOutputStream fileOut =
new FileOutputStream("/tmp/employee.ser");
ObjectOutputStream out = new
ObjectOutputStream(fileOut); out.writeObject(e);
out.close();
fileOut.close();
System.out.printf("Serialized data is saved in
/tmp/employee.ser");
}catch(IOException i)
{
i.printStackTrace();
}
}
}
```

Deserializing an Object

The following DeserializeDemo program deserializes the
Employee object created in the SerializeDemo program.
Study the program and try to determine its output:

```
import java.io.*;
public class DeserializeDemo
{
public static void main(String [] args)
{
Employee e = null;
```

```
try
{
FileInputStream fileIn = new
FileInputStream("/tmp/employee.ser");
ObjectInputStream in = new
ObjectInputStream(fileIn);
e = (Employee) in.readObject();
in.close();
fileIn.close();
}catch(IOException i)
{
i.printStackTrace();
return;
}catch(ClassNotFoundException c)
{
System.out.println("Employee class not found");
c.printStackTrace();
return;
}
System.out.println("Deserialized Employee...");
System.out.println("Name: "+ e.name);
System.out.println("Address: " + e.address);
System.out.println("SSN: " + e.SSN);
System.out.println("Number: "+ e.number);
}
}
```

This will produce the following result:

Deserialized Employee... Name:Reyan Ali

Address:Phokka Kuan, Ambehta Peer

SSN: 0

Number:101

Here are following important points to be noted:

- The try/catch block tries to catch a ClassNotFoundExc eption, which is declared by the readObject() method. For a JVM to be able to deserialize an object, it must be able to find the bytecode for the class. If the JVM can't find a class during the deserialization of an object, it throws a ClassNotFoundException.
- Notice that the return value of readObject() is cast to an Employee reference.
- The value of the SSN field was 11122333 when the object was serialized, but because the field is transient, this value was not sent to the output stream. The SSN field of the deserialized Employee object is 0.

Networking

The term *network programming* refers to writing programs that execute across multiple devices (computers), in which the devices are all connected to each other using a network.

The java.net package of the J2SE APIs contains a collection of classes and interfaces that provide the low-level communication details, allowing you to write programs that focus on solving the problem at hand.

The java.net package provides support for the two common network protocols:

- **TCP:** TCP stands for Transmission Control Protocol, which allows for reliable communication between two applications. TCP is typically used over the Internet Protocol, which is referred to as TCP/IP.
- **UDP:** UDP stands for User Datagram Protocol, a connection-less protocol that allows for packets of data to be transmitted between applications.

This chapter gives a good understanding on the following two subjects:

- **Socket Programming**: This is the most widely used concept in Networking and it has been explained in very detail.

URL Processing

URL stands for Uniform Resource Locator and represents a resource on the World Wide Web, such as a Web page or FTP directory.

This chapter shows you how to write Java programs that communicate with a URL. A URL can be broken down into parts, as follows:

protocol://host:port/path?query#ref

Examples of protocols include HTTP, HTTPS, FTP, and File. The path is also referred to as the filename, and the host is also called the authority.

The following is a URL to a web page whose protocol is HTTP:

http://www.amrood.com/index.htm?language=en#j2se

Notice that this URL does not specify a port, in which case the default port for the protocol is used. With HTTP, the default port is 80.

URL Class Methods

The **java.net.URL** class represents a URL and has a complete set of methods to manipulate URL in Java.

The URL class has several constructors for creating URLs, including the following:

Methods with Description

- **public URL(String protocol, String host, int port, String file) throws MalformedURLException** Creates a URL by putting together the given parts.
- **public URL(String protocol, String host, String file) throws MalformedURLException** Identical to the previous constructor, except that the default port for the given protocol is used.
- **public URL(String url) throws MalformedURLExcepti on** Creates a URL from the given String.
- **public URL(URL context, String url) throws Malformed URLException** Creates a URL by parsing together the URL and String arguments.

The URL class contains many methods for accessing the various parts of the URL being represented. Some of the methods in the URL class include the following:

Methods with Description

- **public String getPath()** Returns the path of the URL.
- **public String getQuery()** Returns the query part of the URL.

- **public String getAuthority()** Returns the authority of the URL.
- **public int getPort()** Returns the port of the URL.
- **public int getDefaultPort()** Returns the default port for the protocol of the URL.
- **public String getProtocol()** Returns the protocol of the URL.
- **public String getHost()** Returns the host of the URL.
- **public String getHost()** Returns the host of the URL.
- **public String getFile()** Returns the filename of the URL.
- **public String getRef()** Returns the reference part of the URL.
- **public URLConnection openConnection() throws IOException** Opens a connection to the URL, allowing a client to communicate with the resource.

Example

The following URLDemo program demonstrates the various parts of a URL. A URL is entered on the command line, and the URLDemo program outputs each part of the given URL.

```java
// File Name : URLDemo.java
import java.net.*;
import java.io.*;
public class URLDemo
{
public static void main(String [] args)
{
try
{
URL url = new
```

```
URL("http://www.amrood.com/index.htm?language=en#j2se")
 System.out.println("URL is " + url.toString());
 System.out.println("protocol is " +
 url.getProtocol()); System.out.println("authority
 is " + url.getAuthority());
 System.out.println("file name is " +
 url.getFile()); System.out.println("host is " +
 url.getHost()); System.out.println("path is " +
 url.getPath()); System.out.println("port is " +
 url.getPort()); System.out.println("default port
 is " + url.getDefaultPort());
 System.out.println("query is " + url.getQuery());
 System.out.println("ref is " + url.getRef());
 }catch(IOException e)
 {
 e.printStackTrace();
 }
 }
 }
```

A sample run of the this program will produce the following result:

URL is http://www.amrood.com/index.htm?language=en#j2se protocol is http authority

file name is /index.htm?language=en hostis www.amrood.com

path is /index.htm port is -1

default port is 80 query is language=en ref is j2se

URLConnections Class Methods

The openConnection() method returns a **java.net.URLConnection**, an abstract class whose subclasses represent the various types of URL connections.

For example:

- If you connect to a URL whose protocol is HTTP, the openConnection() method returns an HttpURLConnection object.
- If you connect to a URL that represents a JAR file, the openConnection() method returns a JarURLConnection object, etc.

The URLConnection class has many methods for setting or determining information about the connection, including the following:

Methods with Description

- **Object getContent()** Retrieves the contents of this URL connection.
- **Object getContent(Class[] classes)** Retrieves the contents of this URL connection.
- **String getContentEncoding()** Returns the value of the content-encoding header field.
- **int getContentLength()** Returns the value of the content-length header field.
- **String getContentType()** Returns the value of the content-type header field.
- **int getLastModified()** Returns the value of the last-modified header field.
- **long getExpiration()** Returns the value of the expired header field.

- **long getIfModifiedSince()** Returns the value of this object's if ModifiedSince field.
- **public void setDoInput(boolean input)** Passes in true to denote that the connection will be used for input. The default value is true because clients typically read from a URLConnection.
- **public void setDoOutput(boolean output)** Passes in true to denote that the connection will be used for output. The default value is false because many types of URLs do not support being written to.
- **public InputStream getInputStream() throws IOException** Returns the input stream of the URL connection for reading from the resource.
- **public OutputStream getOutputStream() throws IOException** Returns the outputstream of the URL connection for writing to the resource.
- **public URL getURL()** Returns the URL that this URL-Connection object is connected to.

Example

The following URLConnectionDemo program connects to a URL entered from the command line.

If the URL represents an HTTP resource, the connection is cast to HttpURLConnection, and the data in the resource is read one line at a time.

```
// File Name : URLConnDemo.java
import java.net.*;
```

```java
import java.io.*;
public class URLConnDemo
{
public static void main(String [] args)
{
try
{
URL url = new URL("http://www.amrood.com");
URLConnection urlConnection =
url.openConnection(); HttpURLConnection
connection = null; if(urlConnection instanceof
HttpURLConnection)
{
connection = (HttpURLConnection) urlConnection;
}
else
{
System.out.println("Please enter an HTTP URL.");
return;
}
BufferedReader in = new BufferedReader(
new
InputStreamReader(connection.getInputStream()));
String urlString = "";
String current;
while((current = in.readLine()) != null)
{
urlString += current;
}
System.out.println(urlString);
}catch(IOException e)
{
e.printStackTrace();
}
}
}
```

A sample run of this program will produce the following result:

```
$ java URLConnDemo
    .....a complete HTML content of home page of amrood.com.....
```

Socket Programming

Sockets provide the communication mechanism between two computers using TCP. A client program creates a socket on its end of the communication and attempts to connect that socket to a server.

When the connection is made, the server creates a socket object on its end of the communication. The client and the server can now communicate by writing to and reading from the socket.

The java.net.Socket class represents a socket, and the java.net.ServerSocket class provides a mechanism for the server program to listen for clients and establish connections with them.

The following steps occur when establishing a TCP connection between two computers using sockets:

- The server instantiates a ServerSocket object, denoting which port number communication is to occur on.
- The server invokes the accept() method of the Server-Socket class. This method waits until a client connects to the server on the given port.

- After the server is waiting, a client instantiates a Socket object, specifying the server name and the port number to connect to.
- The constructor of the Socket class attempts to connect the client to the specified server and the port number. If communication is established, the client now has a Socket object capable of communicating with the server.
- On the server side, the accept() method returns a reference to a new socket on the server that is connected to the client's socket.

After the connections are established, communication can occur using I/O streams. Each socket has both an OutputStream and an InputStream. The client's OutputStream is connected to the server's InputStream, and the client's InputStream is connected to the server's OutputStream.

TCP is a two-way communication protocol, hence data can be sent across both streams at the same time. Following are the useful classes providing complete set of methods to implement sockets.

ServerSocket Class Methods

The **java.net.ServerSocket** class is used by server applications to obtain a port and listen for client requests.

The ServerSocket class has four constructors:

Methods with Description

- **public ServerSocket(int port) throws IOException** Attempts to create a server socket bound to the specified port. An exception occurs if the port is already bound by another application.
- **public ServerSocket(int port, int backlog) throws IOException** Similar to the previous constructor, the backlog parameter specifies how many incoming clients to store in a wait queue.
- **public ServerSocket(int port, int backlog, InetAddress address) throws IOException** Similar to the previous constructor, the InetAddress parameter specifies the local IP address to bind to. The InetAddress is used for servers that may have multiple IP addresses, allowing the server to specify which of its IP addresses to accept client requests on.
- **public ServerSocket() throws IOException** Creates an unbound server socket. When using this constructor, use the bind() method when you are ready to bind the server socket.

If the ServerSocket constructor does not throw an exception, it means that your application has successfully bound to the specified port and is ready for client requests.

Following are some of the common methods of the Server-Socket class:

Methods with Description

- **public int getLocalPort()** Returns the port that the server socket is listening on. This method is useful if you passed in 0 as the port number in a constructor and let the server find a port for you.

- **public Socket accept() throws IOException** Waits for an incoming client. This method blocks until either a client connects to the server on the specified port or the socket times out, assuming that the time-out value has been set using the setSoTimeout() method. Otherwise, this method blocks indefinitely.
- **public void setSoTimeout(int timeout)** Sets the time-out value for how long the server socket waits for a client during the accept().
- **public void bind(SocketAddress host, int backlog)** Binds the socket to the specified server and port in the SocketAddress object. Use this method if you have instantiated the ServerSocket using the no argument constructor.

When the ServerSocket invokes accept(), the method does not return until a client connects. After a client does connect, the ServerSocket creates a new Socket on an unspecified port and returns a reference to this new Socket. A TCP connection now exists between the client and the server, and communication can begin.

Socket Class Methods

The **java.net.Socket** class represents the socket that both the client and the server use to communicate with each other. The client obtains a Socket object by instantiating one, whereas the server obtains a Socket object from the return value of the accept() method.

The Socket class has five constructors that a client uses to connect to a server:

Methods with Description

- **public Socket(String host, int port) throws UnknownHostException, IOException.** This method attempts to connect to the specified server at the specified port. If this constructor does not throw an exception, the connection is successful and the client is connected to the server.
- **public Socket(InetAddress host, int port) throws IOException** This method is identical to the previous constructor, except that the host is denoted by an InetAddress object.
- **public Socket(String host, int port, InetAddress localAddress, int localPort) throws IOException.** Connects to the specified host and port, creating a socket on the local host at the specified address and port.
- **public Socket(InetAddress host, int port, InetAddress localAddress, int localPort) throws IOException.** This method is identical to the previous constructor, except that the host is denoted by an InetAddress object instead of a String.
- **public Socket()** Creates an unconnected socket. Use the connect() method to connect this socket to a server.

When the Socket constructor returns, it does not simply instantiate a Socket object but it actually attempts to connect to the specified server and port. Some methods of interest in the Socket class are listed here. Notice that both the client and the server have a Socket object, so these methods can be invoked by both the client and the server.

Methods with Description

- **public voidconnect(SocketAddress host, int timeout) throws IOException** This method connects the socket to the specified host. This method is needed only when you instantiate the Socket using the no-argument constructor.
- **public InetAddress getInetAddress()** This method returns the address of the other computer that this socket is connected to.
- **public int getPort()** Returns the port the socket is bound to on the remote machine.
- **public int getLocalPort()** Returns the port the socket is bound to on the local machine.
- **public SocketAddress getRemoteSocketAddress()** Returns the address of the remote socket.
- **public InputStream getInputStream() throws IOException** Returns the input stream of the socket. The input stream is connected to the outputstream of the remote socket.
- **public OutputStream getOutputStream() throws IOException** Returns the output stream of the socket. The output stream is connected to the input stream of the remote socket.
- **public void close() throws IOException** Closes the socket, which makes this Socket object no longer capable of connecting again to any server.
- **InetAddress Class Methods** This class represents an

Internet Protocol (IP) address. Here are following usefull methods which you would need while doing socket programming:

Methods with Description

- **static InetAddress getByAddress(byte[] addr)** Returns an InetAddress object given the raw IP address.
- **static InetAddress getByAddress(String host, byte[] addr)** Creates an InetAddress based on the provided host name and IP address.
- **static InetAddress getByName(String host)** Determines the IP address of a host,given the host's name.
- **String getHostAddress()** Returns the IP address string in textual presentation.
- **String getHostName()** Gets the host name for this IP address.
- **static InetAddress InetAddress getLocalHost()** Returns the local host.
- **String toString()** Converts this IP address to a String.

Socket Client Example

The following GreetingClient is a client program that connects to a server by using a socket and sends a greeting, and then waits for a response.

```
// File Name GreetingClient.java
import java.net.*;
import java.io.*;
public class GreetingClient
```

```
{
public static void main(String [] args)
{
String serverName = args[0];
int port = Integer.parseInt(args[1]);
try
{
System.out.println("Connecting to " + serverName
+ "on port " + port);
Socket client = newSocket(serverName, port);
System.out.println("Just connected to "
+ client.getRemoteSocketAddress());
OutputStream outToServer =
client.getOutputStream(); DataOutputStream out =
new DataOutputStream(outToServer);
out.writeUTF("Hello from "
+ client.getLocalSocketAddress()); InputStream
inFromServer = client.getInputStream();
DataInputStream in =
new DataInputStream(inFromServer);
System.out.println("Server says "+ in.readUTF());
client.close();
}catch(IOException e)
{
e.printStackTrace();
}
}
}
```

Socket Server Example

The following GreetingServer program is an example of a server application that uses the

Socket class to listen for clients on a port number specified by a command-line argument:

```java
// File Name GreetingServer.java importjava.net.*;
import java.io.*;
public class GreetingServer extends Thread
{
private ServerSocket serverSocket;
public GreetingServer(int port) throws IOException
{
serverSocket = new ServerSocket(port);
serverSocket.setSoTimeout(10000);
}
public void run()
{
while(true)
{
try
{
System.out.println("Waiting for client on port " +
serverSocket.getLocalPort() + "..."); Socket
server = serverSocket.accept();
System.out.println("Just connected to "
+ server.getRemoteSocketAddress());
DataInputStream in =
new DataInputStream(server.getInputStream());
System.out.println(in.readUTF());
DataOutputStream out =
new DataOutputStream(server.getOutputStream());
out.writeUTF("Thank you for connecting to "
+ server.getLocalSocketAddress() + "\nGoodbye!");
server.close();
}catch(SocketTimeoutException s)
{
System.out.println("Socket timed out!");
break;
}catch(IOException e)
{
```

```
e.printStackTrace();
break;
}
}
}
public static void main(String [] args)
{
int port = Integer.parseInt(args[0]);
try
{
Thread t = new GreetingServer(port);
t.start();
}catch(IOException e)
{
e.printStackTrace();
}
}
}
```

Compile the client and the server and then start the server as follows:

$ java GreetingServer 6066

Waiting for client on port 6066...

Check the client program as follows:

$ java GreetingClient localhost 6066

Connecting to localhost on port 6066

Just connected to localhost/127.0.0.1:6066

Server says Thank you for connecting to /127.0.0.1:6066

Goodbye!

Sending e-Mail

To send an e-mail using your Java Application is simple enough but to start with you should have **JavaMail API** and **Java Activation Framework (JAF)** installed on your machine.

- You can download latest version of JavaMail (Version 1.2) from Java's standard website.
- You can download latest version of JAF (Version 1.1.1) from Java's standard website.

Download and unzip these files, in the newly created top level directories you will find a number of jar files for both the applications. You need to add **mail.jar** and **activation.jar** files in your CLASSPATH.

Send a Simple E-mail

Here is an example to send a simple e-mail from your machine. It is assumed that your **localhost** is connected to the Internet and capable enough to send an e-mail.

```java
// File Name SendEmail.java
import java.util.*;
import javax.mail.*;
import javax.mail.internet.*;
import javax.activation.*;
public class SendEmail
{
public static void main(String [] args)
{
// Recipient's email ID needs to be mentioned.
String to = "abcd@gmail.com";
// Sender's email ID needs to be mentioned
String from = "web@gmail.com";
// Assuming you are sending email from localhost
String host = "localhost";
// Get system properties
Properties properties = System.getProperties();
// Setup mail server
properties.setProperty("mail.smtp.host", host);
// Get the default Session object.
Session session =
Session.getDefaultInstance(properties);
try{
// Create a default MimeMessage object.
MimeMessage message = new MimeMessage(session);
// Set From: header field of the header.
message.setFrom(new InternetAddress(from));
// Set To: header field of the header.
message.addRecipient(Message.RecipientType.TO,
new InternetAddress(to));
// Set Subject: header field
message.setSubject("This is the Subject Line!");
// Now set the actual message
message.setText("This is actual message");
// Send message
Transport.send(message);
System.out.println("Sent message
```

```
successfully....");
}catch (MessagingException mex) {
mex.printStackTrace();
}
}
}
```

Compile and run this program to send a simple e-mail:

```
$ java SendEmail
Sent message successfully....
```

If you want to send an e-mail to multiple recipients then the following methods would be used to specify multiple e-mail IDs:

```
void addRecipients(Message.RecipientType type,
Address[] addresses)throws MessagingException
```

Here is the description of the parameters:

- **type:** This would be set to TO, CC or BCC. Here CC represents Carbon Copy and BCC represents Black Carbon Copy. Example*Message.RecipientType.TO*
- **addresses:** This is an array of e-mail ID. You would need to use InternetAddress() method while specifying email IDs.

Send an HTML E-mail

Here is an example to send an HTML e-mail from your machine. Here it is assumed that your **localhost** is connected to the Internet and capable enough to send an e-mail.

This example is very similar to the previous one, except here we are using setContent() method to set content whose second argument is "text/html" to specify that the HTML content is included in the message.

Using this example, you can send as big as HTML content you like.

```java
// File Name SendHTMLEmail.java
import java.util.*;
import javax.mail.*;
import javax.mail.internet.*;
import javax.activation.*;
public class SendHTMLEmail
{
public static void main(String [] args)
{
// Recipient's email ID needs to be mentioned.
String to = "abcd@gmail.com";
// Sender's email ID needs to be mentioned
String from = "web@gmail.com";
// Assuming you are sending email from localhost
String host = "localhost";
// Get system properties
Properties properties = System.getProperties();
// Setup mail server
properties.setProperty("mail.smtp.host", host);
// Get the default Session object.
Session session =
Session.getDefaultInstance(properties);
try{
// Create a default MimeMessage object.
```

```java
MimeMessage message = new MimeMessage(session);
// Set From: header field of the header.
message.setFrom(new InternetAddress(from));
// Set To: header field of the header.
message.addRecipient(Message.RecipientType.TO,
new InternetAddress(to));
// Set Subject: header field
message.setSubject("This is the Subject Line!");
// Send the actual HTML message, as big as you
like message.setContent("<h1>This is actual
message</h1>", "text/html" );
// Send message
Transport.send(message);
System.out.println("Sent message
successfully....");
}catch (MessagingException mex) {
mex.printStackTrace();
}
}
}
```

Compile and run this program to send an HTML e-mail:

```
$ java SendHTMLEmail
   Sent message successfully....
```

Send Attachment in E-mail

Here is an example to send an e-mail with attachment from your machine. Here it is assumed that your **localhost** is connected to the internet and capable enough to send an e-mail.

```java
// File Name SendFileEmail.java
import java.util.*;
import javax.mail.*;
import javax.mail.internet.*;
import javax.activation.*;
public class SendFileEmail
{
public static void main(String [] args)
{
// Recipient's email ID needs to be mentioned.
String to = "abcd@gmail.com";
// Sender's email ID needs to be mentioned
String from = "web@gmail.com";
// Assuming you are sending email from localhost
String host = "localhost";
// Get system properties
Properties properties = System.getProperties();
// Setup mail server
properties.setProperty("mail.smtp.host", host);
// Get the default Session object.
Session session =
Session.getDefaultInstance(properties);
try{
// Create a default MimeMessage object.
MimeMessage message = new MimeMessage(session);
// Set From: header field of the header.
message.setFrom(new InternetAddress(from));
// Set To: header field of the header.
message.addRecipient(Message.RecipientType.TO,
new InternetAddress(to));
// Set Subject: header field
message.setSubject("This is the Subject Line!");
// Create the messagepart
BodyPart messageBodyPart = new MimeBodyPart();
// Fill the message
messageBodyPart.setText("This is message body");
// Create a multipar message
```

```
Multipart multipart = new MimeMultipart();
// Set text message part
multipart.addBodyPart(messageBodyPart);
// Part two is attachment messageBodyPart = new
MimeBodyPart(); String filename = "file.txt";
DataSource source = new FileDataSource(filename);
messageBodyPart.setDataHandler(new
DataHandler(source));
messageBodyPart.setFileName(filename);
multipart.addBodyPart(messageBodyPart);
// Send the complete message parts
message.setContent(multipart );
// Send message
Transport.send(message);
System.out.println("Sent message
successfully....");
}catch (MessagingException mex) {
mex.printStackTrace();
}
}
}
```

Compile and run this program to send an HTML e-mail:

$ java SendFileEmail

Sent message successfully....

User Authentication Part

If it is required to provide user ID and Password to the e-mail server for authentication purpose, then you can set these properties as follows:

```
props.setProperty("mail.user", "myuser");
props.setProperty("mail.password", "mypwd");
```

Rest of the e-mail sending mechanism would remain as explained above.

Multithreading

Java is a *multi-threaded programming language* which means we can develop multi- threaded program using Java. A multi-threaded program contains two or more parts that can run concurrently and each part can handle a different task at the same time making optimal use of the available resources specially when your computer has multiple CPUs.

By definition, multitasking is when multiple processes share common processing resources such as a CPU. Multi-threading extends the idea of multitasking into applications where you can subdivide specific operations within a single application into individual threads. Each of the threads can run in parallel. The OS divides processing time not only among different applications, but also among each thread within an application.

Multi-threading enables you to write in a way where multiple activities can proceed concurrently in the same program.

Life Cycle of a Thread

A thread goes through various stages in its life cycle. For

example, a thread is born, started, runs, and then dies. The following diagram shows the complete life cycle of a thread.

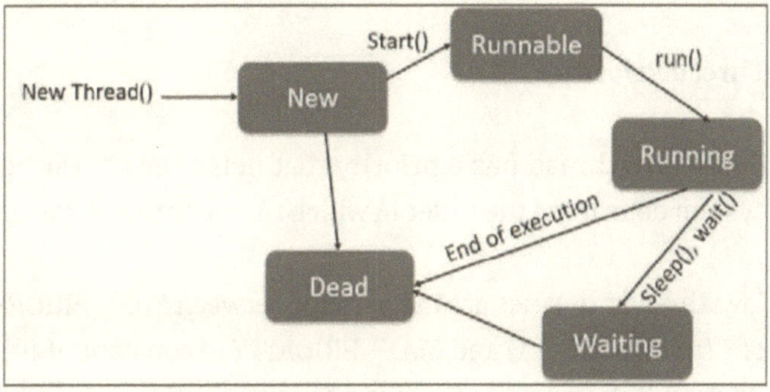

Following are the stages of the life cycle:

- **New:** A new thread begins its life cycle in the new state. It remains in this state until the program starts the thread. It is also referred to as a **born thread**.
- **Runnable:** After a newly born thread is started, the thread becomes runnable. A thread in this state is considered to be executing its task.
- **Waiting:** Sometimes, a thread transitions to the waiting state while the thread waits for another thread to per-form a task. A thread transitions back to the runnable state only when another thread signals the waiting thread to continue executing.
- **Timed Waiting:** A runnable thread can enter the timed waiting state for a specified interval of time. A thread in this state transitions back to the runnable state when that time interval expires or when the event it is waiting

for occurs.

- **Terminated (Dead):** A runnable thread enters the terminated state when it completes its task or otherwise terminates.

Thread Priorities

Every Java thread has a priority that helps the operating system determine the order in which threads are scheduled.

Java thread priorities are in the range between MIN_PRIORITY (a constant of 1) and MAX_PRIORITY (a constant of 10). By default, every thread is given priority NORM_PRIORITY (a constant of 5).

Threads with higher priority are more important to a program and should be allocated processor time before lower-priority threads. However, thread priorities cannot guarantee the order in which threads execute and are very much platform dependent.

Create a Thread by Implementing a Runnable Interface

If your class is intended to be executed as a thread then you can achieve this by implementing a **Runnable** interface. You will need to follow three basic steps:

Step 1

As a first step, you need to implement a run() method provided by a **Runnable** interface. This method provides an entry point for the thread and you will put your complete business logic inside this method. Following is a simple syntax of the run() method:

```
public void run()
```

Step 2

As a second step, you will instantiate a **Thread** object using the following constructor:

```
Thread(Runnable threadObj, String threadName);
```

Where, *threadObj* is an instance of a class that implements the **Runnable** interface and **threadName** is the name given to the new thread.

Step 3

Once a Thread object is created, you can start it by calling **start( )** method, which executes a call to run( ) method. Following is a simple syntax of start() method:

```
void start( );
```

Example

Here is an example that creates a new thread and starts running it:

```java
class RunnableDemo implementsRunnable {
private Thread t;
private String threadName;
RunnableDemo( String name){
threadName = name;
System.out.println("Creating " + threadName );
}
public void run() {
System.out.println("Running " +  threadName );
try {
for(int i = 4; i > 0; i--) {
System.out.println("Thread: " + threadName + ", "
+ i);
// Let the thread sleep for a while.
Thread.sleep(50);
}
} catch (InterruptedException e) {
System.out.println("Thread " + threadName + "
interrupted.");
}
System.out.println("Thread " + threadName + "
exiting.");
}
public void start ()
{
System.out.println("Starting " +  threadName );
if (t == null)
{
t = new Thread (this, threadName);
t.start ();
}
}
}
public class TestThread {
public static void main(String args[]) {
RunnableDemo R1 = newRunnableDemo( "Thread-1");
R1.start();
```

```
RunnableDemo R2 = newRunnableDemo( "Thread-2");
R2.start();
}
}
```

This will produce the following result:

Creating Thread-1

Starting Thread-1

Creating Thread-2

Starting Thread-2

Running Thread-1

Thread: Thread-1, 4

Running Thread-2

Thread: Thread-2, 4

Thread: Thread-1, 3

Thread: Thread-2, 3

Thread: Thread-1, 2

Thread: Thread-2, 2

Thread: Thread-1, 1

Thread: Thread-2, 1

Thread Thread-1 exiting. Thread Thread-2 exiting.

Create a Thread by Extending a Thread Class

The second way to create a thread is to create a new class that extends **Thread** class using the following two simple steps. This approach provides more flexibility in handling multiple threads created using available methods in Thread class.

Step 1

You will need to override **run( )** method available in Thread class. This method provides an entry point for the thread and you will put your complete business logic inside this method. Following is a simple syntax of run() method:

```
public void run()
```

Step 2

Once Thread object is created, you can start it by calling **start( )** method, which executes a call to run( ) method. Following is a simple syntax of start() method:

```
void start( );
```

Example

Here is the preceding program rewritten to extend the Thread:

```
class ThreadDemo extends Thread {
private Thread t;
private String threadName;
ThreadDemo( String name){
threadName = name;
System.out.println("Creating " + threadName );
}
public void run() {
System.out.println("Running " +  threadName );
try {
```

```
for(int i = 4; i > 0; i--) {
System.out.println("Thread: " + threadName + ", "
+ i);
// Let the thread sleep for a while.
Thread.sleep(50);
}
} catch (InterruptedException e) {
System.out.println("Thread " + threadName + "
interrupted.");
}
System.out.println("Thread " + threadName + "
exiting.");
}
public void start ()
{
System.out.println("Starting " +  threadName );
if (t == null)
{
t = new Thread (this, threadName);
t.start ();
}
}
}
public class TestThread {
public static void main(String args[]) {
ThreadDemo T1 = new ThreadDemo( "Thread-1");
T1.start();
ThreadDemo T2 = new ThreadDemo( "Thread-2");
T2.start();
}
}
```

This will produce the following result:

Creating Thread-1

Starting Thread-1

Creating Thread-2

Starting Thread-2

Running Thread-1

Thread: Thread-1, 4

Running Thread-2

Thread: Thread-2, 4

Thread: Thread-1, 3

Thread: Thread-2, 3

Thread: Thread-1, 2

Thread: Thread-2, 2

Thread: Thread-1, 1

Thread: Thread-2, 1

Thread Thread-1 exiting. Thread Thread-2 exiting.

Thread Methods

Following is the list of important methods available in the Thread class.

Methods with Description

- **public void start()** Starts the thread in a separate path of execution, then invokes the run() method on this Thread object.
- **public void run()** If this Thread object was instantiated using a separate Runnable target, the run() method is invoked on that Runnable object.
- **public final void setName(String name)** Changes the name of the Thread object. There is also a getName() method for retrieving the name.
- **public final void setPriority(int priority)** Sets the priority of this Thread object. The possible values are

between 1 and

- **public final void setDaemon(boolean on)** A parameter of true denotes this Thread as a daemon thread.
- **public final void join(longmillisec)** The current thread invokes this method on a second thread, causing the current thread to block until the second thread terminates or the specified number of milliseconds passes.
- **public void interrupt()** Interrupts this thread, causing it to continue execution if it was blocked for any reason.
- **public final boolean isAlive()** Returns true if the thread is alive, which is any time after the thread has been started but before it runs to completion.

The previous methods are invoked on a particular Thread object. The following methods in the Thread class are static. Invoking one of the static methods performs the operation on the currently running thread.

Methods with Description

- **public static void yield()** Causes the currently running thread to yield to any other threads of the same priority that are waiting to be scheduled.
- **public static void sleep(long millisec)** Causes the currently running thread to block for at least the specified number of milliseconds.
- **public static boolean holdsLock(Object x)** Returns true if the current thread holds the lock on the given Object.
- **public static Thread currentThread()** Returns a reference to the currently running thread, which is the thread that invokes this method.

- **public static void dumpStack()** Prints the stacktrace for the currently running thread, which is useful when debugging a multithreaded application.

Example

The following ThreadClassDemo program demonstrates some of these methods of the

Thread class. Consider a class **DisplayMessage** which implements **Runnable**:

```
// File Name : DisplayMessage.java
// Create a thread to implement Runnable
public class DisplayMessage implements Runnable
{
private String message;
public DisplayMessage(String message)
{
this.message = message;
}
public void run()
{
while(true)
{
System.out.println(message);
}
}
}
```

Following is another class which extends the Thread class:

```java
// File Name : GuessANumber.java
// Create a thread to extentd Thread public class
GuessANumber extends Thread
{
private int number;
public GuessANumber(int number)
{
this.number = number;
}
public void run()
{
int counter = 0;
int guess = 0;
do
{
guess = (int) (Math.random() * 100 + 1);
System.out.println(this.getName()
+ " guesses " + guess);
counter++;
}while(guess != number);
System.out.println("** Correct! " + this.getName()
+ " in "+ counter + " guesses.**");
}
}
```

Following is the main program, which makes use of
the above-defined classes:

```java
// File Name : ThreadClassDemo.java public class
ThreadClassDemo
{
public static void main(String [] args)
{
Runnable hello = new DisplayMessage("Hello");
Thread thread1 = new Thread(hello);
thread1.setDaemon(true);
thread1.setName("hello");
System.out.println("Starting hello thread...");
thread1.start();
```

```java
Runnable bye = new DisplayMessage("Goodbye");
Thread thread2 = new Thread(bye);
thread2.setPriority(Thread.MIN_PRIORITY);
thread2.setDaemon(true);
System.out.println("Starting goodbye thread...");
thread2.start();
System.out.println("Starting thread3..."); Thread
thread3 = new GuessANumber(27); thread3.start();
try
{
thread3.join();
}catch(InterruptedException e)
{
System.out.println("Thread interrupted.");
}
System.out.println("Starting thread4..."); Thread
thread4 = new GuessANumber(75);
thread4.start(); System.out.println("main() is
ending...");
}
}
```

This will produce the following result. You can try this example again and again and you will get a different result every time.

Starting hello thread... Starting goodbye thread... Hello

Hello Hello Hello Hello Hello Goodbye Goodbye Goodbye Goodbye Goodbye

....

Major Java Multithreading Concepts

While doing Multithreading programming in Java, you would need to have the following concepts very handy:

- What is thread synchronization?
- Handling interthread communication
- Handling thread deadlock
- Major thread operations

Thread Synchronization

When we start two or more threads within a program, there may be a situation when multiple threads try to access the same resource and finally they can produce unforeseen result due to concurrency issues. For example, if multiple threads try to write within a same file then they may corrupt the data because one of the threads can override data or while one thread is opening the same file at the same time another thread might be closing the same file.

So there is a need to synchronize the action of multiple threads and make sure that only one thread can access the resource at a given point in time. This is implemented using a concept called **monitors**. Each object in Java is associated with a monitor, which a thread can lock or unlock. Only one thread at a time may hold a lock on a monitor.

Java programming language provides a very handy way of creating threads and synchronizing their task by using **synchronized** blocks. You keep shared resources within this block. Following is the general form of the synchronized statement:

```
synchronized(objectidentifier) {
// Access shared variables and other shared
resources
}
```

Here, the **objectidentifier** is a reference to an object whose lock associates with the monitor that the synchronized statement represents. Now we are going to see two examples, where we will print a counter using two different threads. When threads are not synchronized, they print counter value which is not in sequence, but when we print counter by putting inside synchronized() block, then it prints counter very much in sequence for both the threads.

Multithreading Example without Synchronization

Here is a simple example which may or may not print counter value in sequence and every time we run it, it produces a different result based on CPU availability to a thread.

```
class PrintDemo {
public void printCount(){
try {
for(int i = 5; i > 0; i--) {
System.out.println("Counter   --- "+ i );
}
} catch (Exception e) {
System.out.println("Thread interrupted.");
}
}
}
```

```java
class ThreadDemo extends Thread {
private Thread t;
private String threadName; PrintDemo PD;
ThreadDemo( String name, PrintDemo pd){
threadName = name; PD= pd;
}
public void run() { PD.printCount();
System.out.println("Thread "+ threadName + "
exiting.");
}
public void start ()
{
System.out.println("Starting "+  threadName );
if (t == null)
{
t = new Thread (this, threadName);
t.start ();
}
}
}
public class TestThread {
public static void main(String args[]) {
PrintDemo PD= new PrintDemo();
ThreadDemo T1 = new ThreadDemo( "Thread - 1 ", PD
); ThreadDemo T2 = new ThreadDemo( "Thread - 2 ",
PD );
T1.start(); T2.start();
// wait for threads to end try {
T1.join(); T2.join();
} catch( Exception e) {
System.out.println("Interrupted");
}
}
}
```

This produces a different result every time you run this

program:

```
Starting Thread - 1

Starting Thread - 2

Counter —- 5

Counter —- 4

Counter —- 3

Counter —- 5

Counter —- 2

Counter —- 1

Counter —- 4

Thread Thread - 1 exiting.

Counter

—-

3

Counter

—-

2

Counter

—-

1

Thread Thread - 2 exiting.
```

Multithreading Example with Synchronization

Here is the same example which prints counter value in sequence and every time we run it, it produces the same result.

```
class PrintDemo {
public void printCount(){
```

```java
try {
for(int i = 5; i > 0; i--) {
System.out.println("Counter  --- "+ i );
}
} catch (Exception e) {
System.out.println("Thread interrupted.");
}
}
}
class ThreadDemo extends Thread {
private Thread t;
private String threadName; PrintDemo PD;
ThreadDemo( String name, PrintDemo pd){
threadName = name; PD= pd;
}
public void run() {
synchronized(PD) { PD.printCount();
}
System.out.println("Thread "+ threadName + "
exiting.");
}
public void start ()
{
System.out.println("Starting " +  threadName );
if (t == null)
{
t = new Thread (this, threadName);
t.start ();
}
}
}
public class TestThread {
public static void main(String args[]) {
PrintDemo PD= new PrintDemo();
ThreadDemo T1 = new ThreadDemo( "Thread - 1 ", PD
);
ThreadDemo T2 = new ThreadDemo( "Thread - 2 ", PD
```

```
);
T1.start(); T2.start();
// wait for threads to end try {
T1.join(); T2.join();
} catch( Exception e) {
System.out.println("Interrupted");
}
}
}
```

This produces the same result every time you run this program:

```
Starting Thread - 1

Starting Thread - 2

Counter —- 5

Counter —- 4

Counter —- 3

Counter —- 2

Counter —- 1

Thread Thread - 1 exiting. Counter —- 5

Counter —- 4

Counter —- 3

Counter —- 2

Counter —- 1

Thread Thread - 2 exiting.
```

Interthread Communication

If you are aware of interprocess communication then it will be easy for you to understand interthread communication. Interthread communication is important when you develop an application where two or more threads exchange some information.

There are three simple methods and a little trick which makes thread communication possible. All the three methods are listed below:

Methods with Description

- **public void wait()** Causes the current thread to wait until another thread invokes the notify().
- **public void notify()** Wakes up a single thread that is waiting on this object's monitor.
- **public void notifyAll()** Wakes up all the threads that called wait( ) on the same object.

These methods have been implemented as **final** methods in Object, so they are available in all the classes. All three methods can be called only from within a **synchronized** context.

Example

This examples shows how two threads can communicate using **wait()** and **notify()** method. You can create a complex system using the same concept.

```
class Chat {
boolean flag = false;
public synchronized void Question(String msg) {
if (flag) {
```

```java
try {
wait();
} catch (InterruptedException e) {
e.printStackTrace();
}
}
System.out.println(msg);
flag = true;
notify();
}
public synchronized void Answer(String msg) {
if (!flag) {
try {
wait();
} catch (InterruptedException e) {
e.printStackTrace();
}
}
System.out.println(msg);
flag = false;
notify();
}
}
class T1 implements Runnable { Chat m;
String[] s1 = { "Hi", "How are you ?", "I am also
doing fine!"};
public T1(Chat m1) {
this.m = m1;
new Thread(this, "Question").start();
}
public void run() {
for (int i = 0;i < s1.length; i++) {
m.Question(s1[i]);
}
}
}
class T2 implements Runnable { Chat m;
```

```
String[] s2 = { "Hi", "I am good, what about
you?", "Great!" };
public T2(Chat m2) {
this.m = m2;
new Thread(this, "Answer").start();
}
public void run() {
for (int i = 0;i < s2.length; i++) {
m.Answer(s2[i]);
}
}
}
public class TestThread {
public static void main(String[] args) { Chat m =
new Chat();
new T1(m);
new T2(m);
}
}
```

When the above program is complied and executed, it produces the following result:

```
Hi

Hi

How are you ?

I am good, what about you? I am also doing fine!

Great!
```

Thread Deadlock

Deadlock describes a situation where two or more threads are blocked forever, waiting for each other. Deadlock occurs when multiple threads need the same locks but obtain them in different order. A Java multithreaded program may suffer from the deadlock condition because the **synchronized** keyword causes the executing thread to block while waiting for the lock, or monitor, associated with the specified object. Here is an example.

Example

```
public class TestThread {
public static Object Lock1 = new Object();
public static Object Lock2 = new Object();
public static void main(String args[]) {
ThreadDemo1 T1 = new ThreadDemo1(); ThreadDemo2
T2 = new ThreadDemo2(); T1.start();
T2.start();
}
private static class ThreadDemo1 extends Thread {
public void run() {
synchronized (Lock1) {
System.out.println("Thread 1: Holding lock 1...");
try { Thread.sleep(10); }
catch (InterruptedException e) {}
System.out.println("Thread 1: Waiting for lock
2...");
synchronized (Lock2) {
System.out.println("Thread 1: Holding lock 1 &
2...");
}
}
}
}
private static class ThreadDemo2 extends Thread {
public void run() {
synchronized (Lock2) {
System.out.println("Thread 2: Holding lock 2...");
try { Thread.sleep(10); }
```

```
catch (InterruptedException e) {}
System.out.println("Thread 2: Waiting for lock
1..."); synchronized (Lock1) {
System.out.println("Thread 2: Holding lock 1 &
2...");
}
}
}
}
}
```

When you compile and execute the above program, you find a deadlock situation and following is the output produced by the program:

Thread 1: Holding lock 1... Thread 2:

Holding lock 2... Thread 1: Waiting for lock 2...

Thread 2: Waiting for lock 1...

The above program will hang forever because neither of the threads in position to proceed and waiting for each other to release the lock, so you can come out of the program by pressing CTRL+C.

Deadlock Solution Example

Let's change the order of the lock and run of the same program to see if both the threads still wait for each other:

```
public class TestThread {
public static Object Lock1 = new Object();
```

```java
public static Object Lock2 = new Object();
public static void main(String args[]) {
ThreadDemo1 T1 = new ThreadDemo1(); ThreadDemo2
T2 = new ThreadDemo2(); T1.start();
T2.start();
}
private static class ThreadDemo1 extends Thread {
public void run() {
synchronized (Lock1) {
System.out.println("Thread 1: Holding lock 1...");
try { Thread.sleep(10); }
catch (InterruptedException e) {}
System.out.println("Thread 1: Waiting for lock
2..."); synchronized (Lock2) {
System.out.println("Thread 1: Holding lock 1 &
2...");
}
}
}
}
private static class ThreadDemo2 extends Thread {
public void run() {
synchronized (Lock1) {
System.out.println("Thread 2: Holding lock 1...");
try { Thread.sleep(10); }
catch (InterruptedException e) {}
System.out.println("Thread 2: Waiting for lock
2...");
synchronized (Lock2) {
System.out.println("Thread 2: Holding lock 1 &
2...");
}
}
}
}
```

So just changing the order of the locks prevent the program in going into a deadlock situation and completes with the following result:

Thread 1: Holding lock 1...

Thread 1: Waiting for lock 2...

Thread 1: Holding lock 1 & 2...

Thread 2: Holding lock 1...

Thread 2: Waiting for lock 2...

Thread 2: Holding lock 1 & 2...

The above example is to just make the concept clear, however, it is a complex concept and you should deep dive into it before you develop your applications to deal with deadlock situations.

Thread Control

Core Java provides complete control over multithreaded program. You can develop a multithreaded program which can be suspended, resumed, or stopped completely based on your requirements. There are various static methods which you can use on thread objects to control their behavior. Following table lists down those methods:

Methods with Description

- **public void suspend()** This method puts a thread in the suspended state and can be resumed using resume() method.
- **public void stop()** This method stops a thread com-

pletely.

- **public void resume()** This method resumes a thread, which was suspended using suspend()method.
- **public void wait()** Causes the current thread to wait until another thread invokes the notify().
- **public void notify()** Wakes up a single thread that is waiting on this object's monitor.

Be aware that the latest versions of Java has deprecated the usage of suspend( ), resume(), and stop( ) methods and so you need to use available alternatives.

Example

```java
class RunnableDemo implementsRunnable {
public Thread t;
private String threadName;
boolean suspended = false;
RunnableDemo( String name){
threadName = name;
System.out.println("Creating " + threadName );
}
public void run() {
System.out.println("Running " +  threadName );
try {
for(int i = 10; i > 0; i--) {
System.out.println("Thread: " + threadName + ", "
+ i);
// Let the thread sleep for a while.
Thread.sleep(300);
synchronized(this) {
while(suspended) {
wait();
}
```

```java
}
}
} catch (InterruptedException e) {
System.out.println("Thread " + threadName + "
interrupted.");
}
System.out.println("Thread " + threadName + "
exiting.");
}
public void start ()
{
System.out.println("Starting " +  threadName );
if (t == null)
{
t = new Thread (this, threadName);
t.start ();
}
}
void suspend() {
suspended = true;
}
synchronized void resume() {
suspended = false;
notify();
}
}
public class TestThread {
public static void main(String args[]) {
RunnableDemo R1 = newRunnableDemo( "Thread-1");
R1.start();
RunnableDemo R2 = newRunnableDemo( "Thread-2");
R2.start();
try { Thread.sleep(1000); R1.suspend();
System.out.println("Suspending First Thread");
Thread.sleep(1000);
R1.resume();
System.out.println("Resuming First Thread");
```

```
R2.suspend();
System.out.println("Suspending thread Two");
Thread.sleep(1000);
R2.resume();
System.out.println("Resuming thread Two");
} catch (InterruptedException e) {
System.out.println("Main thread Interrupted");
}
try {
System.out.println("Waiting for threads to
finish."); R1.t.join();
R2.t.join();
} catch (InterruptedException e) {
System.out.println("Main thread Interrupted");
}
System.out.println("Main thread exiting.");
}
}
```

The above program produces the following output:

```
Creating Thread-1

Starting Thread-1

Creating Thread-2

Starting Thread-2

Running Thread-1

Thread: Thread-1, 10

Running Thread-2

Thread: Thread-2, 10

Thread: Thread-1, 9

Thread: Thread-2, 9

Thread: Thread-1, 8

Thread: Thread-2, 8

Thread: Thread-1, 7
```

Thread: Thread-2, 7

Suspending First Thread

Thread: Thread-2, 6

Thread: Thread-2, 5

Thread: Thread-2, 4

Resuming First Thread Suspending thread Two Thread: Thread-1, 6

Thread: Thread-1, 5

Thread: Thread-1, 4

Thread: Thread-1, 3

Resuming thread Two

Thread: Thread-2, 3

Waiting for threads to finish. Thread: Thread-1, 2

Thread: Thread-2, 2

Thread: Thread-1, 1

Thread: Thread-2, 1

Thread Thread-1 exiting. Thread Thread-2 exiting. ain thread exiting.

Applet Basics

java.applet package package has been deprecated in Java 9 and later versions,as applets are no longer widely used on the web.

An applet is a Java program that can be embedded into a web page. It runs inside the web browser and works at client side. An applet is embedded in an HTML page using the APPLET or OBJECT tag and hosted on a web server. Applets are used to make the website more dynamic and entertaining.

Important points :

- All applets are sub-classes (either directly or indirectly) of *java.applet.Applet* class.
- Applets are not stand-alone programs. Instead, they run within either a web browser or an applet viewer. JDK provides a standard applet viewer tool called applet viewer.
- In general, execution of an applet does not begin at main() method.
- Output of an applet window is not performed by *System.out.println()*. Rather it is handled with various AWT methods, such as *drawString()*.

Life cycle of an applet :

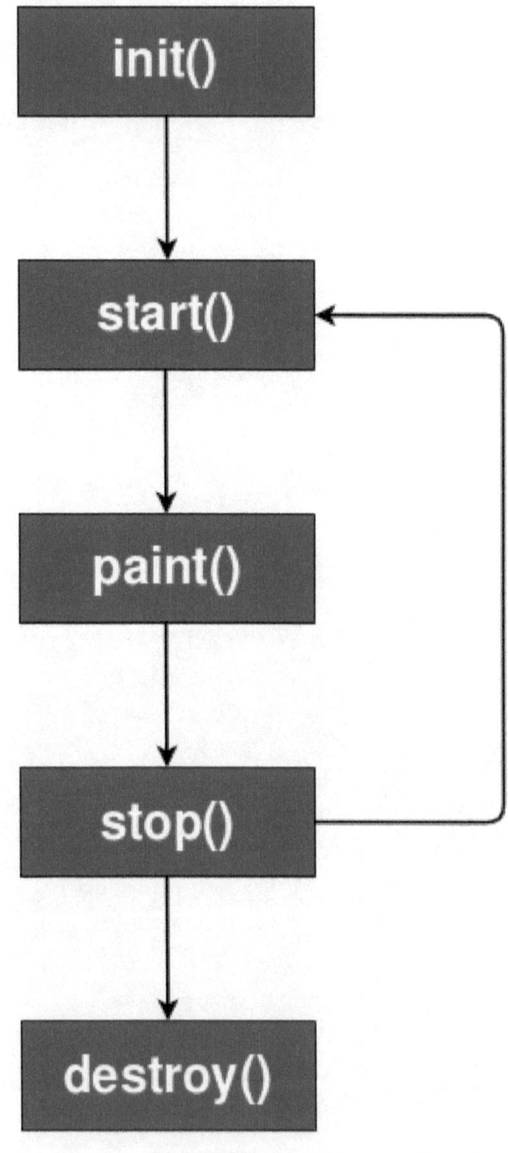

init()
start()
paint()
stop()
destroy()

It is important to understand the order in which the various methods shown in the above image are called. When an applet begins, the following methods are called, in this sequence:

- init( )
- start( )
- paint( )

When an applet is terminated, the following sequence of method calls takes place:

- stop( )
- destroy( )

Let's look more closely at these methods.

- **init( ) :** The **init( )** method is the first method to be called. This is where you should initialize variables. This method is called **only once** during the run time of your applet.
- **start( ) :** The **start( )** method is called after **init( )**. It is also called to restart an applet after it has been stopped. Note that **init( )** is called once i.e. when the first time an applet is loaded whereas **start( )** is called each time an applet's HTML document is displayed onscreen. So, if a user leaves a web page and comes back, the applet resumes execution at **start( )**.
- **paint( ) :** The **paint( )** method is called each time an

AWT-based applet's output must be redrawn. This situation can occur for several reasons. For example, the window in which the applet is running may be overwritten by another window and then uncovered. Or the applet window may be minimized and then restored. **paint( )** is also called when the applet begins execution. Whatever the cause, whenever the applet must redraw its output, **paint( )** is called.

The **paint( )** method has one parameter of type **Graphics**. This parameter will contain the graphics context, which describes the graphics environment in which the applet is running. This context is used whenever output to the applet is required.

Note: This is the only method among all the method mention above, which is parameterized. It's prototype is public void paint(Graphics g) where g is an object reference of class Graphic.

Now the **Question Arises:**

Q. In the prototype of paint() method, we have created an object reference without creating its object. But how is it possible to create object reference without creating its object?

Ans. Whenever we pass object reference in arguments then the object will be provided by its caller itself. In this case the caller of paint() method is browser, so it will provide an object. The same thing happens when we create a very basic program in normal Java programs. For Example:

```
public static void main(String []args){}
```

Here we have created an object reference without creating its object but it still runs because it's caller,i.e JVM will provide it with an object.

- **stop( )** : The **stop( )** method is called when a web browser leaves the HTML document containing the applet—when it goes to another page, for example. When **stop( )** is called, the applet is probably running. You should use **stop( )** to suspend threads that don't need to run when the applet is not visible. You can restart them when **start( )** is called if the user returns to the page.
- **destroy( )** : The **destroy( )** method is called when the environment determines that your applet needs to be removed completely from memory. At this point, you should free up any resources the applet may be using. The **stop( )** method is always called before **destroy( )**.

Creating Hello World applet :

Let's begin with the HelloWorld applet :

- Java

```java
// A Hello World Applet
// Save file as HelloWorld.java

import java.applet.Applet;
import java.awt.Graphics;

// HelloWorld class extends Applet
public class HelloWorld extends Applet
{
    // Overriding paint() method
    @Override
    public void paint(Graphics g)
    {
        g.drawString("Hello World", 20, 20);
    }
}
```

Explanation:

- The above java program begins with two import statements. The first import statement imports the Applet class from applet package. Every AWT-based(Abstract Window Toolkit) applet that you create must be a subclass (either directly or indirectly) of Applet class. The second statement import the **Graphics** class from AWT package.

- The next line in the program declares the class HelloWorld. This class must be declared as public because it will be accessed by code that is outside the program. Inside HelloWorld, **paint( )** is declared. This method is defined by the AWT and must be overridden by the applet.

- Inside **paint( )** is a call to *drawString( )*, which is a member of the **Graphics** class. This method outputs a string beginning at the specified X,Y location. It has the following general form:

```
void drawString(String message, int x, int y)
```

Here, message is the string to be output beginning at x,y. In a Java window, the upper-left corner is location 0,0. The call to *drawString( )* in the applet causes the message "Hello World" to be displayed beginning at location 20,20.

Notice that the applet does not have a **main( )** method. Unlike Java programs, applets do not begin execution at **main( )**. In fact, most applets don't even have a **main( )** method. Instead, an applet begins execution when the name of its class is passed to an applet viewer or to a network browser.

Running the HelloWorld Applet :

After you enter the source code for HelloWorld.java, compile in the same way that you have been compiling java programs(using *javac* command). However, running HelloWorld with the *java* command will generate an error because it is not an application.

```
java HelloWorld

Error: Main method not found in class HelloWorld,
please define the main method as:
```

```
    public static void main(String[] args)
```

There are **two** standard ways in which you can run an applet :

- Executing the applet within a Java-compatible web browser.
- Using an applet viewer, such as the standard tool, applet-viewer. An applet viewer executes your applet in a window. This is generally the fastest and easiest way to test your applet.

Each of these methods is described next.

- **Using java enabled web browser :** To execute an applet in a web browser we have to write a short HTML text file that contains a tag that loads the applet. We can use APPLET or OBJECT tag for this purpose. Using APPLET, here is the HTML file that executes HelloWorld :

```
<applet code="HelloWorld" width=200 height=60>
</applet>
```

The width and height statements specify the dimensions of the display area used by the applet. The APPLET tag contains several other options. After you create this html file, you can use it to execute the applet.

NOTE : Chrome and Firefox no longer supports NPAPI

(technology required for Java applets).

- **Using appletviewer :** This is the easiest way to run an applet. To execute HelloWorld with an applet viewer, you may also execute the HTML file shown earlier. For example, if the preceding HTML file is saved with

RunHelloWorld.html, then the following command line will run HelloWorld :

```
appletviewer RunHelloWorld.html
```

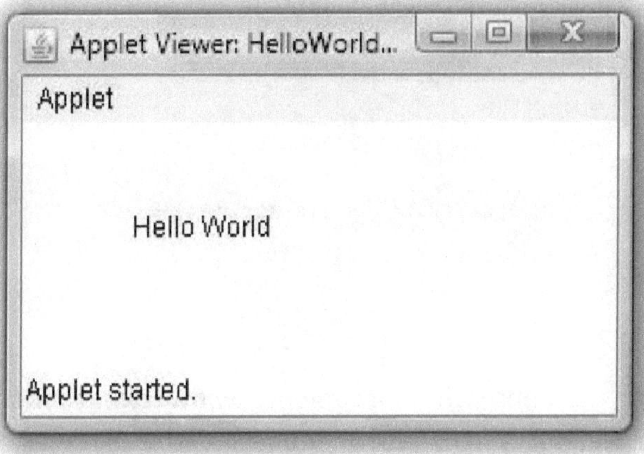

- **appletviewer with java source file :** If you include a comment at the head of your Java source code file that contains the APPLET tag then your code is documented with a prototype of the necessary HTML statements, and you can run your compiled applet merely by starting the applet viewer with your Java source code file. If you use this method, the HelloWorld source file looks like this :

```java
// A Hello World Applet
// Save file as HelloWorld.java
import java.applet.Applet;
import java.awt.Graphics;
/*
<applet code="HelloWorld" width=200 height=60>
</applet>
*/
// HelloWorld class extends Applet
public class HelloWorld extends Applet
{
    // Overriding paint() method
    @Override
    public void paint(Graphics g)
    {
        g.drawString("Hello World", 20, 20);
    }
}
```

With this approach, first compile HelloWorld.java file and then simply run the below command to run applet :

```
appletviewer HelloWorld
```

To prove above mentioned point,i.e paint is called again and again.

To prove this, let's first study what is "Status Bar" in Applet:

"Status Bar" is available in the left bottom window of an applet. To use the status bar and write something in it, we use method showStatus() whose prototype is public void showStatus(String)

By default status bar shows "Applet Started" By default background color is white.

To prove paint() method is called again and again, here is the code:

Note: This code is with respect to Netbeans IDE.

```
//code to illustrate paint
//method gets called again
//and again
import java.applet.*;// used
//to access showStatus()
import java.awt.*;//Graphic
//class is available in this package
import java.util.Date;// used
//to access Date object
public class GFG extends Applet
{
public void paint(Graphics g)
{
Date dt = new Date();
super.showStatus("Today is" + dt);
//in this line, super keyword is
// avoidable too.
}
}
```

Note:- Here we can see that if the screen is maximized or minimized we will get an updated time. This shows that paint() is called again and again.

Features of Applets over HTML

- Displaying dynamic web pages of a web application.
- Playing sound files.
- Displaying documents
- Playing animations

Restrictions imposed on Java applets

Due to security reasons, the following restrictions are imposed on Java applets:

- An applet cannot load libraries or define native methods.
- An applet cannot ordinarily read or write files on the execution host.
- An applet cannot read certain system properties.
- An applet cannot make network connections except to the host that it came from.
- An applet cannot start any program on the host that's executing it.

Documentation Comments

The Java comments are the statements in a program that are not executed by the compiler and interpreter.

Types of Java Comments

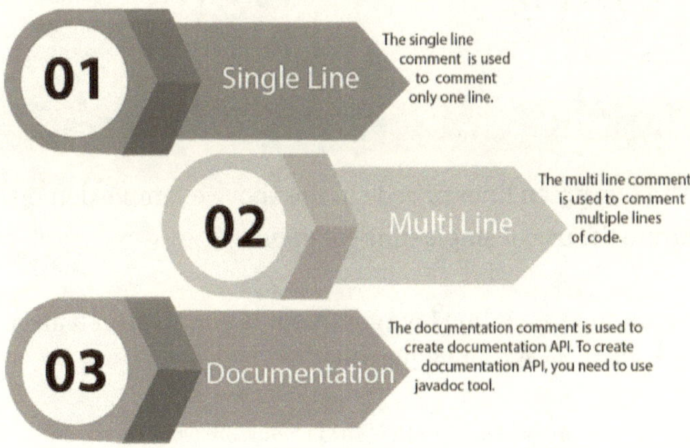

Single line Java comment example

Inline comments, also known as single-line Java comments, begin with two slashes, and only impact the code on the line in which they appear.

The following is an example of a single-line comment in Java:

```java
public class JavaCommentsExample {
  // This is a single-line Java comment

  public static void main(String[] args) {

    System.out.println("This line will run.");
    //System.out.println("This line will not
    run.");

  }
}
```

The two green lines of code in the above example demonstrate the use of single-line comments.

Sometimes an inline Java comment is placed after a piece of code to be executed, like this:

```java
int number = 10;  //initialize number to 10
```

A single-line comment only affects the code that comes after it, not any code that precedes it.

Java block comment example

Inline comments in Java only effect the line of code on which they appear.

But sometimes developers want to comment out multiple lines of code at once. A developer might even want to comment out an entire method.

This is where Java block comments, or multi-line comments, come in handy. Using a slash star (/*), star slash (*/) syntax, a block comment in Java can span multiple lines, and include both code and text.

Here is an example of how to use Java block comments:

```java
public class JavaCommentsExample {
  /* This block comment spans only one line. */
  public static void main(String[] args) {
    System.out.println("This line will run.");

    /* This block comment spans multiple lines.
       System.out.println("This line will not
       run.");
       System.out.println("This line will not
       run.");
       None of the code in this Java block
       comment will run.
    */

  }
}
```

JavaDoc comments in Java

JavaDoc comments, which use a slash-star-star, star-slash (/** ... */) syntax, serve a different purpose from inline comments and multi-line Java comments.

Whereas inline and block Java comments are read by other developers who maintain the code, JavaDoc comments are for developers who use your code.

You can only place JavaDoc comments before the class declaration or a method declaration. Also, they describe the purpose of the class or method and how it might be used.

Unlike block and single-line Java comments, JavaDoc does not include any implementation details.

When Java code is ready to ship, a special JavaDoc utility processes the JavaDoc comments on every file in the codebase, and generates documentation for users of your code to read.

JavaDoc comment example

The following code includes two JavaDoc comments, along with both inline and block Java comments to demonstrate that it is allowable to mix all three types together:

```
/** This JavaDoc comment should describe the
class. */
public class JavaCommentsExample {

  /** This JavaDoc comment should describe the
  method. */
  public static void main(String[] args) {

    System.out.println("This line will run.");
    // Java comment
    /* System.out.println("This is in a Java
    block comment."); */

  }
}
```

How to use Java comments

To use Java comments effectively, follow these steps:

1. If the comment describes how to use the code, use JavaDoc comments /** */
2. If the comment only spans one line, use an inline comment //
3. If the comment spans multiple lines, use a block comment /* */

There's an old saying: good code comments itself. This sentiment has some merit. But at the same time, good programmers comment their code. Add Java comments to your code judiciously, when and where makes sense. This helps others understand the code you write.

References

- Effective Java" by Joshua Bloch
- This book offers valuable insights into writing better Java code and provides best practices for Java developers.
- "Java: The Complete Reference" by Herbert Schildt
- A comprehensive reference book for Java that covers the language's features, libraries, and usage in detail.
- "Head First Java" by Kathy Sierra and Bert Bates
- A user-friendly introduction to Java that combines learning with a fun, interactive approach.
- "Java Concurrency in Practice" by Brian Goetz
- Focuses on Java's concurrency features and provides practical guidance for writing multi-threaded programs.
- "Clean Code: A Handbook of Agile Software Craftsmanship" by Robert C. Martin
- While not specific to Java, this book emphasizes writing clean, maintainable code, which is crucial for any Java developer.
- "Java Performance: The Definitive Guide" by Scott Oaks
- Offers insights into optimizing Java applications for

better performance, a critical aspect of Java development.

- "Java 8 in Action" by Raoul-Gabriel Urma, Mario Fusco, and Alan Mycroft
- Explores the new features introduced in Java 8, such as lambdas and streams, in a practical manner.
- "Java Design Patterns: A Hands-On Experience with Real-World Examples" by Vaskaran Sarcar
- Covers essential design patterns in Java and demonstrates their application through real-world examples.
- "Java Generics and Collections" by Maurice Naftalin and Philip Wadler
- Focuses on Java's generic types and collections framework, helping developers harness the power of generics.
- "Java EE 8 and Angular" by Prashant Padmanabhan, Vijay Garg
- Explores building modern, full-stack web applications using Java EE 8 and Angular.

www.ingramcontent.com/pod-product-compliance
Lightning Source LLC
Chambersburg PA
CBHW051206130726
47988CB00001B/3